Changing
Social Security in
Latin America

Changing
Social Security in
Latin America

Toward Alleviating the
Social Costs of Economic Reform

Carmelo Mesa-Lago

Lynne Rienner Publishers • Boulder & London

Published in the United States of America in 1994 by
Lynne Rienner Publishers, Inc.
1800 30th Street, Boulder, Colorado 80301

and in the United Kingdom by
Lynne Rienner Publishers, Inc.
3 Henrietta Street, Covent Garden, London WC2E 8LU

Library of Congress Cataloging-in-Publication Data
Mesa-Lago, Carmelo, 1934–
    Changing social security in Latin America : toward alleviating the
    social costs of economic reform / Carmelo Mesa-Lago.
    Includes bibliographical references and index.
    ISBN 1-55587-486-X
    1. Social security—Latin America. 2. Structural adjustment
(Economic policy)—Latin America. I. Title.
HD7130.5.M445   1994
368.4'0098—dc20   93-38662
                                                          CIP

British Cataloguing in Publication Data
A Cataloguing in Publication record for this book
is available from the British Library.

Printed and bound in the United States of America

⊗   The paper used in this publication meets the requirements
    of the American National Standard for Permanence of
    Paper for Printed Library Materials Z39.48-1984.

Contents

v

List of Tables

Preface

The economic crisis of the 1980s in Latin America and the Caribbean (LAC) was the worst since the Great Depression and halted development for a decade. The magnitude of the debt crisis was compounded by the process of economic reform (adjustment and restructuring) that several LAC countries introduced at the time (Chile started the process in the 1970s). I distinguish here between the two policy instruments of the reform: *adjustment* refers to short-term measures geared to the reduction of domestic disequilibrium, whereas *restructuring* pertains to medium- and long-run policies that aim at a change in development strategy (from inward to outward oriented), increase in domestic and international competition, privatization, and deregulation. By 1993 most LAC countries had introduced adjustment programs, but the majority still faced the restructuring process.

The economic crisis and reform have had severe social costs that have afflicted a considerable segment of the population. These costs include an increase in open unemployment, a decline in real wages, a reduction in social services, the elimination or reduction of subsidies for consumer goods, rising prices, and higher taxes, mostly of a regressive nature. Overall the main negative outcomes have been an expansion of poverty in the region and deterioration in social protection. The burden of social costs has not been equally distributed across society, but has particularly harmed labor and the lowest income strata.

So far the long-term outcomes of economic reform appear to be positive in most countries that have thoroughly implemented it: together with an economic recovery and stability, there has been an improvement in social indicators, which in a few countries have recuperated or surpassed the levels of 1980. But such positive results do not justify the unequal distribution of the burden; compensatory policies are still required to protect the most vulnerable groups during the transition. There have been varying lengths of time for the transitions and diverse approaches to social costs.

To alleviate the hardship some countries have implemented such ad hoc policies as safety nets, targeting of the most vulnerable groups, and social pacts to achieve a more equitable distribution of the burden and the eventual fruits of economic recovery. Because most LAC countries still have to undergo the restructuring process, the handling of social costs and compensatory policies will become even more important in the rest of the 1990s, a point now stressed by several international and regional lending and development agencies. The democratization process in LAC, if it continues, suggests that moderate and social-cost-conscious approaches will prevail in the future.

Social security should play a crucial role in compensating for the social costs of economic reform. It broadly embraces a variety of programs designed to help individuals cope with social risks that affect the income and health of the labor force and the population as a whole—such as old-age, disability, death, common sickness, maternity, occupational hazards, and unemployment. Specific programs are (1) social insurances, which include pensions for retirement, disability, and survivors; monetary and medical care in case of common sickness and maternity; similar benefits for occupational accidents and diseases; unemployment compensation; and family allowances; (2) public assistance for the segment of the population not covered by social insurances; and (3) public health and other social services. Theoretically all these programs should be coordinated or integrated to provide universal protection to the population and should be countercyclical, i.e., expand in times of economic recession.

Unfortunately, few countries in LAC have developed an all-encompassing social security umbrella; most of them cover only a minority of the population through some social insurances that are not normally integrated, and even fewer countries provide interconnected public assistance and health programs to assist the noninsured majority. The oldest, most advanced social security systems in the region began to suffer serious financial and administrative problems in the 1960s and 1970s that became aggravated by the economic crisis of the 1980s. The result was a decline in revenues and a rise in expenditures that worsened the financial disequilibrium of the social security system. Eventually these problems became widespread in the region, and by the early 1990s there was a social security crisis in most LAC countries.

The structural limitations of these systems, compounded by the worsening macroeconomic environment in the 1980s, made social security incapable of alleviating the social distress derived from the economic crisis and the reform. For instance, neither the increasing number of unemployed and informal workers nor the poor have found protection in the current system, because social insurance does not normally cover these groups and because public assistance and public health programs were cut as part of the adjustment policy. Furthermore, the systems face growing financial deficits because of declining payroll contributions, negative investment yields, and increasing evasion, payment delays, and state debt. To cope with deficits many social security systems allowed a deterioration in both the real value of their pensions and the quality of their health-care services. As a result, the minority covered by social insurance began to suffer social costs, too.

At the beginning of the 1990s the pressure from international lending agencies, the financial limitations imposed on governments, and the success of the Chilean reform model—a pioneer of privatization—led to a growing movement of social security reform in the region. There is little doubt that the system will change; the question is which model will prevail: the continuation of a public social security program (although modified in key aspects), privatization, or a mixed model combining elements of both. The reform should also help make social security (or alternative institutions) better able to cope with the social costs of economic reform.

This book focuses on the process of social security reform in terms of the economic crisis, adjustment/restructuring, and the need to cope with social costs. It does not break new ground on the process of economic reform and its social effects, but it provides a general review of these issues as a base for analyzing the social security crisis and its ongoing transformation.

Chapter 1 summarizes the debt crisis, describes the policies of adjustment/restructuring, and measures social costs according to a series of statistical indicators. Examples are drawn from a number of LAC countries.

Chapter 2 analyzes the problems faced by social security prior to the economic crisis and reform of the 1980s and how the crisis aggravated those problems. Specific issues discussed in this chapter are low population coverage and the difficulties of extending protection to vulnerable groups such as informal, rural, and unemployed workers; high and regressive payroll contributions, noncompliance, and poor investment yields; generous benefits and entitlement conditions that eventually had to be cut; increasing costs of health care; excessive administrative expenditures; and worsening disequilibria of the systems.

Chapter 3 first elaborates a typology of reform models in both pension and health-care programs and then studies in depth the various types of reforms in eight countries: Argentina, Chile, Colombia, Costa Rica, Jamaica, Mexico, Peru, and Uruguay.

The final chapter extracts lessons from the case studies, evaluates the result of the Chilean model of privatization and its replicability in the rest of LAC, and provides recommendations in three areas: (1) redefinition of the roles of the principal social security actors (the state, the private sector, and intermediate bodies); (2) avenues for expanding coverage to the informal and rural sectors and ways to cope with unemployment; and (3) measures needed to ensure financially viable social security systems in the future.

The initial version of this study was prepared for the Social Security Department of the International Labour Office (ILO) in Geneva and completed at the end of 1991. A thorough revision and updating of the manuscript (particularly on the crucial Chapter 3) was undertaken one year later. A third version was completed in mid-1993 in response to valuable criticism and suggestions from an anonymous referee for Lynne Rienner Publishers. The ILO provided copious information to prepare the first version and graciously authorized the publication of the study, but it is not responsible for its content and views. The study also benefited, in its various stages, from a sabbatical leave granted by the University of Pittsburgh for 1990–1991; an Alexander von Humboldt Stiftung Senior Research Prize and the support of the Max-Planck Institut für Ausländisches und Internationales Sozialretch, both for 1991–1992; my participation in the International Conference on Social Security Reform organized by the Institute of the Americas in 1993; and research trips to Argentina, Chile, Colombia, Ecuador, and Mexico from 1990–1993, conducted as part of consultantships with USAID, UNDP, the Inter-American Foundation, the Inter-American Development Bank, the Friedrich-Ebert Stiftung, and CIEDESS-Chile. My research assistant, Rafael Tamayo, provided valuable help in gathering bibliographic information and materials for Chapter 1, and my secretaries, Mimi Ranallo and Jackie Janos, typed several versions of the manuscript. Of course, none of these institutions or persons is responsible for what is said herein.

I gratefully dedicate this book to all the social security technicians and administrators in LAC who provided the valuable information I needed to write it, with the hope that my work may contribute to a reform of social security that makes it more universal, equitable, financially solid, and responsive to the alleviation of the social costs of economic reform in the region.

Carmelo Mesa-Lago

1

The Economic Crisis, Restructuring and Adjustment, and Social Costs

The Antecedents and Implementation of the Economic Reform

In the 1970s economic policies stemming from the Keynesian Revolution, which spread all over the world, resulted in a period of crisis and, in the 1980s, were replaced in many countries by neoliberal policies founded on classical economic theory. The new trends originated in the industrialized countries of North America and Western Europe, and particularly in the United States and Britain, although Chile's reform was also important.

New policies were adopted by international financial agencies and applied to developing countries. The impressive success of the newly industrializing countries in Southeast Asia, largely based on those policies, offered a model for the developing world. The downfall of real socialism in Eastern Europe and the USSR and the introduction of market-oriented policies in all these countries further discredited central planning and state ownership of the means of production, while providing new impetus to the reform. In Western Europe even Social Democratic and Socialist governments (e.g., France, Spain) have adhered to these policies. And some of the remaining bastions of state *dirigisme* and the welfare state have recently shifted course, with the second conservative Swedish government in the last 60 years announcing a dramatic shift toward privatization and a retrenchment from social welfare.

The vast majority of countries in Latin America and the Caribbean (LAC) have followed the new trend. Recent publications from diverse international and regional organizations acknowledge the universalization of these policies and the need for introducing some of them to LAC. But there is no consensus on specific measures, the roles to be played by the state and the market, and the policies' effects and ways to tackle their social costs (IDB 1990; ECLAC 1988; García 1991; World Bank 1991). It has also been noted that the application of these policies is more difficult in LAC than in developed countries (except in Eastern Europe and the former USSR). For example, because LAC economies usually combine modern and traditional sectors, the reform creates dual problems, adversely affecting the modern sector (at least initially) and expanding social exclusion. Further, the debt crisis in LAC has put a heavy burden on their economies, led to a net transfer of resources abroad, and resulted in poor access to fresh credit; despite adjustment policies, inflation increased in the region and in some countries reached the level of hyperinflation; and LAC is less integrated into the world market, as a result of which the magnitude of the reform's adverse consequences are higher (García 1991).

In the 1970s the inward model of development in LAC, based on the increasing economic role of the state and import-substitution industrialization, appeared to be exhausted. Among net-oil-importing countries the oil shocks of 1973 and 1979 dramatically increased import costs; instead of tightening their belts these countries continued their expansionary policies and borrowed heavily, mostly from foreign private banks. Oil-exporting countries thought that the price of oil would keep climbing and increased their investment and expenditures based on external credit. International private banks, overflowing with petro-dollars, moved fast to lend that money to countries in need, disregarding the risks involved. At the turn of the 1980s spiraling international interest rates, a world recession, and declining prices of raw materials (including oil) made the burden of servicing the debt in LAC heavier and the capacity to pay lower. In 1982 the Mexican request to renegotiate its foreign debt created an international panic that led to a virtual halt of new credit for all of LAC. International lending organizations (e.g., IMF, World Bank) became intermediaries for private bank lenders in negotiating the external debt, increased their bargaining leverage with borrowing countries, and conditioned new loans (both private and international) to the introduction of reforms (IDB 1985; ECLAC 1988).

Two different sets of policies were advocated: (1) short-term measures of internal *adjustment* and stabilization geared toward reducing the domestic disequilibrium and abating skyrocketing inflation; and (2) medium- or long-range policies of economic *restructuring* to promote an outward-oriented development strategy based on opening to and insertion into the world economy, increasing domestic and international competition, privatizing, and deregulating. Adjustment policies were initiated by most LAC countries in the first half of the 1980s, whereas restructuring policies (with one exception) began in the second half of the decade: 1975 in Chile; 1985 in Bolivia, Costa Rica, and Mexico; 1989 in Argentina, Jamaica, and Venezuela; and 1990–1991 in Colombia, Peru, Brazil (although some elements were introduced earlier), and Uruguay. The effects of adjustment policies were felt in these countries mostly in the first half of the 1980s, but for most countries (except Chile) the impact of restructuring is just beginning to be felt. In some cases adjustment policies were mixed with some elements of restructuring, making their respective effects difficult to separate. Furthermore, only Chile has passed the transitional stage of restructuring and is now in a consolidation stage, whereas the remaining countries are still in or entering the transitional stage. The full effects of restructuring will be felt in forthcoming years. Only the experience of Chile can be fully evaluated; hence, only preliminary assessments can be made of Bolivia, Costa Rica, and Mexico. Furthermore, the restructuring policies of all these countries, although coinciding on their fundamental elements, have diverged on important aspects: Chile's approach has been the most radical; it used a "shock treatment," and the transition lasted longer and provoked the worst social effects; the other three countries (probably learning from the Chilean experience) applied more gradual, moderate policies, and the transitional stage appears to be shorter and the social costs less (García 1991).

According to the World Bank, the reform must be comprehensive and steady; partial attempts are doomed to fail, and capricious reversals are harmful. But I have already noted that there are diverse reform policies among countries, and I will show later that some countries have modified their policies to correct errors or reduce excessively harmful effects. Furthermore, agreement on some specific policies is not complete among the international agencies supporting the reform. The World Bank also advises policymakers to be realistic in both the sources of financing the reform and expectations about its outcomes (World Bank 1991). However, the reform is expected to be comprehensive and radical, so it will require substantial outside funding not available for most LAC countries. In addition, if the reform outcomes are modest and painful it will be difficult to mobilize support, particularly among those most badly affected, who often constitute the majority of the population. The following pages summarize the main features of both adjustment and restructuring reforms, as advocated by international lending organizations, as well as diverse approaches tried in the region, their social costs, and the overall socioeconomic deterioration suffered by LAC in the 1980s.

The Policies of Economic Reform and Their Effects

Adjustment and Stabilization

A responsible fiscal policy that reduces or eliminates the government deficit is considered essential to reduce inflation to acceptable levels and to form the basis for restructuring and future steady, healthy growth. There is no agreement on whether to achieve that end by tax increases or by reduction in public expenditures. The latter can be implemented more easily and rapidly than a sensible tax reform and hence has been used more extensively. Common measures have been reductions in the public wage bill (by cutting employment, real wages, or both); restrictions in public credit and monetary emission; cuts in state subsidies to cover losses in state-owned enterprises (SOEs) as well as for consumer goods and services; and decreases in public expenditures, particularly social services. These drastic cuts have significantly contributed to rising unemployment, declining real wages, and a worsening situation for the poor. It has recently been acknowledged that the debt overhead is a drag on stabilization and should therefore be reduced. Tax reform is often obstructed in LAC because of inefficiencies in the system of collection and widespread evasion. Important principles of reform are that the tax base should be broad, the system simplified, and its efficacy improved; less emphasis is placed on taxation as a tool of income distribution.

Cuts in public expenditures and social services were widespread in LAC, particularly in the first half of the 1980s. On the revenue side there has been a shift from income to expenditure taxation (in 1990 the value-added tax (VAT) was in effect in 17 out of 25 countries); a reduction in taxes on corporate profits and dividends; an increase in social security contributions (in Chile the employer has not paid any since 1981); and the introduction of user fees, particularly in health-care services (IDB 1990; Williamson 1990; García 1991).

Outward-Oriented Development, Trade Liberalization, and Integration into the Global Economy

Protection of inefficient domestic industry is considered to create costly economic distortions and eventually penalize exports and impoverish the economy. Therefore the new strategy calls for a country to open itself to international capital, goods, and services and to establish an outward-oriented economy with exports (particularly nontraditional ones) as the engine of growth. Increasing competition within the country and from outside is required to make the domestic economy more efficient and promote technological innovation. The incentive system related to relative prices should be changed to favor expansion of investment and production of export goods. Easy access to intermediate inputs at competitive prices (in order to promote exports) and the elimination of taxes on exports are both encouraged. Trade liberalization implies a move away from administrative controls, and common markets should eliminate internal tariffs. Competitive exchange rates (set by market forces) are seen as essential to export development. Restrictions on the entry of foreign direct investment should be eliminated because such investment brings needed capital, technology, and skills, thus contributing to increases in production and employment. Debt-equity swaps are encouraged to reduce the debt and promote foreign investment.

These policies have been adopted by several LAC countries but with varying degrees of rapidity and depth. In Chile there was an abrupt elimination of import restrictions that, after decades of protectionism, led to widespread industrial shutdowns (resulting in huge unemployment and trade deficits); in the 1980s, because of the crisis, tariffs were increased somewhat and the Chilean government reduced them later when the economy improved; the exchange rate policy was changed several times as well. Other countries (e.g., Costa Rica) have shown more caution by reducing tariffs gradually, giving the state a key role in supporting new technologies and penetrating external markets, and avoiding drastic deindustrialization (and huge unemployment) by reconverting traditional industry with the aid of credit. Concerning foreign investment, Chile not only has enforced the most liberal policy but also has been a pioneer in debt-equity swaps—an approach that eventually reduced the external debt. Previous policies involving excessive regulation of foreign direct investment appear to be gone, and there is considerably less discrimination between foreign and domestic investment; some countries are giving preference to foreign capital that fills a domestic void. Recently Mexico modified its foreign investment law, allowing an increase in the share of foreign ownership and opening areas previously reserved for state or private domestic capital. Although Mexico is also supporting debt-equity swaps, the extent to which it does so and the corresponding debt reduction are much less than in Chile (Williamson 1990; World Bank 1991; García 1991).

Restructuring the Public Sector: Privatization and Deregulation

According to the World Bank, both the market and the government have important roles to play in the new model; hence, the supposed dichotomy between interventionist and laissez-faire approaches is judged to be false. Nevertheless, restructuring involves a withdrawal of the state from those areas in which the market performs well (e.g., production, delivery of goods and certain services) and a shift of public action to areas where the market proves to be inadequate (e.g., protecting the poor). Under a "market-friendly" approach the government should allow the markets to function properly by creating an "enabling environment," or stable macroeconomic foundation (e.g., infrastructure, laws, institutions), and restoring confidence in the private sector. Privatization of SOEs is justified on the belief that private enterprises are managed more efficiently because of competition, the threat of bankruptcy, and the profit incentive, whereas SOEs are often heavily subsidized and do not face competition. In addition, privatization can help reduce subsidies and balance the budget, generate short-run revenue needed for higher state priorities (e.g., modernization, paying the debt), and prevent inefficient investment in the long run. However, privatization should not be an end by itself but rather a means to use scarce resources more efficiently. This in turn requires state intervention both to curtail the formation of private monopolies and the improper operation of private enterprises and to promote competition. Furthermore, privatization must be accompanied by such other measures as deregulation, trade liberalization, correction of distortions, etc. The government should stop fixing prices of goods and services, the interest rate, and the exchange rate, all of which should be set by the market. Deregulation of the domestic financial system relies on the interest rate as its key mechanism; market-fixed interest rates should help prevent a misallocation of capital that results from a bureaucratic allocation of credit based on arbitrary criteria. Deregulation of the labor market makes it more flexible, thereby facilitating labor mobility, reducing labor costs, and allowing technological innovation.

Chile has been at the vanguard of privatization since the mid-1970s; SOEs were sold in the mid-1980s at prices below market value, with the government providing 95 percent of credit at zero real interest. Privatization has not been limited to SOEs but has extended to social security (pensions) and health care. In other countries privatization has been delayed or been more limited or selective. Jamaica's divestment of SOEs began in 1981. Costa Rica started the process in 1985 and by the end of the decade had privatized 35 enterprises of CODESA but retained the rest. Mexico's 1,155 SOEs in 1983 were reduced to 310 by 1990, but only half were privatized (accounting for about 20 percent of the SOEs' total assets), and the rest were transferred to state and local governments or merged with other public institutions; many of the remaining SOEs have been made more efficient. In Uruguay a few SOEs were shut down, and there has been a reprivatization of financial institutions. The process began in Argentina only in 1990–1991. Deregulation of the labor market was profound in Chile, aided by an authoritarian government that drastically reduced union power, prohibited strikes, and suspended or intervened in collective bargaining. Bolivia also curtailed unions and suspended collective bargaining, although to a lesser extent. Other countries have approached this issue in a more democratic manner, facilitated by a social consensus (Williamson 1990; World Bank 1991; García 1991).

Social Costs, Distribution of the Burden, and Compensatory Policies

I have previously noted the difficulties involved in separating the effects of adjustment and restructuring policies and in assessing their impact in countries that are still in the transition stage. But it is widely recognized that both sets of policies have induced substantial social costs that have not been equitably distributed among various sectors of society. For instance, capital and business have benefitted from labor market flexibility, elimination or reduction of corporate taxes and employers' social security contributions, and the sale of SOEs at very low prices and with credit facilities. (Another business sector, however, has been adversely affected by the elimination of protectionism.) Labor and the poor have suffered from cuts in employment and easier dismissal of non-needed workers, the elimination of subsidies for consumer goods, price increases for essential consumer goods, a reduction in social services, the introduction of user fees, shifts in taxation (usually toward more regressive consumer taxes), and a decline in real wages (aggravated in authoritarian countries by the control of unions and suspension of collective bargaining). The rationale behind these policies is that they are needed to solve the crises and as a precondition for reaching future high rates of growth, productive employment, and income. So far the experiences of a few countries that have applied both radical and moderate types of policies (Chile, Costa Rica, Mexico) suggest that the outcome is eventually positive. However, that fact does not justify the heavy burden imposed on labor and the poor.

Recently some international lending agencies have acknowledged the social costs of the reform and recommended policies to ameliorate them: (1) cushion the negative effects of adjustment on the most adversely affected groups (particularly the poor) through special programs of assistance and through maintenance or expansion of selective social programs; (2) distribute the burden of adjustment more equitably between labor and business, preferably through a social pact or, if that fails, by direct state action; (3) develop a long-run policy of "investment in people" because the market alone does not generally ensure a safety net for certain parts of society (especially the poorest); hence, the government should invest in nutrition, education, health care, family planning, and poverty alleviation; and (4) increase the degree of equality in distribution (particularly in countries with pronounced inequalities), not through income transfers (except in the case of safety nets for vulnerable groups) but by specific public social services (IDB 1990; World Bank 1991).

As stated earlier, LAC countries show important differences in the length of the transition, the magnitude of the social costs, and the distribution of the burden. In Chile the transition took approximately 10 years, and costs in terms of social exclusion and unemployment were very high (thus imposing the heaviest burden on labor and the poor). These negative effects were partly associated with the authoritarian nature of the regime but also with the excessive rapidity, depth, and number of errors of its policies. On the other hand, the eventual outcome of the Chilean reform— in economic growth, creation of productive employment, and recuperation of prereform wage levels—has been the best so far. An accurate comparison of the effects of the reform in Chile with those of other countries is not possible at this time because only Chile has completed the process. But so far in Costa Rica (and to a lesser extent in Mexico and Bolivia) the length of the transition appears to be shorter, the social costs lighter, and the burden more equitably distributed. Not only has restructuring in these countries been implemented in a more gradual and moderate fashion, but it has also been accompanied by compensatory policies to alleviate social costs and/or attempts to reach social consensus. (However, the economic recuperation—in terms of growth rates and productive employment creation—does not appear as vigorous in these countries as in Chile.) Costa Rica launched an employment program; strengthened existing health care, nutrition, and welfare programs for marginal urban and rural groups; introduced a housing program; and adjusted salaries of the lowest income groups proportionally higher than those of middle and high income groups (the minimum wage has not declined during restructuring). Bolivia established an emergency social fund to help poor groups. In Mexico a social pact was signed between business, labor, and the government to better distribute costs, and support has been given to the "social sector" (e.g., self-managed enterprises, cooperatives) to reduce social costs. (It should be noted that substantial international aid to Mexico facilitated a simultaneous process of restructuring and expansion, thus helping to reduce social costs.) Actually, after the crisis of 1981–1983 Chile adopted more moderate policies (e.g., increase in tariffs, state intervention in banks and some enterprises to avoid bankruptcy), launched special social programs targeted to help the poor (e.g., emergency employment, minimal social protection), and shifted public expenditures toward nutrition and primary health care, targeting the low-income mother/infant group. These policies helped alleviate costs somewhat and since 1990 have been expanded by the new democratic government that has also enacted a tax reform and tried to increase social consensus.

With the process of democratization virtually universal in LAC, the possibility of replicating the radical Chilean approach of 1974–1989 throughout the region appears slim; therefore the more gradual, moderate, social-cost-conscious approach should be more feasible unless the positive trends in economic recovery already achieved are reversed in the future.

In summary, although more time and research are needed to reach sound conclusions, the available evidence indicates that adjustment, and particularly restructuring, can be applied so as to minimize their negative effects on the most vulnerable sectors of society. Social security should play an important role in compensating the social costs of adjustment, but it should be implemented judiciously to avoid harming the process of economic recovery.

The Deterioration of Socioeconomic Conditions in LAC from 1980 to 1990

Table 1.1 presents a series of indicators that show both the seriousness of the economic crisis in LAC and its effects. I do not attempt herein to

separate the effects of the crisis itself from those of adjustment and restructuring policies but only to show the deteriorating socioeconomic conditions in the region from 1980–1990.

One important cause of the crisis has been the rapid growth of the external debt and the heavy burden of its service. In 1985 the average dis-
bursed debt was three and a half times higher than the value of exports
and services. Although such burden had declined in 1990 relative to 1985,
in 41 percent of the countries the burden in 1990 was about twice as high
as that in 1980, and in 23 percent it was from three to six times higher. To
service the debt and follow adjustment programs, the states sharply reduced their expenditures: the average growth rate of government consumption dramatically slowed down in 90 percent of the countries in the
1980s, and the rate was actually negative in one-third of them. The decline in private consumption followed a similar pattern. There was not
only a sharp cut in gross domestic investment (from 23 percent to 16 percent from 1980–1984) but also a negative net transfer of LAC capital
abroad that from 1982–1990 amounted to U.S. $234 billion, compared
with a positive net transfer to LAC of U.S. $95 billion from 1973–1981
(ECLAC 1990a). As a result, the real regional GDP per capita declined by
9.6 percent from 1981–1990, regressing to the 1976–1977 level; 77 percent of the LAC countries suffered a decrease in GDP per capita, and in
two-thirds of them the loss was worse than the regional average.

The regional average rate of inflation increased 26 times from
1980–1990. Whereas in 1980 only one-third of the LAC countries had an
annual rate higher than 25 percent, in 1990 two-thirds exceeded that rate
and four countries suffered from hyperinflation. Those most affected by
inflation have been the lowest income groups, particularly in urban areas.
Real wages shrank: in 1989 the average wage in two-thirds of the countries was below the 1980 level, and the minimum wage (affecting the lowest income strata) was below the 1980 level in 83 percent of the countries.
The regional average open urban unemployment rate rose from 7.3 percent to 10.5 percent from 1980–1985, and although it declined to 8.3 percent in 1989 it was still above the 1980 level; in two-thirds of the countries the 1989 rate was above that of 1980. The jobless situation would
have been worse if it were not for an expansion of informal employment
from 23.8 percent to 29.5 percent of the nonagricultural labor force, or
from 29 percent to 30 percent of the urban labor force. In 1989 half of the
employment was concentrated in informal and macroenterprises (Tokman
1986; García 1991). Similarly underemployment that had declined from
1950–1980 worsened in the 1980s. According to the Inter-American Development Bank (IDB), even if the gross domestic product (GDP) were to
reach 3 or 4 percent per year in the 1990s (three to four times the average
of the 1980s), open unemployment would continue to be serious and underemployment difficult to reverse.

Table 1.1   Effects of the Economic Crisis, Adjustment, and Restructuring in LAC: 1980–1990

Countries	Disbursed Debt (% of Exports & Services)			Consumption: Average Annual Growth (%)				GDP p/c (cumulative %)
				Government		Private		
	1980	1985	1990	1965–1980	1981–1989	1965–1980	1981–1989	1981–1990
Argentina	275	491	499	3.2	-1.3	2.8	0.3	-24.3
Barbados	92[b]	154[b]	506[b,c]	•	•	•	•	8.0
Bolivia	227	458	389	8.2	-1.9	3.1	1.7	-23.3
Brazil	323	379	351	6.8	7.1	8.7	2.4	-5.5
Chile	188	457	167	4.0	-0.2	0.9	1.1	9.2
Colombia	128	314	209	6.7	3.6	5.8	2.9	16.2
Costa Rica	184	307	155	6.8	0.9	5.1	3.0	-5.0
Dominican Rep.	171	281	205	0.2	1.8	7.8	0.8	-2.2
Ecuador	144	246	363	12.2	-2.2	7.2	1.9	-4.6
El Salvador	97	219	253	7.0	3.1	4.2	0.3	-15.3
Guatemala	61	232	200	6.2	2.4	5.1	0.5	-18.0
Haiti	95	178	336	1.9	-1.4	2.4	0.3	-22.3
Honduras	147	309	316	6.9	4.8	4.8	2.2	-14.2
Jamaica	198[b]	661[b]	451[b,c]	9.7	0.1	2.9	2.1	1.9
Mexico	244	357	258	8.5	2.1	5.9	0.7	-8.4
Nicaragua	369	1433	2250	6.1	9.5	2.2	-5.6	-40.8
Panama	141	197	•	7.4	1.0	4.6	1.4	-18.3
Paraguay	152	163	143	5.1	4.8	6.6	1.9	0.4
Peru	207	362	416	6.3	-1.5	4.9	1.6	-30.2
Trinidad & Tobago	32[b]	69[b]	142[b,c]	8.9	1.4	3.4	-7.3	-13.8
Uruguay	140	391	338	3.2	1.2	2.3	0.0	-6.7
Venezuela	148	218	161	•	1.8	•	0.7	-19.9
Average	222	352	292	•	•	•	•	-9.6

Sources: Based on ECLAC 1990a; IDB 1990; World Bank 1991.
Notes: a. Worst point.
b. Percent of exports only.
c. 1989.
d. Rio de Janeiro.
e. 1988.
f. 1977.
g. 1984
• Signifies data not available.

Table 1.1   continued

Inflation Rate (%) (December–December)			Real Wages (1980=100)				Urban Unemployment (% of Labor Force)			Poverty Incidence (% of Total Population)	
			Average		Minimum						
1980	1985	1990	1985	1989	1985	1989	1980	1982–1986[a]	1989	1979–1981	1986–1988
87.6	385.4	1832.5	107.2	81.5	113.1	69.9	2.6	6.1	7.8	10	16
16.1	2.4	1.9	104.9	108.6	•	•	10.8	18.7	16.5	•	•
23.9	8170.5	17.8	96.1	95.6	33.2	37.2[d]	7.1	8.5	7.0	•	•
95.3	228.0	2359.9	112.7[d]	107.2[d]	83.9	68.6	6.2	7.1	3.3	45	45
31.2	26.4	29.4	93.5	102.9	63.4	63.5	11.7	20.0	7.2	•	•
26.5	22.3	31.0	114.6	119.1	108.0	105.0	9.7	14.0	9.6	42	42
17.8	11.1	22.4	92.2	85.7	112.2	110.2	6.0	9.9	3.8	24	27
4.6	28.4	75.9	79.1	60.8	80.2	77.8	•	•	•	•	•
14.5	24.4	48.3	•	•	60.8	43.7	5.7	10.4	14.3	•	•
18.6	30.8	19.9	•	•	63.4	35.6	•	•	•	•	•
9.1	31.5	50.1	94.7	83.3	94.0	78.5[e]	2.2	14.2	7.2	71	73
15.3	17.4	13.2	•	•	88.3	97.6	•	•	•	•	•
11.5	4.2	25.3	•	•	90.7	74.0	8.8	11.7	13.0	•	•
28.6	23.9	17.2[c]	•	•	•	•	13.8	12.5	8.7[e]	•	•
29.8	63.7	30.2	76.6	75.8	67.0	46.9	4.5	6.6	2.9	40[f]	37[g]
24.8	334.3	8500.0	•	•	47.3	•	18.3	•	•	•	•
14.4	0.4	0.8	•	•	100.8	99.8	10.4	15.7	20.0	42	41
8.9	23.1	42.7	89.7	108.3	99.4	136.5	3.9	5.1	6.1	•	•
										53	60
59.7	158.3	8291.5	77.6	41.5	54.2	23.2	7.1	10.1	7.9		
16.6	6.6	10.8	125.0	89.9	•	•	9.9	13.7	•	•	•
42.8	83.0	129.8	68.1	72.8	94.1	78.6	7.4	15.5	8.6	15	20
19.6	5.7	32.2	•	•	95.3	77.1	6.6	14.3	9.7	25	32
56.1	274.1	1491.5	•	•	84.2	75.4	7.3	10.5	8.3	35	37

The burden of adjustment fell disproportionately on the poor, the aged, women, and the young. The number of poor in Latin America increased 34 percent from 1980–1989 (ECLAC 1990b). The incidence of poverty rose in 10 countries from 35 percent at the end of the 1970s to 37 percent in 1986–1988; in almost two-thirds of them the incidence was above the regional average. These data exclude seven of the least developed countries, where poverty should be worse.

The adjustment-induced retrenchment in public expenditures for social services (particularly in the first half of the 1980s) reduced the safety net for the most vulnerable segments of the population. Although some recovery in outlays took place at the end of the decade, there was still a reduction in the overall level of and access to social services and a deterioration in their quality (IDB 1990). Data available for only 10 LAC countries show that in 60 percent of them the share of central government expenditures in social security, welfare, health care, and similar public services was lower in 1989 than in 1972 (World Bank 1991). But if the situation at the end of the 1970s (when expenditures were higher than in 1972) were compared with the period 1984–1985 (when the crisis was worse) the picture would probably be worse. For instance, from 1980–1985 the health-care share of public expenditures fell from 9 percent to 5.5 percent; furthermore, from 1978–1984 public health expenditures per capita by the central government (excluding social insurance) declined in 22 out of 24 LAC countries (Musgrove 1986). Scattered data from individual countries confirm the decline in the share of social service expenditures in total central government expenditures: Chile by -16.4 percent from 1980–1983; Colombia from 39.7 percent to 30.1 percent from 1984–1988 (social security plus health declined from 15.2 percent to 12.9 percent); Costa Rica from 54.3 percent to 41.5 percent from 1979–1984 (social security plus health went from 36.2 percent to 26.3 percent); Jamaica from 35.1 percent to 24.2 percent from 1979/80–1985/86 (social security plus health went from 9.1 percent to 7.8 percent); and Mexico from 2.2 percent to 0.6 percent from 1981–1983 (IDB 1988; Meller 1990; Williamson 1990; Boyd 1988).

Some data on health status in LAC (life expectancy, infant mortality) suggest continuous improvement between 1970 and 1989. However, this might be the result of inaccuracies in the data, too short a period of observation, or lag times in responding to the decline in investment and health-care maintenance (IDB 1990; World Bank 1991). Furthermore, a comparison of such indicators in 1980 and 1989 might reveal a deterioration. A PAHO study has offered evidence of worsening health among vulnerable groups of the population in terms of health indicators, e.g., a rise in infant mortality caused by diarrhea and either an increase in the infant mortality rate or a slowdown in the rate of decrease (Musgrove 1989).

This chapter has shown the grave deterioration of economic and social conditions in LAC during the 1980s. The rest of this study analyzes the impact of the crisis, readjustment, and restructuring on social security and discusses ways that social security can alleviate social costs without harming economic recovery in the 1990s.

2

Social Security: The Problems of Coping with Social Costs

Historical and Evolutionary Framework

After the industrialized countries, the LAC region was the first to introduce social security programs, ahead of most other developing countries in Asia and Africa. Table 2.1 shows that the first contingency to be covered was occupational accidents and diseases: by 1920, 11 LAC countries had such a program, and by 1970 only three countries—from the non-Latin Caribbean (NLC)—lacked it. The timing of sickness/maternity and pension programs was similar: by 1950 close to half of the countries had such schemes in operation, and by 1989 all countries (with the exception of two in the Caribbean concerning sickness/maternity) had introduced both programs. Family allowances and unemployment compensation did not begin until the late 1930s and by 1989 were functioning in only seven countries (all of them in Latin America, with the exception of one unemployment program in the NLC). In general, social security programs in Latin America appeared much earlier than in the NLC.

Three groups of LAC countries can be identified in the process of the historical evolution of social security: pioneer, intermediate, and latecomer (this section is based on Mesa-Lago 1989c, 1991b, 1991c).

Pioneer Group

In five Latin American countries—the most developed of the region (Chile, Uruguay, Argentina, Cuba, and Brazil, which together account for 15 percent of the total number of LAC countries)—pension programs were established in the 1920s and 1930s. These programs originally protected the best-organized occupational groups or sectors of the labor force but gradually incorporated wider and less powerful groups; currently their population coverage is about 70 percent or higher and is virtually universal if noncontributory programs for the indigent are taken into account.

Table 2.1   Historical Inception of Social Security Programs in LAC: 1920–1989
(Number of Countries with Programs in Operation)

	Implementation of First Law								
Programs	1920	1930	1940	1950	1960	1970	1980	1989	No Program
Occupational Risks	11	19	24	26	28	30	30	30	3[a]
Sickness/Maternity[b]	0	2	7	16	19	22	30	32	2[a]
Old age, Disability/ Survivors	0	4	7	13	16	27	34	34	0
Family Allowances	0	0	1	3	6	7	7	7	26
Unemployment	0	0	1	2	3	5	5	7	26

Source: Based on US-SSA 1990 and ISSA 1990–1991.
Notes: a. Excludes Suriname for lack of data.
b. Cash or medical care or both.

Chile and Brazil were also pioneers in the introduction of sickness insurance at about the same time as pensions (as were Chile and Cuba in maternity programs). Both programs were delayed in Argentina and Uruguay (and sickness insurance delayed in Cuba) until as late as the 1960s, partly because of the strong development of health care through mutual aid societies, cooperatives, and trade unions. With the exception of Cuba, all these countries established unemployment and family-allowance programs between the 1930s and 1960s, most of them following the same pattern of evolution as the other schemes. Therefore the social security systems in these countries evolved in a fragmented manner, leading to numerous independent subsystems (in terms of both covered risks and population), each with its own laws, administration, financing, and benefits and each lacking overall coordination.

There were important and usually unjustified differences among all the subsystems (e.g., in terms of their degrees of coverage, conditions for entitlement, benefits available, state subsidies), resulting in considerable stratification. The overall system coverage had a pyramidal shape: relatively small groups were well protected at the apex and to a lesser extent at the center, whereas the majority of the population, at the base, endured the worst protection. As groups in the center became better organized they were able to obtain some benefits previously reserved for those at the top. The cost of these programs became excessive—22–56 percent of wages and 9–11 percent of GDP—because of the universalization of coverage, the generous conditions and benefits, maturation of the pension programs (the bulk of social security expenditures goes to pensions), aging of the population, and high life expectancy. All of these factors led to actuarial and financial imbalances in many subsystems.

Several technical studies recommended the unification and standardization of the subsystems as well as the eradication of costly privileges, but the needed reform was blocked by the powerful pressure groups. In the 1960s, 1970s, and 1980s political changes in the pioneer countries reinforced the power of the state vis-à-vis those groups, thus facilitating the reform. In Cuba and Brazil almost the entire system was unified; in Argentina and Uruguay a new central agency integrated or coordinated the various groups into a uniform system; and in Chile a new private system was created while most of the remains of the old system were coordinated and standardized and the old privileges virtually eliminated. Chile's model of privatization has been influential in the region but has not been replicated in toto so far.

All countries in this group have moved from partially funded pension programs to pay-as-you-go programs and are heavily subsidized by the state; Chile's new system, however, is fully funded. The cited reforms occurred before the economic crisis and adjustment/restructuring policies of the 1980s, but the deteriorating financial conditions of several of these programs, combined with the state incapacity to continue the subsidies, have made such programs targets of the adjustment/restructuring process.

Intermediate Group

In a second group of nine Latin American countries (26 percent of LAC countries, the second largest group) pension and sickness/maternity programs were founded mostly in the 1940s (except for two in the mid-1930s and one each in the 1950s and 1960s). Although Mexico was relatively industrialized, the other intermediate-group countries had poor industrial development and a predominant rural sector: Bolivia, Colombia, Costa Rica, Ecuador, Panama, Paraguay, Peru, and Venezuela. (The first three launched family allowances programs and two—Ecuador and recently Venezuela—unemployment programs.) This group was influenced by the new trends inspired by the ILO and the Beveridge Report of the 1940s and tried to avoid the errors suffered by the pioneers. In each country a general institute was charged with the task of eventually covering the entire population, but its action was initially limited to the capital and major cities (currently population coverage ranges from 13–60 percent in different countries). Furthermore, independent programs protecting the most powerful groups (particularly for pensions) evolved either before or after the creation of the general system. Still, fewer independent funds were formed than in the pioneer countries, so the degree of stratification in the intermediate group was smaller. Costa Rica was originally part of this group (because its system was introduced in the 1940s, its pension program has not matured completely, and its population is relatively young), but now Costa Rica is more like a member of the pioneer group because its population coverage is virtually universal, the financial burden of the system is quite heavy (36 percent of wages and 9 percent of GDP), and the life expectancy of its population is high.

Because pension programs in this group were introduced later, they are less mature and the bulk of social security expenditures goes to sickness/maternity. In addition, because of their relative unity and uniformity and their lower coverage of risks and population, these systems have only recently confronted the financial difficulties of the pioneers (their costs are lower: 16–24 percent of wages and 3–4 percent of GDP). Therefore they did not need radical reforms. Nevertheless, the countries heading this group (those with the widest coverage, growing maturity of pensions, and highest costs) began to face financial problems in the 1980s that were accelerated by the economic crisis. All but one country in this group use the scaled premium method in pensions (one uses the alternative method of assessment of constituent capitals), but some (like Peru and Mexico) are practically on pay-as-you-go. Currently most of them are experiencing actuarial disequilibrium, and some face financial imbalance in the short run. State subsidies to independent programs in the public sector, generous benefits, and liberal entitlement conditions have been targeted by adjustment policies in most of these countries.

Latecomer Group

This group embraces the majority of countries in LAC (59 percent of the total), including all in the NLC but only six in Latin America. Common characteristics are the late inception of their programs relative to the rest of the region and their relatively high degree of unity and uniformity.

The six Latin American countries in this group are among the least developed and most rural in the region: Haiti, Honduras, Nicaragua, El Salvador, Guatemala, and the Dominican Republic. Most of their pension programs were founded in the late 1960s or early 1970s (but one each in the 1940s and 1950s), so they are the least mature in the region. Their sickness/maternity schemes were launched in the late 1940s and 1950s (Haiti's law has not been enforced) and absorb the bulk of social security expenditures. None of these countries has unemployment or family-allowance programs. The general institute in each country covers all the insured (although civil servants and the armed forces may have independent programs), but population coverage is very low: it ranges from 4–13 percent, except for one case of 38 percent coverage. Furthermore, entitlement conditions in this subgroup tend to be the strictest in the region, benefits the most frugal, population the youngest, and life expectancy the lowest. Because of these factors the burden of social security financing is relatively light (11–18 percent of wages and 1–2 percent of GDP), and the majority of countries in this group did not face serious financial difficulties until recently. Their major problem is determining how to extend population coverage; a few of them (e.g., Nicaragua, Guatemala) have made

significant efforts to achieve that goal. Pension programs in these countries tend to use scaled premium methods, but there is not enough information to determine whether some of them are shifting to a pay-as-you-go
approach. In any case the economic crisis of the 1980s, aggravated by severe political instability in some cases, has induced actuarial disequilibrium and financial problems in several of these programs.

The NLC subgroup is made up of 14 countries that won their independence in the 1960s and 1970s. They have varying levels of development but are usually ahead of their Latin American counterparts; some
even surpass the level of countries in the intermediate group. Practically
all of these countries established a national health-care system prior to independence (following the British model) and social insurance programs
thereafter (including pensions and cash benefits for sickness/maternity in
most of them). Many of these systems show similarities with Costa Rica:
recent establishment of pensions, universal population coverage, relatively
young populations, and high life expectancy. Conversely, because the
NLC systems are even newer, their benefits usually meager, and investment more efficient than Costa Rica's, these NLC systems exhibit some
different features: their contributory burden is lighter (5–14 percent of
wages), their costs are lower, and some enjoy a sounder financial status.
However, the economic crisis and recent liberal social security policies in
some of them have created financial difficulties.

Major Problems Faced by Social Security

This section reviews the problems that LAC's social security systems confronted in the 1980s and discusses how they have been aggravated by the
economic crisis and reform. Specific problems to be analyzed herein are
(1) poor population coverage and lack of protection for the informal and
rural sectors, the unemployed, and other vulnerable groups; (2) burden-
some and regressive contributions, compounded with noncompliance; (3)
inefficient investment policies that have contributed to the decapitalization of funds; (4) liberal and unequitable benefits that ultimately had to be
curtailed; (5) high and increasing health-care costs; (6) heavy administrative expenditures and other managerial deficiencies; and (7) worsening actuarial and financial deficits. These problems made social security increasingly unable to cope with social costs and eventually led to the crisis
and the urgent need for reform.

Poor Coverage and Difficulties in Extending It

*Low population coverage and negative effects of the economic crisis and
reform.* In half of Latin America the social insurance sickness/maternity

scheme covers all the salaried employed labor force, whereas in the other half it covers only some of the employees, usually those in the public sector and in industry, mining, commerce, and financial services, excluding agriculture. In Cuba and Nicaragua all residents are covered, and in Chile and Costa Rica virtually the whole population is covered (through a combination of social insurance and welfare programs), except for those with high incomes who do not work. In the rest of Central America the statutory coverage is normally limited to the capital and the larger cities. In 13 countries the law protects the self-employed (with compulsory protection in only four and voluntary in nine), in 12 countries domestic servants are covered (compulsorily in nine), and practically all countries cover the dependents of insured persons (normally the wife or common-law wife and children, except in Haiti and Ecuador) and pensioners. In virtually all of the NLC (plus Cuba and Nicaragua) all residents have the legal right to medical and hospital care under either a national health system or the public health sector. In addition, social insurance provides monetary benefits for sickness/maternity in all but four countries. However, the law grants monetary benefits to the self-employed in only six countries (compulsorily in four) and to domestic servants in five countries.

Legal coverage for other risks is more restricted. All salaried employees are legally covered by pensions in almost two-thirds of the 34 countries in LAC, but only some of them are covered in the remaining one-third (once again, excluding agriculture). In 21 countries the law includes the self-employed (but compulsorily in only nine), and in 17 countries it covers domestic servants as well (compulsorily in 15). In eight countries the noninsured population is eligible for welfare (i.e., noncontributory pensions), compulsorily in six of them. For occupational risks 18 LAC countries provide coverage to all salaried employees and 12 to only some of them (agriculture and microenterprises are usually excluded). Only eight countries cover domestic servants and seven the self-employed (but completely and compulsorily in only two). Unemployment compensation programs, available in seven countries, cover all salaried employees in only two countries and only some in the rest; the self-employed and domestic servants are always excluded, as are agricultural workers in two countries. Family allowances (in seven countries) cover all salaried employees in five countries, but the self-employed and domestic servants are excluded (though the latter are included in one country).

Table 2.2 summarizes the legal exclusion of six important groups of workers from sickness/maternity (the program with the largest coverage). The unemployed and family workers are excluded in all countries but one; the self-employed, domestic servants, and temporary/casual workers are excluded in half of the countries; and rural salaried workers are excluded in two-fifths of the countries. Because most agricultural work is not salaried and permanent (but rather seasonal, self-employed, etc.) the bulk

Table 2.2   Groups of Workers Not Legally Covered by Social Insurance in LAC:
1987–1988

| | (Number of Countries) | | | | |
| | Legally Covered[a] | | | Legally | |
Groups of Workers	Mandatory	Voluntary	Total	Excluded[b]	Total
Unemployed	0	0	0	34	34
Unpaid Family	0	1	1	33	34
Self-employed	6	11	17	17	34
Domestic Servants	14[c]	2	16	18	34
Temporary/Casual	16	0	16	18	34
Rural	21[d]	0	21[d]	13[d]	34

Source: Mesa-Lago 1992c.
. Notes: a. Coverage in terms of (1) cash benefits in countries with national health systems
(all types of work are covered on benefits in kind) and (2) both cash and in-kind benefits in
countries with social insurance systems.
   b. In three Latin American countries "indigents" have the right to welfare benefits in kind.
   c. Only for maternity in two countries.
   d. Salaried employment; other forms of agricultural work (self-employment, small land-
owners, sharecropping, seasonal) usually excluded.

of the agricultural work force is not protected. With the exception of rural
workers, the groups in Table 2.2 are informal workers.

Table 2.3 presents the most recent and reliable statistics on coverage
of the economically active population (EAP) for pensions and of the total
population for sickness/maternity. Based on coverage of the EAP from
various years during the 1980s, the countries are ranked as follows:
80–100 percent in Cuba, Barbados, Jamaica, Brazil, and the Bahamas;
60–79 percent in Chile, Uruguay, Costa Rica (these three countries would
show a higher coverage if welfare programs were included), and Panama;
40–59 percent in Venezuela and Mexico; 20–39 percent in Peru,
Nicaragua, Colombia, Guatemala, and Ecuador; and 1–19 percent in Bolivia, Paraguay, Honduras, El Salvador, and the Dominican Republic.
Rankings in terms of coverage of the total population from 1985–1988 are
as follows: 80–100 percent in Brazil and Costa Rica (there are no statistics for the Bahamas, Barbados, Cuba, and Jamaica, but these four countries probably fit in this rank); 60–79 percent in Argentina, Uruguay,
Chile (if coverage of indigents and mutual aid societies were taken into
account, these three countries would show higher percentages); 40–59
percent in Mexico, Panama, and Venezuela; 20–39 percent in Peru,
Nicaragua, and Bolivia; and 1–19 percent in Paraguay, Colombia,
Guatemala, Honduras, El Salvador, and the Dominican Republic.

As previously noted, the highest coverage is found in the most developed countries, which also have the oldest programs (except in the NLC).
In 1980 the overall coverage of the population of Latin America was

Table 2.3   Total and Economically Active Population Covered by Social Security
in LAC: 1970–1988
(in Percentages)

	Economically Active Population			Total Population	
Countries	1970	1980	1985–88	1980	1985–88
Argentina	68.0	69.1	79.1[a]	78.9	74.3[a]
Bahamas	•	85.3	85.9	•	•
Barbados	75.3	79.8	96.9	•	•
Bolivia	9.0	18.5	16.9	25.4	21.4
Brazil	27.0	87.0	•	96.3	•
Chile	75.6	61.2	79.2	67.3	•
Colombia	22.2	30.4	30.2	15.2	16.0
Costa Rica	38.4	68.3	68.7	84.4[b]	83.1[b]
Cuba	88.7[c]	93.0[c]	•	100.0[c]	•
Dominican Rep.	8.9	11.6	10.2	•	4.2
Ecuador	14.8	21.3	25.8	9.2	13.4
El Salvador	8.4	11.6	•	6.2	•
Guatemala	27.0	33.1	27.1	14.2	13.1
Honduras	4.2	14.4	12.8[a]	7.3	10.3[a]
Jamaica	58.8	80.9	93.2	•	•
Mexico	28.1	42.0	40.2	53.4	53.7
Nicaragua	14.8	18.9	31.5	9.1	37.5
Panama	33.4	52.3	59.8	49.9	57.4
Paraguay	10.7	14.0	•	18.2	•
Peru	35.6	37.4	32.0[d]	15.7[d]	22.2[d]
Uruguay	95.4	81.2	73.0	57.9	60.5
Venezuela	24.4	49.8	54.3	45.2	49.9[e]

Source: Mesa-Lago 1991b, 1991c, 1992c.
Notes: a. 1984.
b. Includes coverage of the dispossessed (indigents).
c. Estimate based on legal coverage and population censuses.
d. Adjusted official figures.
e. 1983.
• Signifies data not available.

estimated to be 61 percent, but when Brazil (which accounts for more than half of the insured of the subregion) was excluded from the calculations, coverage dropped to less than 43 percent. Furthermore, in about half of the countries, coverage from 1985–1988 extended to less than one-third of the population and in seven countries less than one-fourth. Overall, though, the region leads the developing world in level of population coverage, and several of the LAC countries have reached levels similar to those of the developed world. But half of the Latin American countries have very low coverage, and based on the annual average rate of coverage expansion from 1960–1988 it would take 11 Latin American countries from 45 to 540 years to reach universal coverage.

Table 2.3 also indicates the negative impact of the economic crisis and the adjustment/restructuring on population coverage. From 1970–

1980 the covered EAP expanded in 19 countries and declined in two (Chile and Uruguay, because of the reform of their systems). Conversely, during the 1980s there were increases in eight countries, stagnation in four, and declines in six, and there was no spectacular expansion in coverage except for one country. Furthermore, the table does not show the trough in coverage because this trough occurred in the early years of the decade, when the crisis was at its worst. For instance, total population coverage in Costa Rica fell from 84.4 percent to 76.9 percent from 1980 to 1981 and in Uruguay from 57.9 percent to 53.7 percent from 1980–1984; total population coverage in the Dominican Republic decreased from 11.5 percent to 9.7 percent from 1980–1982 (Mesa-Lago 1992c). Legal mandates to extend coverage (such as in Peru from 1985–1987) have not been implemented because of the severity of the crisis. The table's data for the late 1980s show some recuperation in coverage but without a return to the precrisis level in many countries. Although some of these figures may be affected by statistical deficiencies, it is safe to conclude that significant increases in the openly unemployed and informal workers (those not legally covered by social insurance) as well as growing tax evasion were the major culprits in the declines in population coverage in the 1980s.

Structural barriers to extending coverage to informal and rural sectors. A structural barrier to the extension of coverage is the Bismarckian model of social insurance financed with wage contributions. The most developed countries, where the majority of the labor force is salaried, have been able to reach or approximate universal coverage; but the least developed countries, where the majority of the labor force is not salaried (i.e., self-employed, domestic servants, unpaid family workers, owners of macroenterprises, small farmers, and peasants), cannot expand coverage beyond the small proportion in the urban formal and rural modern sectors. As the informal sector grew in the 1980s, the possibility of expanding social insurance coverage became more remote. The cost of reaching universal coverage under the current model of social insurance (i.e., adding protection for the informal and rural sectors) would be unfeasible in many countries: from 11–39 percent of GDP in 13 of them (Mesa-Lago 1991c).

• Informal Sector. According to Table 2.4, the informal sector accounts for 20–62 percent of the EAP in nine LAC countries. I have shown that as a result of the crisis and adjustment/restructuring in the 1980s, the informal sector expanded in LAC and by 1985 reached almost one-third of the urban labor force. The percentage of coverage for the self-employed (one of the major components of the informal sector) ranges from 0.6–4 percent among five countries (Colombia, Mexico, Panama, Jamaica, and Peru) and from 12–48 percent among three others (Chile, Barbados, and

Table 2.4   Coverage of the Informal Sector by Social Insurance in Selected
Countries of LAC: 1980–1987

Countries	% EAP in the Informal Sector[a]	% Coverage Informal Sector[b]	% of Income Paid for Coverage	
			Salaried	Self-employed
Bahamas	•	48.4	1.7–3.4	6.8–8.8
Barbados	•	24.8	4.6–5.5	8.0
Chile	20.1[c]	11.9–17.5	20.6–27.2	20.6–27.2
Colombia	22.3[c]	0.6	4.5–6.2	15–20
Costa Rica	21.6	2.0/93.0[d]	9.0	12.2–19.5
Jamaica	37.7	4.0	2.5	5.0
Mexico	30.9	0.8	3.75	13.57
Panama	20.9[c]	1.5	7.25	18–22
Peru	61.9	4.0	6.0	18.0

Source: Mesa-Lago 1990.
Notes: Informal sector includes self-employed, domestic servants, and unpaid family workers.
a. Self-employed workers, plus domestic servants, plus unpaid family workers within the EAP; excludes informal wage earners.
b. Only self-employed.
c. All the informal sector.
d. The lower figure relates to pensions and the higher to health care; the latter includes noncontributory coverage to indigents.
• Signifies data not available.

the Bahamas), and it reaches 93 percent in one (Costa Rica) because of the coverage of indigents. Although coverage of the self-employed is mandatory in Jamaica, only 4 percent of them are actually covered.

One of the reasons for the low coverage of this sector is the heavy contributory burden. The required percentage of income paid by the self-employed is from two to four times the percentage paid by the salaried worker; the only exception is Chile, where both types have similar percentage contributions. This largely explains not only the low coverage of this group but the high degree of evasion and payment delays in countries with mandatory coverage.

Another problem is the high cost of detecting, inspecting, and collecting from the large number of self-employed, domestic servants, and wage earners in microenterprises. In some countries the administrative cost of incorporating this sector is higher than the revenue actually collected. For these reasons the proportion of noncompliance is very high: in Peru 65 percent of the enterprises are not registered, and in Jamaica 44 percent of the registered enterprises delay their payments.

A third problem is that the benefits available for this group are usually very poor and reduce incentives for affiliation even more. In Jamaica the average pension for the self-employed in 1986 was one-fifth of the national income per capita, and the process for requesting the benefit was so complex and prolonged that only half of those eligible actually applied.

Informal workers in Lima said in 1988 that they were not interested in affiliation because of the low level of pensions, the poor quality of health care, and the time they lost waiting in line for the services.

Data are lacking on salaried workers in small informal enterprises, but a key question is whether if these workers had a real option to join social insurance (to which they may be legally entitled) they would do so. Scattered information suggests a negative answer because the cost of joining the system is too high for them. In any case the informal employer (through savings of social insurance and other taxes as well as lower wages and fringes) reduces production costs and successfully competes with formal enterprises. This may lead to a shutdown of formal enterprises and a labor transfer to the informal sector, which would in turn reduce both coverage by and revenue for social insurance. However, forcing informal employers to fulfill their obligations to social insurance (assuming enforcement is feasible, which it seldom is) would substantially reduce their small profits and potentially shut down enterprises and create additional unemployment (Mesa-Lago 1990).

With the growth of the informal sector in the 1980s it is even more important to study alternative ways to protect this sector, whether conventionally (e.g., social insurance) or unconventionally (e.g., mutual aid societies, collective insurance policies with low premiums, solidarity groups). Chapter 3 reviews the approach taken by Costa Rica in this context.

• Rural Sector. Because of a rapid process of urbanization, from 1960–1989 the average rural population in LAC declined from 51 percent to 30 percent of the total population. However, in 1989, in 10 out of 25 countries the rural share of the population ranged from 31–49 percent and in 6 countries from 50–73 percent (IDB 1990). At the beginning of the 1980s the agricultural population in six Latin American countries had the lowest social insurance coverage among all economic branches (as low as 4.6 percent in Colombia and 5.5 percent in Peru).

Numerous factors can explain the low coverage of the rural sector by social security. *Physical and demographic* factors include dispersion and low density of the population, isolation due to topographical barriers, and large rural areas with population pockets far away from urban centers, all of which result in higher medical and administrative costs. *Cultural* factors include large indigenous populations who speak a dialect different than that of the national language and have divergent cultures and values, closed societies that resist integration and are suspicious of modern medicine, and illiteracy; these factors limit access to services. *Socioeconomic* factors are important because rural populations generally have considerably lower living standards than the urban population (e.g., lower income, higher infant mortality, worse housing and nutrition) and are more afflicted by disease. *Public service infrastructure* factors include nonexistent or poor roads, communications, transportation, health care, sanitation, potable water, education, mailing, and other public services that make extending coverage even more difficult and costly. *Special labor* features are important because the majority of the labor force is usually nonsalaried and works under multiple arrangements (e.g., self-employment, sharecropping, seasonal work), the same individual changes jobs during the year (e.g., from a personal subsistence plot to a salaried job during harvest), and work is often done by unpaid family members; this diversity and instability make it impossible to apply conventional and uniform methods. *Administrative complexity* is another problem because there is a lack of employment registration, payroll, and/or records of hirings and dismissals; payment is often partly in kind (e.g., a share of the crop, housing), making it difficult to evaluate the contributory capacity, collect contributions, prove the number of years of work, and assess the proper amount of monetary benefits; medical personnel are generally reluctant to live in poor, isolated areas unless significant incentives are offered; and unions and associations—which could function as intermediaries between the population and social security institutions—are poorly developed in most cases. Another problem is that the Bismarckian approach to social insurance excludes the rural population because it is nonsalaried; when protection is granted it is usually on a voluntary basis and, because the worker lacks an employer, the contributory burden on the worker is too heavy; revenues generated through traditional financing methods are insufficient to cover expenditures and require transfers from the state or the urban sector.

A recent study by the International Social Security Association (ISSA) notes that although these problems have been discussed in many international meetings, few Latin American countries have been able to overcome them. Granting that social security coverage is largely determined in the long run by the socioeconomic development of the rural sector, the study rejected policy inertia and conversely argued that there is an urgency in the short run to extend minimum protection to that sector under either the general or special systems (ISSA 1991; Mesa-Lago 1992c).

There are some LAC countries that have been successful in expanding social security coverage (mostly for health care) to the rural sector with different approaches: national health systems in the NLC, Cuba, and Nicaragua; sickness/maternity insurance programs that protect the rural dispossessed as welfare cases in Costa Rica (which has also noncontributory pensions) and Chile; social insurance programs (health care and pensions) with fewer benefits than in urban areas in Argentina; dual systems that expand social insurance health care (mainly primary care) to rural populations in Brazil, Ecuador, Mexico, and Panama; and an extension of sickness/maternity insurance coverage to rural, underdeveloped regions in Guatemala—with a planned expansion to the southeast coast in the early 1990s that is expected to incorporate a population equal to 80 percent of that already covered.

In 1986–1988, 49 percent of the rural population was covered in Costa Rica (even more if noncontributory programs are taken into account), 55 percent in Uruguay, and 56 percent in Mexico. A combination of many positive factors explains the advances in the first two countries: their territories and populations are small and without insurmountable topographical barriers, both countries rank among those with higher income and living standards in the region, their social service infrastructures are well developed, their respective populations speak the same language and are not divided by significant cultural differences, the percentage of salaried employment is high, their agricultural sectors are relatively modern (Uruguay's has the smallest proportion of rural population, but Costa Rica's is well above the regional average), their social security systems grant mandatory coverage to that sector, and rural unions and cooperatives are fairly well developed. Mexico does not share many of the above advantages but has compensated with an innovative, relatively successful program of expanding coverage to isolated rural populations (Mesa-Lago 1992c). The models of expansion in Costa Rica and Mexico will be analyzed in Chapter 3; herein I summarize the experiences of Brazil and Ecuador.

In Brazil the social security system, SINPAS, extended coverage to rural areas in the 1970s through two programs: one of social insurance, FUNRURAL, and another, PIASS, operated through the federal ministry of health (MH) and states' health services. FUNRURAL began independently in 1971, granting assistance pensions and health care to the rural population and towns with less than 20,000 inhabitants; it had a network of facilities (health posts and centers, polyclinics, and hospitals) developed through agreements with trade unions, states, municipalities, and private institutions. In 1977 FUNRURAL became part of the social insurance system and was financed by three taxes: 2.4 percent on the payroll of urban enterprises (this tax generated 63 percent of total revenue in 1980); 2.5 percent on rural production, collected by the producer and paid by the buyer (35 percent of total revenue); and 0.036 percent paid by rural employers based on the value of agricultural production or the value of noncultivated farms (2 percent of total revenue). From 1978 through the 1980s the program operated at a deficit (11 percent of revenue in 1981) that resulted from tax evasion estimated to be from one-third to one-half of the potential revenue of the three taxes combined. To help finance the program, FINSOCIAL was created in 1982 with a contribution of 0.5 percent of the revenue of all enterprises in the nation. In addition to its financial imbalance, FUNRURAL had the following flaws: a basically curative model not adapted to the sector needs; predominance in the allocation of resources to urban over rural zones and developed over underdeveloped regions; insufficient and deteriorated equipment and low quality of services; scarcity of medicines; and restricted access to hospitals and high user fees that prevented the lowest income group from using the services.

PIASS was created in 1976 to provide primary health care to rural zones and small towns and rapidly extended throughout the nation, first under the MH and later depending on the states. In 1979 the program suffered a grave financial crisis and was rescued by social insurance at the price of a change in its approach; it became predominantly curative and offered less community participation. At the beginning of the 1980s there was a plan to create a national health system that would integrate all existing programs (including FUNRURAL and PIASS). Features of the plan were a two-fold increase in federal government financing, priority given to primary health care, and an increase in the role of community assistants. By the end of the 1980s the integration had been achieved, and the special programs disappeared as such (since 1990 all health services are unified under the ministry of health and all pensions under the ministry of labor and social insurance). Integrated health action (AIS) units are reportedly trying to eliminate differences between urban and rural health services; however, the rural population cannot use the social insurance facilities but instead have to develop agreements with public- and private-sector facilities. Reportedly the economic crisis of the 1980s affected not the percentage of the population covered but the quality of the services provided (ISSA 1991; Mesa-Lago 1992c).

In Ecuador the peasant social insurance program (SSC) began in 1968 as part of the social insurance institute (IESS) and was pushed forward in 1973 and 1981. Eligible are peasants (and their dependent families) organized in cooperatives and agrarian associations; affiliation is voluntary, based on agreements between the IESS and the peasant groups. Although the SSC-insured population increased more than six-fold from 1980–1991, the SSC covered only 14 percent of the rural population in 1991. Emphasis is on primary health care at a low cost (there are pensions for old age and disability for the head of the household), and the services are based at a rural post built on community land, with a basic structure supplied by the IESS and erected through community work. A traveling physician offers medical, maternity, and dental care at the post, and auxiliary permanent personnel provide prenatal care, health education, and immunization. Those patients who cannot be cured at the rural post should be referred to more complex IESS facilities. The program is financed with a 1 percent contribution on the payroll of all those insured through the IESS (paid in equal parts by the insured, the employer, and the state) plus the equivalent of 1 percent of the national minimum wage paid by the participant peasant (in 1985 the minimum wage increased two-fold, thus theoretically making the peasant contribution very heavy; however, it is said that the actual contribution is very small). It is not possible to estimate either the SSC costs or its financial stability, but scattered information suggests that it faces a deficit and that hospitalization costs are high. Coverage has increased at a low rate for 20 years, and there are indicators of discrimination against the poorest and most isolated peasant population, a low number of referrals to higher levels of attention, and different treatment between peasants and the insured at IESS facilities. Furthermore, the SSC is not coordinated with the rural health system of the ministry, its number of immunizations is small, and it merely pays lip service to basic sanitation. There is no information on whether the economic crisis of the 1980s has negatively affected this program (ISSA 1991; Mesa-Lago 1992b).[1]

Limited protection of the unemployed. As noted in Chapter 1, open urban unemployment dramatically increased in the 1980s, particularly in the first half. Reasons include the reduction in public employment resulting from the fiscal crisis, widespread bankruptcy in the industrial sector (because it lost most of its protection and could not compete with cheaper imports), the decline in domestic investment and net capital inflows, measures taken to make the labor market more flexible, and changing world technological trends. There are few programs to help individuals cope with unemployment in LAC; as noted in Table 2.1, unemployment (together with family allowances) is the contingency least covered by social security in the region. Only seven countries provide such protection (compared with 30 to 34 countries for occupational risks, sickness/maternity, and pensions), and four of them are among the most developed (see Table 2.5).[2] Furthermore, existing programs have considerable limitations in terms of population coverage, level of benefits, and entitlement conditions.

In Argentina only the construction sector is covered; a 1985 decree expanding this scheme to all the employed labor force has not been implemented. In Brazil there are three programs: (1) the old unemployment assistance payable in case of employer's bankruptcy, enterprise shutdown, or massive layoffs (reportedly used very little); (2) the new unemployment insurance introduced in 1986 and summarized in Table 2.5 (in its first year of operation only 12.6 percent of the total unemployed received this benefit); and (3) the length-of-service guaranty fund established in 1965 and financed with an 8 percent wage contribution, paid by employers, that goes into individual accounts for those insured; the funds can be withdrawn in case of dismissal but also for marriage, a house purchase, and other instances (many workers who became unemployed in the 1980s had already used their funds for other purposes). In Chile there are conflicting estimates on coverage and level of benefits. According to one source, during the worst years of the crisis more than 50 percent of the unemployed received no benefits at all (the majority in the lowest income group), 20 percent received compensation equivalent to 30 percent of the minimum liquid income; and the remaining 30 percent received 60 percent of that minimum. Another source reports that coverage increased from 25 percent to 33 percent of all unemployed workers from 1980–1983 and then declined; the unemployment benefits decreased from 77 percent

Table 2.5   Features of Unemployment Insurance/Assistance Programs in LAC: 1989

Countries	First and Current Laws	Coverage for Salaried Employees		Contributions (% Salary)			Conditions (Months of Previous Insurance or Contributions)	Benefits		
		All	Some	Insured	Employer	State		% Earnings	Pay't Period (Weeks)	Waiting Period (Days)
Argentina	1967		x[a]	0	4.0	0	12	b	26	0
Barbados	1982		x[c]	0.5	0.5	0	12	60	2	3
Brazil[d]	1965, 1986	x		0	0	e	36	50	17	60
Chile	1937, 1981	x		0	0	e	12	f	26–52	0
Ecuador	1951, 1988		x[g]	2.0	1.0	0	24	f	•	60
Uruguay	1944, 1981		x[h]	0	0	e	6	50	52	0
Venezuela	1989		x[i]	0.25	0.85	0	12	50	13–26	30

Source: Based on US-SSA 1990, supplemented with IDB 1987, Dixon and Scheurell 1990, and ISSA 1989 to 1990.

Notes: a. Construction only.

b. Refund of contributions.

c. From 16 to 64 years of age; excludes government employees, who have their own programs.

d. Data in the table refers to the 1986 program; there are two others described in the text.

e. Whole cost; in Uruguay theoretically financed out of general contributions, but in practice from state transfers or taxes; in Brazil financed by the state, at least in its first year.

f. Fixed monthly sum.

g. Industry, commerce, agriculture and government; excludes transportation, construction, domestic service.

h. Private salaried employment; excludes banking, agriculture, domestic service.

i. Private- and public-sector employees with fixed-term contracts who are covered by social security; excludes domestic servants.

• Signifies data not available.

to 67 percent of the minimum wage from 1983–1985. In any event, based on the law, in 1986 the monthly benefit was equivalent to U.S. $30 during the first 90 days of compensation and was halved after 180 days. In Ecuador only one-fourth of the labor force is covered by social insurance, and the proportion of the total unemployed benefiting from this program is probably very small; they receive a monthly fixed sum, but data are lacking on whether it is sufficient to maintain previous living standards or even meet basic needs. In Uruguay the proportion of the total unemployed receiving benefits increased from 20 percent to 30 percent from the late 1970s to early 1980s, but declined to 10 percent by 1985, and the benefit was well below the minimum wage; daily workers are entitled to an even smaller compensation, and the number of applicants is virtually nil. There is no information available on coverage in Venezuela. All but one of these programs require from one to three years of previous insurance, employment, or contributions to entitle a worker to the benefits, a fact that considerably limits eligibility. In two countries workers involved in a strike are not eligible for these benefits (IDB 1987; Dixon and Scheurell 1990; Meller 1990).

More widespread than unemployment insurance/assistance in LAC are programs established by labor legislation that, in addition to protection against unjustified dismissals, provide severance pay or lump sums at dismissal, usually financed by the employer. Some countries that have this program are Argentina, Barbados, Bolivia, Brazil, Colombia, Honduras, Mexico, Panama, Peru, and Venezuela (US-SSA 1990; Bronstein 1990). In most cases the severance payments can be simultaneously collected with insurance benefits (Brazil is an exception). Finally, there are or have been special employment programs in Brazil, Chile, Costa Rica, Panama, and Peru; more modest or temporary programs operate in other countries. These are financed by the state, and the beneficiary must be engaged in productive work. In general, these programs are good in recession periods and are rapid, flexible, and targeted to the neediest (IDB 1987).

At first glance the cost of unemployment insurance/assistance in LAC does not seem to be excessive. In 1983, in the midst of the crisis, the proportions of total benefit expenditures spent on the programs were relatively small—3.2 percent in Barbados, 3.6 percent in Chile, 4.5 percent in Uruguay, and 5.7 percent in Ecuador—and by 1986 these percentages had declined in most countries (ILO 1988, 1991a). Such low percentages are explained by the significant limitations in coverage, level of benefits, and entitlement conditions. But data available from two countries (Barbados and Uruguay) indicate that costs have risen significantly, and such experience is important for other LAC countries.

In Barbados the cost of the program increased two-fold in each year of the 1983–1986 period for the following reasons: (1) an increment of open unemployment from 10.8 percent in 1981 to 18.7 percent in 1985 (the rate declined to 17.9 percent in 1987 and 16.5 percent in 1989 but was still considerably higher than in 1981, before the program began); (2) a two-fold expansion of the payment period, from 13 to 26 weeks; and (3) an increase in the rate of salary replacement from 40 percent to 60 percent. The last two measures were taken in 1985 at the time the unemployment rate peaked, in the midst of an electoral campaign; in addition, the contribution rate was cut in half. The unemployment share of total benefit expenditures increased from 3.2 percent to 14.2 percent from 1983–1986, thus becoming the largest after pensions. The program generated a surplus from 1982–1985, but it operated at a deficit in 1986 that was projected to increase two-fold in 1987; the reserves of the program declined 14 percent in 1986 (in nominal terms) and were expected to be depleted by 1990. To cut costs and minimize payments to persons who have returned to work, the benefit period has been reduced from 26 weeks to two weeks (Mesa-Lago 1987a; ISSA 1990).

In Uruguay in 1982, after the unemployment program was generalized, the number of unemployed workers receiving benefits reached a historic peak of 24,546 in the month of December; the number declined to 9,002 in 1986 as unemployment declined but rose again to 14,236 in 1990, although the number of jobless workers declined slightly. The deficit in the program reached a peak in 1982 equivalent to 0.4 percent of GDP; in real pesos the deficit declined to 0.1 percent of GDP in 1986 but rose again to 0.2 percent in 1990 (BPS 1986–1990).

In view of the few existing programs (the majority of which are in the most developed LAC countries), their low coverage and level of benefits, and relatively high costs, one has to question if it is feasible and advisable to expand unemployment insurance to other LAC countries or to currently excluded sectors of the labor force in those countries that already have the scheme in operation. The difficulties of expanding in the midst of a crisis are highlighted by the fact that only two programs have effectively been implemented in the last 10 years. Legislation enacted in Argentina to expand coverage has not been enforced, and in Venezuela a law passed in 1985 was not put in force until new legislation was enacted in 1989.

Some countries have failed in an attempt to add unemployment insurance to their social security systems. In Costa Rica from 1982–1983, when the unemployment rate reached a historic peak, there were three legal drafts to create unemployment compensation that was to be financed by an additional 8 percent wage contribution paid exclusively by the employers; the fear of a negative impact on employment, combined with opposition from employers, some political leaders, and the World Bank (which at the time was negotiating a structural adjustment loan), led to the defeat of these drafts in the National Assembly. In the Bahamas and Jamaica there were debates in the 1980s on this issue: government officials and employers argued that unemployment was too high, chronic, and seasonal and that costs would be excessive and impossible to finance in the midst of the crisis. They argued that it was better to use scarce resources to promote employment creation; conversely, some union leaders supported unemployment insurance but under tight conditions to reduce costs. No legislative action was taken (Mesa-Lago 1983a, 1987a).

In general, the paralysis of unemployment programs in LAC may be explained by the differences in economic and labor conditions between most LAC countries and market industrialized economies. Unemployment insurance was created in industrialized countries to cope with a cyclical, short-term phenomenon during a recession, to help break the business cycle, and to sustain the level of workers' demands by maintaining part of their income. Recent recessions in developed countries have been characterized by higher unemployment rates and longer jobless periods. These changes have led to a lively debate and to revisions of the existing programs in an attempt (whether successful or not) to support economic recovery and job creation and to curtail unemployment (ILO 1986–1987). But in LAC unemployment is more typically a structural phenomenon: it affects a larger proportion of the labor force and continues for much longer periods of time than in industrialized countries because of higher population growth rates, greater rural-to-urban migration, and the inability of the industrial sector to absorb the labor surplus. Furthermore, the aggravation of unemployment in LAC in the 1980s was more severe and longer lasting than in the developed world; it was largely induced by the prolonged crisis and the adjustment/restructuring of the LAC economies. The most significant difference is that in LAC, seasonal unemployment, underemployment, and informal employment are by far more important than open unemployment. Before the crisis informal employment accounted for an average of 7 percent of the labor force in Latin America; underemployment ranged from 20–29 percent, and the informal sector was estimated to be 24 percent of the regional urban labor force and as high as 40–60 percent in the capitals or major cities of 10 countries. As noted earlier, the crisis led to a notable expansion of both underemployment and informal employment (ILO 1976; Tokman 1986; IDB 1987; Mesa-Lago 1990). Workers affected by these phenomena (e.g., self-employed, wage earners in clandestine microenterprises, subsistence farmers) are not usually covered by social security. Another problem is that a good part of the unemployed in LAC are young new entrants in the labor force and that existing programs exclude them from any benefits. Therefore unemployment insurance not only is restricted within the formal sector but obviously cannot alleviate the predicament of most of the labor force.

The ILO has acknowledged that social protection must be adapted to economic conditions in different countries and to those countries' capacities to provide productive employment to the available labor force; hence, it should not be surprising—the ILO explains—that unemployment programs are absent in developing countries despite the expansion of other branches of social security (ILO 1986–1987). In addition, the ISSA, in a volume devoted to unemployment and social security policies in industrialized countries, has noted the insufficiency of traditional unemployment insurance when trying to cope with massive long-term unemployment in developing countries (ISSA 1985).

The long debate on whether employers' contributions to social security have a negative effect on job creation has not yielded conclusive results; however, industrialized countries have recently stabilized or even reduced such contributions in an attempt to preclude the substitution of capital for labor. An expansion of unemployment insurance in LAC would result in an increase in contributions that are already high in some countries. It has been argued, although not proven, that in LAC the employers' contributions (if actually paid by the employer) reduce the formal sector further and stimulate the expansion of informal employment, thereby leading to a double decrease in social security coverage (see the debate in Mesa-Lago 1985, 1989c). An opposite reaction by employers (reported in Barbados), particularly in small enterprises, is to increase noncompliance (i.e., evasion, payment delays); prosecution of violators is difficult because trade unions and social security institutions fear enterprise shutdowns more than a loss of revenue (Mesa-Lago 1987a).

Unemployment benefits in industrialized countries are usually conditioned to the beneficiary's acceptance of retraining, and the benefits are normally withdrawn when the beneficiary rejects an adequate job offer. These conditions also exist in most LAC countries with unemployment insurance, but the magnitude of unemployment in those countries makes it difficult to find formal jobs (although it does promote entry into the informal sector) or effectively retrain the beneficiary. Other obstacles include poor-quality employment services and placement offices and the difficulty in supervising involuntary unemployment (ILO 1986–1987).

Last but not least is the problem of how to finance an expansion of unemployment insurance in a crisis situation. I will show later that the wage tax burden in some LAC countries has reached unbearable levels. An increase in wage contributions to finance unemployment insurance would aggravate that problem. Furthermore, revenues would go to protect only a small percentage of the labor force, and this might have negative effects on employment creation.

In 1986 a questionnaire was sent by the ILO to member countries concerning the revision of the Unemployment Provision Convention of 1934; it included numerous questions related to the expansion of that program's coverage and benefits. Only three LAC countries answered the survey, and they overwhelmingly supported expansion, although two of them did not and still do not have unemployment insurance. None of the

47 questions in the survey dealt with the issue of financing; the last question asked for any other pertinent issues not included in the survey, but in spite of the severe economic crisis in LAC, the three respondents from the region failed to note the dearth of financing (ILO 1986–1987). Future ILO surveys should not only deal with the crucial issue of financing but question the members, particularly developing countries, on other more urgent priorities in view of the enormous pressure associated with scarce resources.

The inadequate relationship between social insurance and public assistance in protecting disadvantaged groups. Because of the significant proportion of the population not covered by social insurance in half of Latin America and the difficulties in expanding coverage, the role of public assistance for the dispossessed is crucial, as is the coordination of both types of programs. But only the most developed countries of Latin America and some in the NLC have been able to create a combined system of insurance and assistance to cover virtually the entire population in terms of both health care and income maintenance (Isuani 1985).

There are four types of systems in LAC that offer noncash health benefits: (1) integrated national health systems that cover practically the entire population and provide similar treatment to both the insured and the noninsured indigents (as found in the NLC, Cuba, and Nicaragua; in all cases the system is administered by the respective ministry of health); (2) social insurance sickness/maternity programs that, with state aid, cover both the insured and the noninsured indigents who pass a means test (found in Costa Rica); (3) social insurance with dual systems, one providing full benefits to the insured and another offering primary health care to disadvantaged groups (usually in rural areas), with the rest of the poor cared for under the ministry of public health (found in Ecuador, Mexico); and (4) separation of social insurance and public health programs (found in most of Latin America).

The level of insured benefits for income-maintenance programs (basically pensions) is usually higher than that under assistance programs. There are four types of systems: (1) integrated programs administered by social insurance, financed either by separate contributions for insurance and assistance (found in Barbados) or by a contribution for insurance plus state aid (found in the Bahamas), but in both cases with a common fund; (2) social insurance administering two separate programs and funds, one financed with wage contributions for the insured and another financed by state transfers for the dispossessed (found in Costa Rica, Uruguay); (3) separately administered programs, with pensions for the dispossessed mandated and regulated by law (found in Chile); and (4) separate programs in which public assistance is left to government decisions (found in most of LAC). In addition to pensions there are public assistance programs administered by the state that provide modest grants to the elderly, disabled, unemployed, children, and victims of natural disasters, as well as funds for nursing homes, food programs, and so forth.

There is very little information available on what percentage of overall social security benefits goes to public assistance. The ILO triannual survey probably underestimates the percentage because noncontributory pensions for health care are included under the "social insurances and assimilated schemes" category instead of under public assistance (even if the beneficiary is subjected to a means test), as are public health programs that are universal and based on a right of the population (ILO 1988). Data available for only six NLC countries for 1983 show the following shares of public assistance: 17.6 percent for Suriname, 15.7 percent for Jamaica, 7.6 percent for Trinidad and Tobago, 7.3 percent for Guyana, 6.7 percent for Belize, and 5.6 percent for Barbados (ILO 1988).

The following paragraphs summarize the integrated but dual pension programs of the Bahamas, Barbados, Costa Rica, and Uruguay, countries that have achieved virtually universal population coverage. (Health programs will be analyzed in a later section of this chapter and in Chapter 3.)

In the Bahamas and Barbados public assistance was introduced prior to social insurance. In the Bahamas the social insurance system (NIB) was put in charge of both programs in 1974; the public assistance program provides pensions (conditioned to a means test) for old age, disability, and survivors. There is a general wage contribution to the insurance program, and the state allocates a sum that covers only a fraction of the cost of the assistance program; because there is a common fund, revenues from other programs are used to cover the deficit, and a transfer of funds occurs between the insured and the dispossessed. It has a progressive distribution effect but is resented by the insured and criticized by some government officials. The bulk of the pensioners are assistance cases, but their share in the total number declined from 87 percent to 76 percent from 1981–1985; the percentage of benefits going to this program declined from 69 percent to 46 percent in the same period; the fixed assistance pension and the minimum insurance pension were at a very similar level in the first half of the 1980s, but the gap between the two has expanded since 1985. The means test was liberalized (which prompted an increase in assistance cases), and by 1985 the state contribution covered only 11 percent of the cost of assistance; hence, the equilibrium of the program was threatened. Tighter measures were introduced (including revision and termination of many assistance pensions), but data are lacking on the impact of these measures (Mesa-Lago 1987a).

In Barbados the public assistance program provides only old-age pensions. It was put under the social insurance administration (NIO) in 1982 and is financed by a separate wage contribution (2 percent each from the insured and employers). However, NIO revenues are not segregated by contingency and are consolidated in a common fund. Assistance pensions were initially subjected to a means test, but this test was eliminated in 1982 when the statutory age was reduced and the level of the pension increased (these measures took place in the midst of political campaigns), so the number of assistance pensioners boomed. The levels of the fixed assistance pension and the minimum insurance pension are similar, but the average insurance pension is considerably higher. From 1982–1984 expenditures of the assistance program exceeded its contributions, so reserves from the common fund were used to finance the deficit. This situation led to criticism by the trade unions and some government and social security officials. In 1983 the International Monetary Fund (IMF) recommended to separate both programs, but the NIO did not comply; the 1985 actuarial review repeated the recommendation and requested that the means test be restored. As economic conditions improved somewhat in Barbados, the number of assistance pensions declined slightly; conversely, the number of insurance pensioners and the level of their pensions rose. As a result the share of assistance cases in total pensions declined from 65 percent to 58 percent from 1982–1987, and their share of total pension benefits decreased from 53 percent to 40 percent (Mesa-Lago 1987a).

Coverage of noninsured indigents on old-age, disability, and survivors pensions (conditioned to a means test) was introduced in Costa Rica in 1974 and placed under the control of the social insurance institute (CCSS). The pension assistance program has a separate fund and is financed (as is health care for assistance pensioners) through transfers from the family-allowance institute, but if the transfer is insufficient or delayed the CCSS must transfer funds from its other programs. In 1989 the proportion of assistance pensions was 46 percent of all pensions, but if the number of pensioners is used for the calculation (because there may be several beneficiaries of one pension) the proportion declines to 37 percent; furthermore, the ratio of insurance to assistance pensions was 5 to 1. Therefore the assistance share of total benefit expenditures was only 14 percent (Mesa-Lago 1989c; CCSS 1989).

Public assistance pensions were established in Uruguay in 1919; currently they cover old age and disability for those who lack means (or whose income is lower than the old-age pension) and whose close relatives cannot support them. The assistance program is a branch of the social insurance institute (BPS), but it is financed out of general contributions that are insufficient to cover expenditures, so the state has to subsidize the deficit. The share of assistance pensioners in the total number of pensioners was only 9 percent in 1990 and in terms of total benefits was less than 6 percent; the average insurance pension is 2.6 times higher than the assistance pension (BPS 1990).

Table 2.6 compares the major features of the public assistance programs in the four countries. Uruguay's program is the smallest, but it is heavily subsidized by the state. Costa Rica's program is probably the best:

Table 2.6 Social Insurance and Public Assistance Pension Programs in Selected Countries of LAC: 1985–1990

Countries	Contingencies Covered by Assistance			Percent of Assistance in Total:		Ratio of Average Insurance to Assistance Pension	Means Test	Sources of Revenue					
								% of Wages	Transfers from:		Fund		
	OA	D	S	No. of Pensioners	Benefit Expenditures				State	Social Insurance	Common	Separated	
Bahamas (1985)	x	x	x	76.5	45.5	1.5	x[a]	[b]	x	x	x		
Barbados (1986–1987)	x	x		58.5	39.9	1.4		4.0		x	x		
Costa Rica (1989)	x	x	x	36.7	14.2	5.0	x		x[c]	x		x	
Uruguay (1990)	x	x	x	9.3	5.7	2.4	x	[b]	x	x	x		

Sources: Mesa-Lago 1987; CCSS 1989; BPS 1990.
Notes: OA = old age.
D= disability.
S = survivors.
a. Made more flexible in 1982.
b. General wage contributions to social insurance.
c. Transfer from family allowances institute.

it is second in size proportionally; it has a wide difference between insurance and assistance pensions; it has a separated fund; and although transfers are not always sufficient to finance the program, the resulting deficit is not a heavy burden on social insurance. The programs of the Bahamas and Barbados are huge, the levels of the two pensions are similar (although the gap between them is expanding), and there is a common fund for both programs. The wage contribution in Barbados is insufficient to finance the program because the means test has been eliminated and the entitlement conditions liberalized; hence, the resulting deficit must be covered with social insurance reserves. The state transfer to the Barbados program is grossly insufficient to cover its costs, requiring a substantial transfer from social insurance. The large shares of the assistance programs in the Bahamas and Barbados are partly due to the newness of their insurance pension programs and lack of maturity, whereas the small shares for Costa Rica's and particularly Uruguay's programs are influenced by older and more mature insurance pension programs. However, overly liberal conditions in Barbados and inadequate financing in the Bahamas significantly contribute to the difficulties faced by these two programs.

Burdensome, Regressive Contributions and Noncompliance

Financing for social security in LAC is based mostly on a percentage of the payroll contribution, payable by the insured and the employer. In some countries the state pays a third-party contribution (in addition to that as an employer), whereas in others it subsidizes the system through special taxes or by covering all or part of the costs or deficit. In the few countries where the self-employed are covered, they pay a percentage contribution (on an estimated income) equal to the sum of the percentages paid by employees and their employers. The percentage contributions from payrolls in 25 countries at the end of the 1980s are shown in Table 2.7.

High payroll contributions. The older a social security system is, the higher the total percentage contribution from the payroll. Thus in the pioneer countries the percentage ranges from 22–56 percent. (The only exception is Cuba, where only the employer [i.e., the state] pays 10 percent, but the state directly subsidizes half of the cost of the system). These percentages are similar to those of Europe and Japan. In countries in the intermediate group, the total percentages range from 16–24 percent, higher than those of Canada and the United States (Paraguay's and Peru's percentages are close to that of the United Kingdom). In the latecomer Latin American group (excluding Haiti) the total percentages vary from 11–18 percent (similar to those of the United States and Canada), but in the NLC (excluding Barbados and Grenada) the percentages range from 5–10 percent (the lowest in LAC).[3] It should be noted that population coverage is very low in all Latin American countries of

Table 2.7 Contributions to Social Security in LAC: 1989–1990 (in Percentages of Wages or Income)

Countries[a]	Insured			State[b]				Total Contributions[d]	Ranking[c]
	Salaried	Self-employed	Employer	%	Taxes	Covers Deficit	Others[c]		
Argentina	16	21	31[f]	9.2		x		56.2	1
Bahamas	1.7–3.4	6.8–8.8	5.4–7.1				x	8.8	26
Barbados	6.665	9.3	7.135		x		x	13.8	18
Bolivia	5		15[g]	1				21	10
Brazil	8.5–10	19.2	17.8–18.8		x	x	x	26.3–31.3	4
Chile	20.6–27.2[h]	20.6–27.2	0.9			x	x	21.5–28.1[h]	5
Colombia	4.5–6.17	15–20	14.5–17.8					19–24	9
Costa Rica	9	12.25–19.5	25.66					35.66	3
Cuba	0	10		1	x			10	23
Dominican Rep.	2.5		9.5	2.5		x	x	14.25	16
Ecuador	8.5–16.35	15.5	7.35–16.85	0.3				15.85–30.5	8
El Salvador	3.23–5.5	8.75	7.57–8.25	0.5				10.8–13.75	20
Grenada	4.0	6.75	4.0					14.75	15
Guatemala	4.5		10	3			x	17.5	13
Guyana	4.8	10	7.2					12	21
Haiti	2–6		4–12					6–18	22
Honduras	3.5		7	3.5		x		14	17
Jamaica	2.5[i]	5[i]	2.5[i]		x			5[i]	29
Mexico	4.5	13.57	15.61				x	21	10
Nicaragua	4		11	0.9				15.5	14
Panama	7.25	18	12.45	0.5	x			19.7	12
Paraguay	9.5		13	1.5				24	6
Peru	6	18	16					23	7
St. Christopher	5		5					10	23
St. Lucia	5		5					10	23
St. Vincent	2.5		3[f]					5.5	28
Trinidad & Tobago	2.8	5.6	5.6[f]				x	8.4	27
Uruguay	13–16		25.5–33.5		x			38.5–49.5	2
Venezuela	4		7.9	1.5			x	12.5–14.5	19

Sources: US-SSA 1990; Mesa-Lago 1991b.

Notes: a. Three NLC countries have fixed sums instead of percentages.

b. State contribution as such, not as employer.

c. Examples include: the costs of welfare, health care, and/or pensions; part of the cost of health services or pensions; the difference in the cost of the minimum guaranteed pension; administrative expenditures; and part of the cost of population-coverage extension.

d. Excludes both the self-employed insured contribution and state payments that are not a percentage of wages. In some countries includes not only the main managing agency but other institutions as well.

e. From high to low; an average has been calculated when there is a range of contributions.

f. Excludes the premium for employment injury; in Argentina also excludes 4% for unemployment insurance for construction workers.

g. Excludes contributions for family allowances and pensioners' health care.

h. The lower sum is in the new system and the higher sum in the old system.

i. Variable percentage contribution according to wages; in addition there is a fixed contribution.

the latecomer group and in most of the intermediate group, whereas the developed countries usually have universal coverage and better benefits. Between 1980 and 1989/1990, the total percentage contribution in Latin America increased in eight countries, was stagnant in eight, and declined in four. Declines took place in Chile, which eliminated the employer contribution in the 1980s (but at the cost of an increasing state subsidy to the old system), and in Bolivia, which cut the employer's contribution (but is edging toward financial disequilibrium). The majority of the pioneers increased the percentage contribution, whereas all the latecomers kept it unchanged.

In two-thirds of the LAC countries in Table 2.7, the percentage contribution paid by the insured is one-third or less of the total, and in nine countries the insured's percentage ranges between one-third and one-half. The principal source of financing is the employer, who contributes two-thirds or more of the total percentage in 19 countries and from one-half to one-third in the rest (except in Chile). In 5 out of 13 countries where the state contributes a percentage of the payroll, the percentage ranges from one-tenth to one-fourth of the total; these calculations do not take into account other state contributions. Data from 26 LAC countries on the 1986 percentage distribution of social insurance plus family-allowances revenue support the above statements. Average contributed shares from the respective sources are as follows: 25 percent from the insured, 53 percent from the employer plus the state, 19 percent from investment, and 3 percent from other sources. These are nonweighted averages, but if they had been weighted (in terms of population) the largest countries (i.e., Argentina, Brazil, and Mexico) would have pushed up the proportion paid by the employer plus the state. The employer plus the state contributes more than 60 percent of total revenue in eight countries (including Argentina and Mexico) and from 50–59 percent in 12 countries (see Table 2.8).

Regressivity of financing. Contributions appear to have a regressive effect on income distribution: (1) the insured's contribution is flat, and in 75 percent of the countries there is a contribution ceiling; (2) although there is no conclusive evidence, it appears that the employer's contribution is transferred to prices, and the state contribution often comes from regressive taxes; and (3) the state contribution, mainly based on regressive taxes, often subsidizes the cost of protection for the middle-income insured. The situation becomes more inequitable in those countries that have a very low population coverage. For instance, in Honduras the population coverage in 1983 was 10 percent; the insured contributed 26 percent of total revenue, and the employer and the state together contributed 55 percent. This arrangement suggests a regressive effect on income distribution: 90 percent of the population is not insured (including the lowest-income group), but they may be financing—through prices and taxes—the bulk of the benefits for those insured.

Table 2.8   Percentage Distribution of Social Insurance Plus Family Allowances[a] Revenue by Sources in LAC: 1986

Countries	Insured	Employer	State & Taxes	Investment	Others	Total
Argentina	31.3	45.6	19.5	3.3	0.3	100.0
Bahamas	26.8	40.7	1.4	30.7	0.5	100.0
Barbados	39.9	41.7	0.0	17.7	0.7	100.0
Belize	9.4	56.4	0.0	33.9	0.3	100.0
Bolivia[c]	25.6	39.4	23.4	8.3	3.2	100.0
Brazil	39.3	52.5	3.9	2.8	1.5	100.0
Chile	30.1	2.0	48.9	18.3	0.7	100.0
Colombia	22.9	52.7	0.0	8.5	15.9	100.0
Costa Rica	25.5	49.2	2.6	11.3	11.3	100.0
Cuba[b]	0.0	44.3	55.7	0.0	0.0	100.0
Dominica	22.6	50.9	0.0	25.4	1.1	100.0
Ecuador	19.9	15.9	6.0	48.9	9.3	100.0
El Salvador	23.2	52.9	0.0	23.3	0.6	100.0
Grenada	40.4	40.4	0.0	19.0	0.2	100.0
Guatemala	26.8	55.9	0.0	0.0	17.2	100.0
Guyana	15.5	23.2	0.0	61.3	0.0	100.0
Honduras	25.7	46.6	5.9	21.3	0.5	100.0
Jamaica	17.3	21.2	2.8	58.5	0.1	100.0
Mexico	18.1	68.8	7.5	0.0	5.5	100.0
Nicaragua[b]	22.8	59.9	3.2	12.9	1.2	100.0
Panama	28.1	47.2	3.5	16.0	5.2	100.0
Peru	31.1	68.9	0.0	0.0	0.0	100.0
St. Lucia	28.6	28.6	0.0	42.7	0.0	100.0
Trinidad & Tobago	16.9	33.9	29.9	19.3	0.0	100.0
Uruguay	33.3	37.2	24.0	0.7	4.7	100.0
Venezuela	20.2	40.4	13.2	26.3	0.0	100.0
Regional Average[d]	24.8	42.0	11.3	18.9	3.0	100.0

Sources: ILO 1991a; Mesa-Lago 1991b.
Notes: a. Family allowances only in six countries.
b. 1983.
c. 1985.
d. Nonweighted

Although to confirm this point one would need to determine who really pays the social security contributions, the above analysis questions the widespread belief that those insured pay for the bulk of the benefits they receive and that there should thus be a close correspondence between contribution and benefit. Such distorted views have (1) increased the obstacles standing in the way of extending coverage in intermediate and

latecomer countries with small employed labor forces (in addition to obstacles of a structural nature); and (2) impeded a solution to the pension
crisis in pioneer countries, such as Argentina and Uruguay, that requires
enormous state subsidies. In only a few countries are there transfers from
the state budget (or from urban employers) to cover marginalized groups
not eligible for social security benefits. In Mexico the state contributes directly (and the insured and employers contribute indirectly) to the operation of the primary health-care program for marginal rural groups. In
Brazil the program of public assistance for health care that covers the
rural sector is financed by taxes on both the payroll of urban enterprises
and the value of agricultural production. In Costa Rica the state contributes to the health-care and pension assistance programs for the very
poor in rural and urban areas.

The adverse impact of the economic crisis on revenues. The crisis and adjust-
ment/restructuring policies of the 1980s reduced real revenue of social security (e.g., by 35 percent in Mexico from 1982–1988), although the economic
recovery of some countries has led to a positive reversal. Chapter 1 showed
that in the vast majority of LAC countries real average and minimum wages
in 1989 were below the 1980 levels, and rates of open unemployment and
informal employment were considerably higher. The jobless and the informal workers (usually not covered) have ceased to contribute, and those still
working are paying less in real terms (in Mexico the average real payroll
contribution declined 42 percent from 1982–1988). Enterprise bankruptcies
have closed another source of contributions. In those countries that impose a
ceiling on payroll contributions or where such contributions are fixed according to income brackets, the rapid increase in inflation (without proper adjustments of ceilings and income brackets) has resulted in a decrease in real contributions. Inflation has also adversely affected real investment yields
because most investments and their interests are not indexed (this point is
discussed in more detail later). Last but not least, private employers' tax evasion and payment delays *(mora),* as well as the state debt, have increased
during the crisis, as discussed below.

Evasion, payment delays, and state debt. Increasing rates of inflation and
hyperinflation in the 1980s have provided an extra incentive to private
employers to delay payments to social security because it is more profitable
to deposit the money in the bank (which pays a higher interest than the pen-
alty rate charged for *mora*) and pay later with devalued currency. The lack of
indexation of employers' debts, combined with low interest rates and soft
fines imposed on delinquent employers, has stimulated payment delays, and
social security revenues have declined. At the end of the decade the interest
(deflated) charged on the debt was negative in many countries: -668 percent
in Bolivia, -134 percent in Peru, and -52 percent in Ecuador. It is not

surprising, therefore, that both evasion and *mora* have reached historical peaks in LAC: 23 percent evasion in Argentina, 44 percent *mora* in Barbados, 60 percent both in Brazil, 44 percent *mora* in Jamaica, 33 percent evasion in Peru, and 27 percent evasion in Uruguay. In 1982 Costa Rica was collecting 70 percent of expected contributions, and in 1988 Uruguay's contributions comprised 52 percent of estimated total obligations. (Among the self-employed, evasion and *mora* ranged from 52–96 percent in the Bahamas, Barbados, and Jamaica.) Debt from both causes in the second half of the 1980s reached U.S. $135 million in Colombia, and the debt for *mora* alone ranged between U.S. $35 million and U.S. $50 million in Ecuador, Guatemala, and Peru. Spiraling inflation has eroded the real value of such debt, e.g., by 85 percent from 1985–1988 in Peru (because of even higher rates of inflation in 1989–1990 the Peruvian debt must have vanished).

However, inflation has only aggravated a previous problem resulting from (1) deficient systems of employer registration, payment processing, and individual account tracking; (2) a very large number of microenterprises (many of them informal), each usually hiring only a few workers but with enormous aggregate employment (these enterprises are difficult to detect, control, and collect from—the administrative cost of such an operation often exceeds the revenue collected); (3) a scarcity of skilled inspectors, who receive low salaries that create incentives for fraudulent deals with the debtors; (4) the lack of an efficient legal and judicial system to collect contributions and a poor record of prosecution and imprisonment of debtors; and (5) government and union pressure to condone or postpone debts to avoid enterprise bankruptcy and unemployment.

Measures to control evasion and late payment have been introduced with mixed results. The Bahamas, Barbados, Jamaica, Peru, and Uruguay have tried computerizing registration, payment records (that can be checked against tax records), up-to-date lists of delinquent employers, and other data to identify underpayment or *mora*. In 1989 Uruguay received a structural adjustment loan (SAL) to replace its obsolete and insufficient computer equipment and to train its personnel, and in 1991 it organized a team to fight evasion. Computerization techniques adopted by Peru in the mid-1980s showed positive results but were largely abandoned in 1988 because of their costs and the economic crisis. In Costa Rica private enterprises are required to show certification from the social insurance institute to prove they are up to date in their contribution in order to participate in public bidding or conduct bank transactions (the central government and decentralized institutions must present similar certification to get their budgets approved). Some countries are fixing both interest rates and fines higher than the inflation rate and commercial interest; others have committed resources to paying the debt and strengthening the inspection system and judicial procedures for collection and execution.

The increasing state debt toward social security in many Latin American countries results from the central government and decentralized institutions not paying their contributions as employers and third parties (and in some countries not transferring employees' contributions), retaining tax payments collected for social security, and failing to reimburse the cost of services provided by social security on behalf of the state to the dispossessed, civil servants, or military personnel. In the 1980s, under increasing pressure to cut expenditures and satisfy more urgent demands (e.g., servicing the external debt), the state debt grew worse and became a major factor in the liquidity crisis of social security in several countries. The state debt reached U.S. $73 million in Costa Rica, U.S. $95 million in the Dominican Republic, U.S. $170 million in Colombia (for only the civil servants fund), U.S. $190 million in Guatemala, U.S. $194 million in Peru, and U.S. $602 million in Ecuador. The combined state and private debt for *mora* alone to Guatemala's social security in 1988 was twice the size of the actual revenue collected. In some countries the state has signed agreements to pay the debt to the social insurance institution. However, both the debt and the interest rate have not been indexed to inflation, so payment is made with devalued currency and the real interest rate is often negative. As a result the real debt has shrunk dramatically; for instance, in Peru it was cut by 99.8 percent from 1981–1988, and in Ecuador it declined by 75 percent from 1973–1985. In Costa Rica state contributions were reduced in the early 1980s in exchange for payment of the past debt in bonds and punctual state delivery of its contributions (Miranda 1991; Mesa-Lago 1991b; BPS 1979–1991; ISSA 1991).

The economic recuperation in some LAC countries since the mid-1980s has led to increases in employment, real wages, and social security revenues; and control of inflation has reduced its pervasive effect on evasion, *mora*, and the debt. With reasonable stabilization achieved, a few countries (e.g., Costa Rica, Mexico) have raised the payroll contribution and augmented revenue. Chile has perhaps the best record in terms of both economic recuperation and increases in social security revenue; such revenue has also increased in Costa Rica since 1983, although a decrease occurred in 1990. However, many LAC countries are not enjoying such a recovery, and in the future many will endure the consequences of restructuring.

Inefficient Investment Policies and Decapitalization

The importance of investment. The historical importance of investment in financing social insurances in LAC is apparent from Table 2.9. The countries have been clustered by groups (pioneer, intermediate, latecomer) and within each group by date of enactment of the pension programs. The rationale is that, in general, the newer the program the higher the reserves and vice versa. I will deal with two indicators: (1) *investment returns,* or the annual payoff or yield generated by the invested reserves of a program; and (2) *average investment share,* or the percentage of program revenue generated by investment

Table 2.9   Percentage of Social Insurance Plus Family Allowances (and Pension) Revenue Generated by Investment Returns in LAC (Investment Shares): 1965–1986

Countries	Year(s) of Pension Program(s)[a]	Investment Returns as Percentage of:						Pensions Only
		Social Insurance Plus Family Allowances						
		1965	1970	1975	1980	1983	1986	1983
Latin America								
Pioneers	*(1920s–1960s)*							
	(1920s–1930s)							
Brazil	1920s–1930s	0.0	0.0	0.0	0.0	0.0	2.8	0.0
Uruguay	1920s–1930s	1.1	•	0.6	1.5	1.6	0.7	2.4
Argentina	1930s–1950s	•	•	1.1	2.2	2.0	3.3	0.2
Cuba	1920s–1950s/1963	0.0	0.0	0.0	0.0	0.0	0.0	0.0
Chile	1924/1981	2.2	1.1	2.0	1.8	15.9	18.3	22.6
Intermediate	*(1940s)*							
Mexico	1941	4.9	2.4	1.6	3.6	5.2	•	8.9
Costa Rica	1943	10.6	12.2	7.6	5.2	4.6	11.3	15.1
Ecuador	1930s–1942	18.6	24.8	20.3[e]	17.7	22.1	48.9	15.9
Panama	1941–1954	19.2	11.3	8.3	10.1	13.3	16.0	23.5
Colombia	1945–1956	0.0	5.1	6.9	7.3	10.7	8.5	19.0
Peru	1936–1962	•	•	•	11.1[f]	10.3	•	20.4
Latecomers	*(mid-1950s–1960s)*							
Nicaragua	1955	4.8	3.6	5.3	2.8	12.9	•	15.0
Bolivia	1959	0.9[b]	2.5[d]	3.4	7.9	12.4	8.3	16.4
Venezuela	1966	—	5.6	12.2	12.7	18.3	26.3	•
Guatemala	1969	—	1.4	0.0	7.7	13.2	•	33.1
El Salvador	1969	2.1	2.4	7.6	13.6	20.0	23.3	45.9
Honduras	1971	2.1	2.8	•	11.5	16.8	21.3	40.8
Non-Latin Caribbean	*(mid-1960s–1970s)*							
Jamaica	1966	14.6	14.8	31.4	43.6	38.5	58.5	•
Barbados	1967	—	16.9	28.6	25.4	22.3	17.7	•
Grenada	1969–1983	—	—	—	66.2	3.3	19.0	•
Guyana	1969	—	12.1	20.4	26.7	48.5	61.3	49.0
St. Lucia	1970	—	—	•	25.3	13.0	42.7	•
Dominica	1970	—	—	•	21.3	26.2	25.4	26.2
Trinidad & Tobago	1971	—	—	12.9	29.3	18.5	19.3	25.4[g]
Antigua-Barbuda	1972	—	—	•	19.8	19.2	—	•
Bahamas	1974	—	—	—	26.1	33.6	30.7	30.7
Belize	1979	—	—	—	3.0	14.3	33.9	14.6

Sources: ILO 1988, 1991a; Mesa-Lago 1991.
Notes: a. Countries ordered by year(s) in which the major pension program(s) was implemented; separation by "/" signifies old program/new program.
b. 1961; c. 1971; d. 1972; e. 1974; f. 1981; g. Social insurance only
• Signifies data not available.
— Signifies program not in force yet.

returns (see Table 2.9). Investment returns should be proportionally higher for the pension program alone than for all the programs combined because the latter include short-term programs with little or no reserves. The average investment shares (in all programs) in 1983 were as follows: 0.9 percent in pioneers (excluding Chile, whose share was 15.9 percent based on the new system introduced in 1981); 11.1 percent in intermediate countries; 15.6 percent in Latin American latecomers; and 23.7 percent in NLC latecomers.

Pension funds in pioneer countries operate under pay-as-you-go methods and basically lack reserves (this is true of Chile's old system, which is not included in the table); intermediate countries rely on partial capitalization methods, mostly scaled premiums, but some (such as Mexico) have in practice shifted to a pay-as-you-go approach; latecomer countries employ partial capitalization methods; and Chile's new system is fully funded.

The trend in the size of the investment share exhibits a similar pattern—the newer the program the higher the reserves and shares, the older the program the lower the reserves and shares. It is basically stagnant in the pioneer group (although small increases are noted in 1986 in two countries); it is erratic in the intermediate group, increasing in some and declining in others; and it is steadily increasing in virtually all countries in the latecomer group.

In summary, pioneer countries (including Chile under its old system) initiated their programs in the 1920s and 1930s, they use pay-as-you-go methods and lack reserves, and their investment shares of revenue averaged 0.9 percent in 1983 and are basically stagnant. (Chile's new system, founded in 1983 and the only fully funded system in the region, generated 15.9 percent of revenue; that value is increasing.) Intermediate countries established their programs mostly in the 1940s; they rely on partial capitalization methods, but some are shifting to pay-as-you-go; and their investment shares averaged 11 percent and do not exhibit a clear trend. Latecomer Latin American countries introduced their programs in the second half of the 1950s and 1960s, they use partial capitalization, and their investment shares averaged 15.6 percent in 1983 and are increasing; the NLC countries established their programs in the second half of the 1960s and 1970s, they employ partial capitalization, and their investment shares averaged 23.7 percent in 1983 and are increasing. These differences can be explained by the different ages or degrees of maturity of the pension programs (which generate the most reserves); the tendency by the programs to replace capitalization with pure assessment methods that lead to a reduction in the size of the reserve and its yield; investment efficiency; and external factors such as inflation.

Inefficient investment policies. Management of the investment of pension funds in LAC has not usually been efficient. In almost all of the region social security agencies are not designed to be financial intermediaries; their personnel have no experience in investments, and no investment plans have been developed. Furthermore, capital markets are poorly developed, and inflation has devalued reserves and made it difficult to generate positive yields.

In Latin America pension fund reserves have commonly been invested in (1) bonds and other state securities, often non-negotiable and rarely indexed to inflation, that in practice have been forced loans to cover state budget deficits, thus flooding social security institutions with nonnegotiable bonds of little value; (2) personal or mortgage loans, generally for the insured, who—aided by inflation (and the lack of indexation in loans and interest)—have obtained capital practically free, thus contributing to a decapitalization of the fund; (3) loans to sickness/maternity programs to help them build hospitals or cover their deficits—a laudable tactic from a social point of view, but not financially profitable; (4) construction of administrative buildings or housing for the insured, which generates very low or no revenues at all because of rent freezing, collection inefficiency, and payments in depreciated money; and (5) stores with subsidized prices for the benefit of the insured, cinemas, theaters, and sports facilities, all of which have also yielded very low or negative returns. Investment in fixed-term bank deposits is probably the most profitable approach in LAC, but it is not a very common one (with some exceptions), and investment in shares is negligible (except in Chile).

In the NLC most of the reserves have been invested in (1) state bonds and securities with higher yields (in some instances) than in Latin America; and (2) fixed-term deposits that also generate high yields. Some countries have also invested profitably in mortgage bonds. Therefore, not only do these countries have the advantage of having the newest programs, but they are also still accumulating sizable reserves; hence, their investments appear to have been managed more efficiently. A problem confronted by some of the NLC countries, however, is that the respective finance ministries (not the social security institutes) control investment and, in some circumstances, have retained part of the investment returns.

The effect of the economic crisis on investment. The crisis of the 1980s had an adverse effect on investment performance in many countries, particularly those with high rates of inflation. I have noted that state securities and personal and mortgage loans are not usually indexed to inflation and so have rapidly devalued. The unpaid state debt in many countries has reduced the level of reserves, and when the state has paid its debts with bonds, these bonds have long terms and are not indexed to inflation. The liberalization of the interest rate in some countries has allowed commercial banks to offer positive real rates, but few Latin American countries except Costa Rica have a significant part of their portfolio in this investment instrument (although

NLC countries do). Real estate values have skyrocketed with inflation, and some countries (e.g., Mexico) have heavily invested in real estate, but they have directed their resources to social security administrative buildings and hospitals, which are not profitable (investment in housing for the insured has been harmed by a lack of indexation).

NLC countries usually have much lower rates of inflation than Latin American countries, so they have suffered less from the above problems. Pioneer countries have had very high rates of inflation (except Chile), but this is irrelevant because they lack reserves. Some intermediate countries (e.g., Bolivia, Mexico, Peru) have been afflicted by hyperinflation that has had a devastating effect on their investment yields. Conversely, inflation rates in Panama, Colombia, Costa Rica (except for two years), Ecuador, and Venezuela have been moderate. Finally, most Latin American late-comers except Nicaragua have had low inflation rates. Therefore investment performance has been affected not only by the age of the programs and efficiency in managing the portfolios but also by an exogenous factor: inflation.

Poor investment yields and their causes. A comparative study of portfolio investment of social insurance funds in eight LAC countries from 1980–1987 confirmed most of the points discussed above (Mesa-Lago 1991a). Invested assets as a percentage of national gross fixed capital formation in 1987 ranged from 67–96 percent in the Bahamas, Barbados and Chile; from 15–29 percent in Costa Rica, Ecuador, and Jamaica; and from 0.2–3.5 percent in Mexico and Peru. (As percentages of GDP the ranges were, respectively, 11–15 percent, 3–6 percent, and 0.04–0.7 percent.) The oldest pension funds, such as that of Peru, are more mature and thus have less resources to invest; the opposite is true of the newest programs, such as those of Chile, the Bahamas, and Barbados. Real (deflated) growth of invested assets from 1981–1987 was as follows: 424 percent in Chile, 62 percent in the Bahamas, 45 percent in Costa Rica, 38 percent in Barbados, -3 percent in Jamaica, -18 percent in Peru, and 3 percent or -73 percent in Mexico, depending on different estimates. Only three countries had annual real positive investment yields from 1980–1987: 13.8 percent in Chile, 2.7 percent in the Bahamas, and 0.7 percent in Barbados. The other countries had negative yields: -4.8 percent in Jamaica, -10 percent in Ecuador, -10.5 percent in Costa Rica, -20.8 percent in Mexico, and between -20.6 percent and -29.4 percent in Peru. The three countries with positive real yields are also those that have the relatively most important invested assets and highest growth rates of those assets. Conversely, the two countries with the worst negative yields are those that have the least significant invested assets and have suffered a real decline in the value of such assets. The positive relationship among the three variables is a logical one because investment returns are influenced by the relative size of the fund and its real growth rate.

Average inflation rates from 1980–1987 for the eight countries were as follows: 6.6 percent in the Bahamas, 7.2 percent in Barbados, 16.6 percent in Jamaica, 24.3 percent in Chile, 25.7 percent in Ecuador, 29.1 percent in Costa Rica, 69.5 percent in Mexico, and 93.4 percent in Peru. In general, the higher the inflation rate the lower the real yield, and vice versa. Because most investment has a fixed interest, high steady inflation rates play a crucial role in turning positive real yields into negative yields and in decreasing the real value of the reserves.

The terms of the investment instruments and the compositions of the portfolios were also important in explaining the yields. A high concentration in instruments with poor performance led to overall negative yields: 91 percent in public bonds in Jamaica, 84 percent in real estate in Mexico, 83 percent in personal and mortgage loans in Ecuador, and 44 percent in public bonds in Costa Rica. On the other hand, 66 percent of the Bahamas' invested assets are concentrated in public bonds, but these bonds have had an interest rate higher than the commercial bank rate, thus largely explaining that country's positive yield. Fixed-term deposits usually pay a high real positive interest, a fact that has helped the performance of the Bahamas, Chile, and Costa Rica (in Costa Rica such deposits have helped partly offset the negative performance of public bonds). Peru had 72 percent of its investment concentrated in fixed-term deposits (mostly in U.S. dollars), but in 1985 the government forcibly converted dollar deposits into *intis*, and the subsequent dramatic devaluation of that currency led to a substantial loss in the fund. Investment in short-term instruments, which offers lower interest than investment in long-term instruments, accounts for 73–77 percent of the total investment of Mexico and Barbados. The proportion of the fund in either fixed or net-current assets is very high in Mexico and Ecuador, thereby reducing the sum invested and contributing to poor returns.

In Mexico the law established that 85 percent of the reserves had to be invested in infrastructure such as hospitals, clinics, administrative buildings, and day-care centers, as well as in equipment and furniture. In 1989, 87 percent of Mexico's investment was in that instrument; the actuary warned that such property could not be sold and that its yield was nil, so it would be impossible to finance pensions in the year 2004. In 1990 the law was modified, establishing that pension reserves should be invested in financial instruments and allowing investment in shares up to 5 percent of total reserves (Soto Pérez 1990; IMSS 1990b).

Costa Rica was moderately successful in improving investment performance in the second half of the 1980s. The average real yield for 1981–1982 (in the midst of the crisis and under very high inflation rates) was -37.6 percent; it improved for 1983–1984 to -3.6 percent and turned positive for 1985–1987 to 2.7 percent. In the second half of the 1980s, as part of a stabilization program, inflation was cut to less than one-fifth of the 1981–1982 peak rate. The state debt was reduced from 23 percent of total reserves in 1977 to 2.6 percent in 1987, and cash surpluses (lost potential investment) were cut from 16 percent to 2.6 percent. The composition of the portfolio also improved: (1) unprofitable loans to the sickness/maternity program declined from 35 percent to zero from 1982–1987 (such loans were prohibited in 1983); (2) fixed-term deposits increased from 5 percent to 35 percent; and (3) mortgage loans and other unprofitable loans declined from 20 percent to 14 percent. Conversely, the share of government bonds increased from 32 percent to 47 percent; because the bonds' real yields were negative, they partially neutralized the increase in positive real yields coming from the above-mentioned improvements.

Experience with investments in the 1980s taught some important lessons: (1) both reduction of inflation and economic stabilization are essential to provide the needed base for any sound investment policy and to generate positive real yields; (2) government interference and investment in state securities should be eliminated or reduced (unless it pays positive yields as in some LAC countries); (3) funds in fixed and net-current assets should be reduced to a minimum; (4) the portfolio should be diversified, giving priority to high-yield instruments such as fixed-term deposits; and (5) interest rates should be indexed to inflation (Mesa-Lago 1991a).

Generous and Inequitable Benefits and Their Erosion

Social security benefits in LAC countries are the most advanced in the Third World, and the sickness/maternity and family-allowance programs are ahead of those in a few industrialized countries such as the United States and Japan. But excessive generosity in both entitlement conditions and benefits, combined with inequalities in benefits for different segments of the population, has pushed costs to intolerable levels in some countries. The crisis and the adjustment/restructuring programs induced a decline in the level and quality of benefits in most of LAC in the first half of the 1980s, although a recuperation might currently be taking place.

In the pioneer countries the highest proportion of benefit expenditures (for social insurances and family allowances) goes to pensions, but in the latecomer countries it is allocated to sickness/maternity (see Table 2.10). The NLC countries appear to be an exception, though, because most of their expenditures go to pensions; this is explained by the exclusion of public health expenditures from the table and the fact that in the NLC the sickness/maternity social insurance schemes pay only monetary benefits. Between 1965 and 1986 the average regional share of benefit expenditures for pensions increased from 34 percent to 56 percent, and the share for sickness/maternity declined from 52 percent to 38 percent. The changing trend is an outcome of the growing maturity of pension programs combined with the aging of the population and the increase in life expectancy.

In the future an even higher proportion of expenditures will go to pensions, and less will be available for the sickness/maternity programs. This situation has been aggravated in many countries by the investment of a sizable portion of the pension reserves in the construction and equipping of hospitals and even in the subsidizing of operation costs. Such an investment is rarely profitable and has contributed to the decapitalization of the pension funds (as described later in this chapter). The eventual maturation of the pension funds has thus led to financial difficulties or bankruptcy in both the pension and sickness/maternity programs.

Generosity in benefits and entitlement conditions. The pioneer countries tend to cover all contingencies and to provide a greater number of benefits: Argentina, Brazil, Chile, and Uruguay are the only countries in LAC that cover all the risks—including unemployment and family allowances. The older systems have granted exceptional and costly benefits as well as more liberal entitlement conditions than those available in countries of the intermediate and latecomer groups. Once these benefits and conditions are set by a law it is very difficult to reduce them or make them stricter. The following paragraphs provide examples of generous entitlement conditions in pension and sickness/maternity programs.

In the pension programs of three pioneer countries (Argentina, Cuba, and Uruguay) the retirement ages are 60 for males and 55 for females, but the life expectancy in these countries is among the highest in the region; therefore the average retirement period is quite long. Brazil has generally higher ages of retirement but allows a seniority pension with 30 years of service regardless of age. Only Chile has retirement ages commensurate with its life expectancy. In Costa Rica the age for early retirement was gradually reduced in the 1970s and 1980s from 65 for both sexes to 57/55 for males/females; in the meantime, life expectancy grew from 65 to 75 years (in 1991 the retirement ages were raised to 60/62); in addition, special programs for some groups of civil servants permit retirement at 50 years of age or with 30 years of service regardless of age. The latter program is also available in Uruguay with only 20 years of service. Under these *special* schemes the average retirement periods (measured by the average life expectancy at time of retirement) for males and females are 24 and 27 years in Brazil, 25 and 29 years in Costa Rica, and 25 and 28 years in Uruguay. In Cuba the average retirement periods under the *general* system are 19 and 25 years. A few countries in the intermediate group have very low ages of retirement as well: Panama has 55/50 for males/females (with average retirement periods of 22 and 28 years, respectively), and Ecuador has 55 for both sexes (with average retirement periods of 20 and 21 years).

In many of these cases the average retirement period is similar to the period of work and contribution, particularly among females.[4] Stricter

Table 2.10 Percentage Distribution of Benefit Expenditures for Social Insurance and Family Allowances in LAC: 1965–1986

		Sickness/ Maternity	Pensions	Employment Injury	Family Allowances	Unemployment
Argentina	1975	14.5	58.3	0.0	27.2	0.0
	1986	•	76.8	0.0	22.4	0.8
Bahamas	1980	27.4	72.5	0.1	0.0	0.0
	1986	24.1	53.1	22.9	0.0	0.0
Barbados	1971	65.4	25.2	9.4	0.0	0.0
	1986	9.8	75.0	0.9	0.0	14.2
Belize	1983	52.7	5.8	41.4	0.0	0.0
	1986	40.9	26.2	33.0	0.0	0.0
Bolivia	1961	55.4	13.7	0.0	30.9	0.0
	1986	55.2	36.4	5.8	2.2	0.3
Brazil	1970	47.2	40.2	3.4	9.2	0.0
	1986	32.1	63.3	0.9	3.7	0.0
Chile	1965	16.6	36.2	0.0	45.9	1.3
	1986	17.4	70.8	2.6	7.0	1.1
Colombia	1965	63.3	0.0	1.2	35.4	0.0
	1986	8.9	84.4	6.7	0.0	0.0
Costa Rica	1965	77.8	4.7	17.5	0.0	0.0
	1986	65.5	26.7	7.8	0.0	0.0
Cuba	1980	13.0	85.2	1.8	0.0	0.0
Dominican Rep.	1977	72.0	25.3	2.7	0.0	0.0
	1986	67.4	32.6	0.0	0.0	0.0
Ecuador	1965	18.9	63.3	0.0	0.0	17.8
	1986	35.8	59.0	1.4	0.0	3.9
El Salvador	1965	91.2	0.0	8.8	0.0	0.0
	1986	65.4	34.5	0.0	0.0	0.0
Guatemala	1970	50.3	0.0	49.7	0.0	0.0
	1986	39.5	26.6	33.8	0.0	0.0
Guyana	1972	25.6	5.3	69.1	0.0	0.0
	1986	6.5	77.2	16.3	0.0	0.0
Honduras	1965	96.3	0.0	3.2	0.0	0.0
	1986	86.2	13.8	0.0	0.0	0.0
Jamaica	1975	0.0	92.0	8.0	0.0	0.0
	1986	12.6	82.4	4.9	0.0	0.0
Mexico	1965	73.3	16.7	10.0	0.0	0.0
	1986	58.6	30.0	11.4	0.0	0.0
Nicaragua	1965	89.4	4.7	5.9	0.0	0.0
	1983	27.9	63.7	8.4	0.0	0.0
Panama	1965	60.4	39.6	0.0	0.0	0.0
	1986	46.8	46.8	6.4	0.0	0.0
Peru	1981	60.0	32.1	7.9	0.0	0.0
	1983	58.7	34.1	7.2	0.0	0.0
Trinidad & Tobago	1975	21.4	71.4	7.2	0.0	0.0
	1986	5.6	91.3	3.0	0.0	0.0
Uruguay	1975	3.6	73.6	1.9	16.9	4.0
	1986	10.1	81.8	0.0	6.7	1.4
Venezuela	1965	79.9	0.0	20.1	0.0	0.0
	1976	65.9	34.1	0.0	0.0	0.0

Sources: Based on ILO 1991a.
Note: Rows may not always total 100% due to rounding.
• Signifies data not available.

conditions exist in a few countries of the intermediate group (e.g., Mexico's age is 65 years for both sexes) and in most countries of the latecomer group (e.g., 65 in Guatemala, the Bahamas, and Barbados; and 65/60 for males/females in El Salvador, Honduras, and Jamaica). Although Mexico has a very high age of retirement, its life expectancy at age 65 almost doubled from 1942–1990 (from 9 to 16 years); in addition, benefits were liberalized without an increase in contributions for almost 50 years (Soto Pérez 1991). The Latin American countries of the latecomer group are the least developed and have the lowest life expectancy, so their average retirement period is the shortest.

The rules for calculating pensions are the most liberal in the pioneer countries, except for Chile and to a lesser extent Cuba; for instance, in Brazil the base salary is computed according to the salary of the last three years, the basic rate is 70 percent, and the maximum rate is 95 percent; in Argentina and Uruguay the conditions are slightly tighter. Costa Rica's civil servant schemes—at least until recently—usually pay 100 percent of the salary earned in the last year or even the last month. Five countries set the maximum pension as 100 percent of the salary average (this appears to be the case in four other countries), and four countries set such maximums from 90–95 percent. In many developed countries a rate of 40–50 percent of the base salary is considered adequate.

The above generous pension conditions offer a strong incentive for premature retirement at the peak of productive activity; retirees receive a pension equal or close to their previous salary and may still perform paid work either legally or, most frequently, in the informal sector. The common allegation that such generosity at least helps alleviate unemployment lacks solid evidence. The important issue of pension readjustment is analyzed later in this chapter.

Benefits and entitlement conditions for sickness/maternity programs are equally liberal, particularly in Latin America. Eight countries require neither a waiting period nor contributions for an individual to be eligible for paid sick leave—it is enough to be employed and insured (this is also true for maternity benefits in two countries). Six countries require a waiting period from four to six weeks to receive paid sick leave. Furthermore, in three countries the sick-leave pay is equal to 100 percent of the salary, and two other countries pay 90 percent (in 11 countries maternity leave is equal to the salary). These conditions are strong incentives for workers to claim sickness and collect paid leave (a problem reported in several countries), thereby significantly increasing the costs of the program. In countries where the only requirements are to be insured or have paid a few contributions, evaders frequently have access to costly health-care treatment by simply registering or paying a small sum and thereafter stopping their contribution. In the NLC the waiting period is usually longer, and paid leave averages 60 percent of the salary; two NLC countries do not have this benefit at all. Some countries (e.g., Ecuador, Peru, Costa Rica until 1982, and Colombia until 1986) provide such expensive benefits as contact lenses, orthodontics, and the cost of travel and treatment abroad when the required treatment is not available at home. In 1982 the cost of treating 131 Peruvian insured persons abroad was U.S. $5 million, or U.S. $38,168 per capita. Finally, some countries provide "social benefits" to the insured and their dependents, such as personal and mortgage loans, low-cost or low-rental housing, special shops with subsidized prices, and free or heavily subsidized recreational and sport activities. These services are very expensive and usually create program deficits.

Inequities in benefits.   Unjustified inequalities in benefits among occupational groups, geographical regions, and age groups pose another problem in LAC. In the 1980s the ratios of average pensions in several occupational groups (often with independent programs) to the average pensions in the general systems of seven Latin American countries were as follows: 2.5–8 for the armed forces; 1.6–6.9 for the police; 1.2–4 for civil servants; 3.4–5.8 for banking; but only 0.8 for rural workers and 0.7 for domestic servants. In Brazil the average privileged pension is triple the standard pension, so 28 percent of total urban pension expenditures go to 9 percent of the pensioners. In Costa Rica 19 independent pension programs for civil servants (9 entirely financed by the state) account for 20 percent of all the nation's pensioners but receive 42 percent of the total pension expenditures. Civil servants in the Bahamas, Barbados, and Jamaica are usually exempt from paying contributions for pensions, can retire 5–10 years earlier than in the general system, and are eligible to receive two pensions (and, in Jamaica, to continue performing paid work). Inequalities in health-care benefits are common in countries with separate programs for special groups. The armed forces normally enjoy some of the best services available and either do not pay any contributions or pay only a token amount; superior state-subsidized programs are also available for petroleum workers and similarly powerful groups who have relatively high incomes. Furthermore, the least developed, poorest, most isolated rural regions (with the highest concentration of Indian population) usually have the lowest health-care coverage and the worst services, whereas the most developed, wealthiest urban regions have the highest coverage and the best services.

Finally, there are disparities related to the population age structure. Thirty percent of the productive-age population of Peru is covered by social security, but only 1.4 percent of the population below 14 years of age; in Colombia the proportions are 15 percent and 3.6 percent, respectively; and Brazilian pensioners make up only 4.3 percent of the population but receive almost one-third of total benefit expenditures. Infant mortality rates among these three countries are among the highest in LAC. A better distribution of social security expenditures by age and to vulnerable groups—for instance, by eliminating seniority pensions and transferring those resources to provide better primary health care to pregnant women and children and to rural areas—could reduce infant mortality rates and increase life expectancy.

Generous and lopsided social security benefits in LAC (particularly in the pioneers) have had a perverse demonstration effect, contributed to escalating costs, produced actuarial and financial disequilibrium, and eventually led to the erosion of real pensions and a deterioration in the quality of health care. Privileged benefits only partly financed by the insured have had a regressive impact on income distribution. In countries of the intermediate and latecomer groups the enormous cost of vertically extending benefits for a minority of insured often makes impossible the horizontal extension (universalization) of such essential benefits as minimum pensions and primary health care to the majority of the population (Mesa-Lago 1991b, 1991c).

The impact of the economic crisis on the erosion of benefits. In the 1980s the decline in real revenues of social security in LAC was aggravated by an increase in expenditures. Prices of medicines and medical/surgical devices, many of which are imported, escalated because of domestic as well as international inflation. High unemployment rates provoked a jump in expenditures by such programs, particularly in Barbados, Uruguay, and Chile. Elderly insured individuals suffering long-term unemployment and entitled to old-age pensions chose to retire, and those lacking that right resorted to public assistance pensions where available (in the Bahamas and Barbados the increase in assistance expenditures depleted resources from the insurance fund). Many insured who used private rather than social security medical services shifted to the latter as their income declined. In countries where social insurance provides free health care for the indigents (e.g., Costa Rica) more people ceased being contributors when they lost their jobs or entered the informal sector, but they became eligible for the welfare programs. The state was expected to reimburse social security for those welfare costs, but as we have seen, it often failed to fulfill that obligation. In countries where sickness/maternity care is available only to the insured, those who lost insurance coverage became dependent on the public health system, the budget of which had been severely cut. Pensions were readjusted to the cost of living (as discussed in more detail later). In countries where salaries of social insurance employees were adjusted to inflation, that expenditure (the largest component of total expenditures) increased, at least for a while. Pressures to adjust benefits to the cost of living also led to increased expenditures, at least for a while.

Facing a liquidity crisis, some countries enacted emergency programs to cut expenditures and increase revenues; a common step was to halt investment, particularly in health-care facilities. From 1974–1981 Chile eliminated most privileged benefits enjoyed by certain occupational groups in the old social security system (including seniority pensions) and introduced a new, uniform system with more reasonable benefits and tighter entitlement conditions. In 1982 Costa Rica launched a successful emergency program that, among other things, cut down employment, salaries, and fringes; eliminated generous benefits (such as orthodontics and contact lenses); established better control on prescriptions; and reduced the basic list of medicines by almost two-thirds. Other emergency programs followed, including one in Peru in 1988. Continuing the reform initiated in the 1970s, Uruguay eliminated various privileged programs in 1987–1988 and set a pension ceiling. However, these reforms have not always been successful, and many generous benefits still remain because politically powerful groups resist their elimination. Seniority and special pension programs, as well as relatively low ages of retirement, are still in place in Brazil, Panama, and Uruguay (in Uruguay an attempt to raise the ages of retirement was defeated in congress); on the other hand, Costa Rica has recently tightened the early retirement program.

Mexico followed a different strategy by partially compensating for the social cost of adjustment by raising contributions without significantly reducing other costs. Some of the compensatory measures are (1) an expansion of health-care coverage to the unemployed from 8 to 26 weeks; (2) extension of emergency care for the noninsured by 10 percent; (3) an increase in minimum pensions (since 1989); (4) provision of health care to pensioners with permanent partial disabilities; (5) cancelation of contribution debts for those with housing needs; and (6) maintenance of support to the social solidarity program. These measures increased costs, but the program to offset such increases was grossly insufficient; it included (1) an attempt to increase installed capacity; (2) increased priority to maintenance and recovery of equipment (to reduce imports); and (3) cancelation of air transport services. The result was a surplus that shrank from 18.8 percent of expenditures in 1982 to 1.9 percent in 1988 (the surplus left after actuarial reserves were provided declined from 15.8 percent to 0.35 percent). A more stern measure was to increase the total contribution for sickness/maternity by 33 percent. However, the actuary still warned that costs would continue to grow and thus would forestall universal coverage and create a serious financial deficit in the pension program at the beginning of the next century; the actuary suggested a gradual increase in total pension contributions: by two-fold from 1991–2011 and three-fold from 1991–2031. At the beginning of 1991 the contribution was legally modified so that it will gradually increase by 33 percent from 1991–1996 (Soto Pérez 1990, 1991; IMSS 1991a).

Most countries have resorted to less direct means to cope with the crisis, allowing real benefits to erode through inflation. From 1965–1975 the real average benefit increased in virtually all LAC countries, in four-fifths

of them by a substantial percentage. From 1980–1982 the trend continued
in about half of the countries but was reversed in the other half; from
1983–1985 more than half of the countries had benefit levels below those
of 1980–1981. The situation improved somewhat in 1986, but in two-
fifths of the countries the average benefit was still below the 1980–1981
level; five countries suffered benefit reductions from one-third to two-
thirds (see Table 2.11). It should be noted that, with one exception, all increases in the benefit level have occurred in the NLC. These countries
were the last in the region to introduce social security, and initially their
benefits were extremely low, but these benefits have been increased to
more reasonable levels in some countries. Another plausible explanation
is that the share of pensions in total benefit expenditures increased very
fast in these countries (e.g., from 5.3 percent to 77.2 percent in Guyana,
5.8 percent to 26.2 percent in Belize, and 25.2 percent to 75 percent in
Barbados—see ILO 1991a; Mesa-Lago 1991b); because the amount paid
for a pension is much higher than that paid for short-term benefits, the
average benefit increased rapidly. However, this issue requires further
investigation.

The impact of the crisis on the quality of health care is difficult to assess. One expert argues that such questions cannot be answered with
available data from most LAC countries, although he reports a reduction
in hospital admissions, curtailment of some hospital services, and difficulties in maintaining basic care (Musgrove 1989). Another expert, based
on data from the Dominican Republic and Peru, reports a clear deterioration of health services: severe cuts in medical supplies, elimination or reduction of meals in hospitals, lack of basic surgical materials, and shar-
ing of one bed by two patients (Mesa-Lago 1992c).

Costly pensions readjustment and their eventual devaluation. Until the crisis of the 1980s cost-of-living adjustments to pensions were generous: in
Argentina pensions were adjusted to 82 percent of the last salary earned and
in Bolivia 90 percent; in Chile pension adjustments among some groups were
based on the adjusted salary of the job the pensioner had prior to retirement
(this method—called *perseguidora*, or "follow up"—was a model copied by
other Latin American countries). Table 2.12 shows that in all but two countries real pensions increased in the second half of the 1970s: by 31 percent in
Costa Rica, 53 percent in Ecuador, and 42 percent in Jamaica (and by 48 percent in Chile, not shown in the table). However, pensions peaked and thereafter declined in Uruguay (with the peak in 1963) and Mexico (with the peak
in 1975).

For a while some countries continued adjusting pensions to the increasing cost of living, e.g., in Barbados and Jamaica until 1981–1982, in
Panama until 1985, in Uruguay until 1982 (still below the 1963 peak,
however), and in Peru from 1984–1988. But in all these countries

Table 2.11   Indices of Annual Average Social Security Benefits Expenditure per
Capita in LAC: 1965–1986
(Adjusted for Cost of Living; 1970 for Old Series and 1980 for New Series)

	1965	1970	1975	1980	1981	1982	1983	1984	1985	1986
Antigua & Barbuda	•	•	•	100	103	85	101	•	•	•
Argentina	•	•	•	100	84	67	73	77	62	62
Bahamas	•	•	•	100	138	169	216	238	269	282
Barbados	•	100	175	100	107	131	153	178	188	228
Belize	•	•	•	•	100	134	611	609	743	729
Bolivia	73	100	131	100	115	82	76	133	706	•
Brazil	138	100	154	100	109	122	98	93	98	104
Chile	21	100	4,753[a]	100	93	121	107	110	104	106
Colombia	39	100	141	100	79	80	87	52	52	55
Costa Rica	50	100	191	100	104	73	71	85	94	94
Dominica	•	•	•	100	100	97	151	271	337	379
Ecuador	75	100	123	100	104	93	111	114	113	120
El Salvador	89	100	104	100	90	79	80	67	59	44
Grenada	•	•	•	•	100	109	109	114	125	122
Guatemala	85	100	105	100	80	87	78	79	70	62
Guyana	127	100	77	100	84	79	76	69	77	120
Honduras	71	100	•	•	100	101	95	102	101	100
Jamaica	100	100	171	100	90	85	110	119	95	94
Mexico	78	100	129	100	109	110	84	93	91	80
Nicaragua	•	•	•	•	100	101	73	•	•	•
Panama	68	100	106	100	106	109	127	142	148	159
Peru	•	•	•	•	100	100	78	29	28	33
St. Lucia	•	•	•	•	100	110	124	247	102	232
Suriname	•	•	90	100	175	200	232	•	•	•
Trinidad & Tobago	86	100	121	100	193	229	322	303	271	285
Uruguay	•	•	•	100	133	140	75	112	96	107
Venezuela	126	100	239	100	61	88	85	85	78	84

Sources: ILO 1988, 1991a.
Note: a. This figure is questionable but has been repeated by the ILO in successive reports.
• Signifies data not available.

pensions later declined. In Colombia, Costa Rica, Ecuador, and Mexico
real pensions declined in the first half of the 1980s. Facing enormous
deficits, the social security ministry in Argentina allowed pensions to go
under the 82 percent statutory adjustment to inflation (as low as 45 percent). This action prompted hundreds of pensioners to sue the ministry,
and they won an appeal to Argentina's supreme court. It was estimated
that if all pensioners had been paid the amount due, the total sum would
have equaled the Argentinean foreign debt. To avoid bankruptcy the government had to enact a law declaring a national social security emergency.
In the second half of the 1980s there was some recuperation in real pensions in several countries, but recent data from most countries are lacking,
so it is not possible to reach any solid conclusion. In 1989 Costa Rica had
almost recovered the 1980 level and Uruguay had exceeded it, but Mexico
was well below (see Table 2.12).

An Uruguayan law enacted in 1987 stipulated that pensions be adjusted to the wage index of the previous year and set a pension ceiling. Inflation was running close to 60 percent at that time; hence, these measures aimed at reducing the cost of pensions. Indeed, in 1989 the real pension declined, but it nevertheless remained 19 percent above its 1980 level. During Uruguay's national election campaign that year practically all political parties supported a constitutional amendment, which was eventually approved, to fully adjust pensions to the cost of living starting in April 1990. It was estimated that the adjustment would require an increase of 8–11 percentage points in either the VAT or the payroll contribution or, should that fail, a 150 percent increase in inflation would occur. The newly elected government, which had endorsed the adjustment policy, confronted a serious problem at the start of its term because the measure contradicted an agreement with an international lending agency to reduce pensions to an affordable level. New earmarked taxes had been already established in 1987 to reduce the deficit in pensions, so the government reluctantly decided to increase the VAT to 22 percent and raise the payroll tax for employers as well. An attempt was made to apply the pension ceilings established in the 1987 law, but eventually the regulation was found unconstitutional and the ceilings were revoked. In spite of the increases in taxes and contributions, inflation rose from 89 percent to 130 percent from 1989–1990. Inflationary pressures would have been worse if not for a drastic fiscal adjustment program, launched by the government in 1990, that was able to cut the public sector deficit significantly but at the cost of increasing unemployment and lowering real wages from 1990–1991 (ECLAC 1990a, 1991a; Mesa-Lago 1991b; BPS 1979–1991).

The experiences of Argentina and Uruguay (countries where the fiscal burden of pensions is enormous) teach the lesson that pension adjustments must be commensurate with the economic capacity of the country to avoid negative effects; such adjustments should not be regulated by laws, much less by a constitution, because laws do not allow the required flexibility. Costa Rica has been more cautious on adjustment policies but has also been helped by having a younger population and a much newer pension program.

High and Increasing Health-Care Costs

The organization of health care and the distribution of resources. Three major types of organizations for health-care services can be identified in LAC. First, some countries have a national health system that is basically operated by the ministry of health and has its own facilities (as in the NLC, except Bermuda, and in Cuba and Nicaragua). Second, in some countries social insurance (with one or more institutes) covers the majority of the population

Table 2.12   Real Values of Pensions in Selected Countries of LAC: 1975–1989
(1980 Value=100)

Countries	1975	1976	1977	1978	1979	1980	1981	1982	1983	1984	1985	1986	1987	1988	1989
Barbados	•	•	•	108.9	103.1	100.0	125.8	120.3	111.7	88.8	98.5	99.0	•	•	•
Colombia[a]	96.8	91.0	102.6	106.4	84.5	100.0	91.9	93.3	92.4	89.9	89.3	•	•	•	•
Costa Rica	76.2	87.2	95.8	94.0	101.2	100.0	84.5	53.5	84.6	88.8	116.4	98.8	111.0	93.6	94.0
Ecuador	65.3	62.3	72.6	64.7	67.3	100.0	90.4	85.0	76.6	66.1	67.0	72.2	•	•	•
Jamaica	70.1	66.9	77.9	69.4	72.3	100.0	107.3	107.4	129.1	100.5	82.4	78.2	•	•	•
Mexico[b]	107.1	106.2	103.9	98.4	98.4	100.0	81.7	59.8	48.7	43.0	47.6	42.1	54.8	34.4	60.2
Panama	102.2	106.6	107.0	108.5	106.3	100.0	105.9	105.8	119.6	124.0	126.4	•	•	•	•
Uruguay[c]	112.3	114.6	105.4	106.4	96.7	100.0	137.0	143.2	110.5	105.0	98.2	113.4	123.1	125.5	118.7

Sources: Mesa-Lago 1991b updated with BPS 1990, CCSS 1989, and IMSS 1990a.
Notes: a. The highest point was 116.7 in 1973.
b. Data from IMSS only; the highest point was in 1975; since 1980 only old-age and disability pensions.
c. The highest point was 199.7 in 1963.

through either direct or indirect systems of delivery, and the ministry of health covers the noninsured and provides other services such as prevention and supervision. Only in Costa Rica and Mexico do the social insurance programs provide most of the services directly. Argentina, Brazil, and Uruguay follow the indirect system through the formation of programs administered by trade unions, private facilities, and mutual aid societies. Venezuela and Panama are somewhere in between the direct and indirect approaches. Third, in some countries the great majority of the population is expected to be covered by the ministry of health, and social insurance covers less than one-fourth of the population through either direct or indirect delivery systems (as in Bolivia, Colombia, the Dominican Republic, Ecuador, El Salvador, Guatemala, Honduras, Paraguay, and Peru). Chile is a special case for which social insurance and the rest of the public sector are difficult to separate and for which there is an increasing private sector. Haiti does not have sickness/maternity social insurance, and its ministry of health is grossly inadequate to cover the population (Castellanos 1986; Mesa-Lago 1992c).

The most important providers within the public sector are the respective ministries of health, which have two major functions: (1) prevention and sanitation (e.g., immunization, environmental sanitation, control of endemic and epidemic diseases, health education, supervision of all health care); and (2) curative medicine. In some Latin American countries there are additional public services delivered by states, departments, provinces, or major cities (e.g., the federal district in Mexico City); in virtually all of these countries there are independent services for the armed forces. The noninsured population (particularly the poor) usually has access only to the ministry of health and similar public services, except in the case of those in the high-income and possibly middle-income strata who pay for private services. The ministry's facilities and services are often the worst in quality, although there are notable exceptions. In the Dominican Republic the very low quality of both the ministry and social security facilities have led to the development of health maintenance organizations (HMOs), or *igualas*.

Social insurance has become the second major provider of health care in LAC, mainly through the sickness/maternity program and to a lesser extent through unemployment, injury, and family-allowance programs focusing on curative services (with important exceptions). The population covered is normally the middle-income strata, and in some countries the upper low-income and lower high-income groups. However, I have noted that in a few cases social insurance provides free health care to all the noninsured dispossessed (as in Costa Rica) or to the rural poor (as in Brazil, Ecuador, and Mexico). Social insurance facilities and services are normally better in terms of quantity and quality than those of the ministry of health.

The private sector, be it nonprofit or for-profit, is mostly involved in providing curative medicine in LAC. It is the smallest of the three sectors (the other two being social insurance and public health), but it is rapidly expanding in many countries. Nonprofit providers are nongovernmental organizations (NGOs) such as religious and charitable organizations, development institutes, and community associations. They have experienced impressive and rapid growth in recent years, both in numbers and in the volume of resources they manage (they obtain 60 percent of their resources by themselves and receive the rest from official aid agencies). NGOs have a number of advantages: they are flexibly organized, they can act in fields not covered by the state and better reach target groups (in some cases they can take over functions that are normally the domain of the state if they are given clear legal and operational frameworks), and their staffs are usually highly motivated and work for lower salaries than those of the public sector.

Within the for-profit private sector, prepaid plans are still incipient and include insurance (individual and group policies) as well as employer, cooperative, and community plans. Most of these operate in large urban areas, but some are found in small cities and agroexport areas. In addition, there are private hospitals, clinics, and medical personnel who tend to individuals not covered by any plan, as well as traditional medicine practitioners (*curanderos*, midwives, etc.). Surveys conducted in Costa Rica, the Dominican Republic, Jamaica, and Uruguay show that from 5–42 percent of the lowest income groups purchase private services at significant personal costs either because they lack institutional protection or because the services offered are poor.

Although in most of Latin America the only health services available to the majority of the population are provided by the ministries of health, these ministries receive considerably smaller shares of the national funds allocated to public health care than social insurance. Table 2.13 contrasts the percentage distributions of population covered and national revenue received between the ministries of health and the social insurance programs in a few Latin American countries for which data are available; the table also shows a ratio of revenue to coverage in each institution. In the Dominican Republic 91 percent of the population (outside of the private sector) is covered by the ministry and 9 percent by social insurance, but the respective shares of the revenues given to each institution are 53 percent and 47 percent, resulting in ratios of 0.58 for the ministry and 5.22 for social insurance. Similarly diverse ratios are shown for Colombia, Ecuador, and Peru. The most equal ratios are registered in Costa Rica and Panama. Most NLC countries have avoided an imbalance because they normally have one national health system. Another difference is that social insurance concentrates on curative medicine, whereas an important proportion of a ministry's resources goes toward preventive medicine and primary health care.

Rising costs of health care: trends, causes, and effects of the economic crisis.
Health-care expenditures in Latin America are relatively high by international standards (the highest in the Third World) and exhibit a growing trend,
following similar behavior in overall social security expenditures. Although
the available data are scarce and sometimes questionable, from 1980–1986
social insurance health expenditures as percentages of GDP were 4.8 percent
in Costa Rica, 2.6 percent in Argentina, 2.6 percent in Chile (combined with
public health), 2.5 percent in Colombia, 1.3 percent in Brazil, 1.2 percent in
Peru, and 0.4 percent in Uruguay (where the bulk of health care is provided
by mutual aid societies). Scattered information from the remaining Latin
American countries suggests that, with the exception of Panama, values there
are 1 percent or less.

The historical trend in social insurance health-care costs as a percentage of GDP is even more difficult to trace because of the absence of data
and changes in methodology. Since 1978 the ILO's international inquiry
excluded health-care expenditures in the public sector from its series, but
it included such expenditures in countries that offer national health services (often of a contributory nature) as part of social insurance. This
change created comparability problems in the series before and after 1978.
Furthermore, this change makes it practically impossible to assess health
costs in NLC countries because they have public health systems that are
not part of social insurance; hence, since 1978 expenditures for med-
ical/hospital care in the NLC are not included in the series. With these
caveats taken into account, social security health expenditures as a percentage of GDP for 10 Latin American countries from 1960–1980 showed
a clear increasing trend in all but one country, and in two countries (Costa
Rica and Panama) there were increases of five or six times in such expenditures (ILO 1988; ILO/PAHO/CPISS 1986).

The high and increasing costs of health care in LAC (as well as the
resulting financial deficits in the social insurance sickness/maternity programs) can be explained by universal causes as well as by peculiarities of
the region. Determining factors are both external (i.e., inflation, demographics) and internal (i.e., health-care philosophy, expansion of population coverage, generosity of benefits, high personnel and supply costs,
lack of integration among health providers, and hospital inefficiency). The
following paragraphs discuss these causes.

• Inflation. I have already noted that escalating inflation in LAC in
the 1980s created increases in real terms in the cost of medicines, medical
equipment, construction, and salaries of medical personnel. Technological
advances in medical/hospital devices and drugs, and the fact that most of
them are usually imported at high prices, has reinforced the increasing
trend in health-care costs. Prices of all these products have usually risen
at a higher rate than the overall inflation level.

Table 2.13   Percentage Distribution of Population Coverage and Revenue
in the Ministries of Health and Social Insurance Systems for Selected
Latin American Countries: 1980[a]

Countries	Ministry of Health			Social Insurance		
	% Population Coverage	% Revenue	Ratio of Revenue to Coverage	% Population Coverage	% Revenue	Ratio of Revenue to Coverage
Colombia	82	38	0.46	18	62	3.44
Costa Rica	15	22	1.47	85	78	0.92
Dominican Rep.	91	53	0.58	9	47	5.22
Ecuador	89	59	0.66	11	41	3.72
Panama	45	34	0.76	55	65	1.18
Peru	76	50	0.66	24	50	2.08

Source: Mesa-Lago 1989a.
Note: a. Excludes private sector; the percentage distributions are based on coverage and
revenue data for the health ministries and insurance systems only.

• Demographics. The most developed LAC countries (e.g., Argentina,
Cuba, Uruguay, and several NLC countries) exhibit demographic features
similar to those in industrialized countries: low rates of population
growth, an aging trend in the population, and high life expectancy. The
rapidly growing older population demands health services for longer periods, as well as increasingly sophisticated and costly treatment. The
pathological profile of these countries also resembles that of developed
countries: the main causes of death are "development diseases" (e.g., car-
diovascular illness, malignancies, traffic accidents), which are difficult
and costly to treat. Costa Rica shares the same pathological profile, in
spite of its relatively young population, because of its rapid expansion of
social security and high health standards. The less developed countries in
the region have young populations and a pathological profile characterized by a predominance of "underdevelopment diseases" (e.g., prenatal,
malnutrition, digestive, respiratory, and contagious conditions). These diseases can effectively be treated with simpler and cheaper techniques (such
as immunization, sanitation, health education, and nutrition supplements)
than development diseases. As LAC countries become more developed the
shift in the morbidity and pathological profiles results in increases in
health-care costs.

• Health-Care Philosophy. The overwhelming predominance of curative medicine over preventive medicine is another cause of high medical

costs. In LAC, and particularly Latin America, the distribution of health resources is abnormally skewed in favor of curative medicine. Priority is given to capital-intensive over labor-intensive services, hospitals over small clinics and rural posts, and physicians over paramedic personnel. The system favors the use of complex and costly equipment (virtually always imported), surgery, laboratory tests, and treatment (such as kidney dialysis, chemotherapy, organ transplants, heart surgery, and nuclear medicine). In the late 1970s or early 1980s the ratio of curative to preventive medicine expenditures were 15 to 1 in Chile, 9 to 1 in Mexico, and 6 to 1 in Brazil. In Brazil in 1949, 13 percent of public health expenditures were in curative medicine and 87 percent in preventive medicine, but by 1982 the proportions had flipped to 85 percent and 15 percent, respectively. The Brazilian government spent more in 1981 for 12,000 patients to receive three costly types of services (renal dialysis, coronary bypasses, and intensive care) than for the preventive medicine geared to 40 million people in the impoverished Northeast. The skewed distribution of health resources obstructs the expansion of basic services to the majority or to important segments of the population in Latin America. The chief actuary of Mexico's general social security institution has acknowledged that the current allocation of health resources leads to increasing costs and impedes universalization; there are pressures to acquire complex technology that is often excessive or unnecessary, to buy costly medicines of dubious value, to construct redundant physical plants, and to duplicate costly equipment and functions (McGreevey 1990; Soto Pérez 1991; Mesa-Lago 1991b, 1992c).

Primary health care (PHC) is a comprehensive approach that combines several techniques such as detection and control of chronic diseases, prevention of and immunization for contagious diseases, improved sanitation (e.g., low-cost excreta disposal and potable water supplies), family planning, nutritional supplements (e.g., powdered milk for infants), health education (e.g., about boiling water and basic hygiene), targeting of vulnerable population groups (e.g., pregnant women, infants) and specific diseases (e.g., acute diarrhea, tuberculosis), and community participation (e.g., in sanitation work and antiparasitical campaigns). In some countries PHC also incorporates some practitioners of traditional medicine (e.g., midwives) as well as herbal medicine and other sound techniques. PHC gives preference to relatively small, low-cost installations at the primary care level (often located in marginal urban and rural areas), minimizes the use of physicians by utilizing lower-paid paramedics, and stresses the incorporation of local people as health promoters or assistants through special training. This approach is considerably less costly than the conventional curative one and uses resources more efficiently to maximize results (e.g, reduce infant mortality, improve nutrition). When a very large majority of a population is below the poverty level, PHC is even more advisable because resources are extremely scarce and the health needs of the population huge. A PHC strategy does not imply abandonment of curative care but rather a more rational and balanced distribution of limited resources according to the most urgent health needs of a given population.

I have noted how in the least developed countries in Latin America the predominant diseases are those typical of underdevelopment, as well as malnutrition. Such illnesses are the main causes of death and are mainly responsible for very high infant mortality rates and low life expectancy. Although the diseases of underdevelopment can drastically be reduced with a relatively modest investment and a PHC approach, the bulk of health-care resources in those countries goes to curative medicine. Furthermore, in most of LAC social security expenditures are concentrated on the productive-age and retired groups of the population, and little is allocated to such vulnerable groups as infants and pregnant women. Several countries in the latecomer and even intermediate groups (e.g., Ecuador, most of the insured in Colombia, and Peru until recently) exclude dependent wives and children (after a few months of age) from sickness coverage.

Shifting a portion of the health-care resources from curative medicine to PHC and from productive-age and retired groups to mother/infant and other vulnerable groups can significantly improve the health status of the population. Under the current crisis situation such a change in emphasis is even more urgent, but it is feasible only through the effective coordination of the health services offered by the two major providers of each country.

There are several successful examples of PHC application in LAC. In Costa Rica since the 1970s, the coordination between ministry of health programs (essentially PHC) oriented toward marginal rural and urban groups and social security programs (essentially curative but providing some preventive services) has significantly contributed to a reduction in infant mortality and an increase in life expectancy. Since the mid-1980s both providers have jointly planned the construction of first-level facilities giving emphasis to PHC. In the 1970s, in spite of a shrinking public health budget in Chile, a reorientation of health resources toward the mother/infant group and a nutritional program also led to a rapid decline in infant mortality (Castañeda 1987). In Mexico the PHC effort to extend coverage to low-income, isolated rural populations has achieved success; a more modest example of rural PHC is the peasant social insurance program in Ecuador. In most countries of the NLC access to health services is free, at least for the poor or people with very low incomes, as well as for certain services or certain age groups of the population regardless of income (the rest of the population often pays user fees). In Jamaica primary health care, diagnosis of contagious diseases, and care for pregnant women are always free. In the Bahamas all children below the age of 14 who attend school are treated for free. In 1985 that country established a special fund (with transfers from the social insurance programs for employment injury and short-term benefits) to improve the public health system. In some countries such basic services as prophylaxis, sanitation, and PHC are exempted from user fees (Mesa-Lago 1987, 1992c). The success stories of Costa Rica, Jamaica, and Mexico will be studied in greater detail in Chapter 3.

• Expansion of Population Coverage. The process of expanding a population's social insurance coverage is another cause of increasing health costs (and growing deficits). Once the urban, salaried sector—with higher levels of income and health—is covered, the incorporation of the informal and rural population—with lower income and health standards—is costlier. This group (in the few countries where it is protected) contributes nothing or relatively little but uses health services more on a per capita basis.[5] In those countries where social insurance cares for the indigents (i.e., Costa Rica and Chile) or partly finances programs for the rural sector (i.e., Brazil and Mexico), health-care expenditures are higher than contributions plus state subsidies (when these materialize).

• Generosity of Benefits and Entitlement Conditions. I have already mentioned the generosity of sickness/maternity benefits and entitlement conditions, particularly in some Latin American countries. In the pioneer countries these exceptional benefits initially covered a relatively small proportion of the population and were easy to finance through direct state subsidies, special taxes, and/or price increases. These programs, however, served as models that were eventually imitated by larger groups of the population. Increasing trade unionism, combined with state intervention and concessions by political parties competing for electoral votes, played a key role in the gradual expansion of some generous benefits and entitlement conditions to an increasing number of insured. But what was financially viable for a minority of insured (although unjustifiable from an equity viewpoint) could not work in the long run for the insured masses.

• High Personnel and Supply Costs. Personnel salaries make up the bulk of administrative expenditures, and physicians' salaries constitute the majority. In some countries there are more physicians than necessary; they exert pressure to be hired and then perform services that could be done at a lower salary by paramedic personnel. Salaries in the ministries of health are normally lower than in social insurance: in Costa Rica from 1982–1985 the cost of personnel in the former declined from 62 percent to 48 percent of the budget, whereas in the latter it increased from 53 percent to 57 percent. In Peru the cost of personnel in social insurance increased from 38 percent to 50 percent from 1982–1985.

After personnel the next highest item in health budgets in LAC is materials and supplies: budget shares for this item ranged from 22–34 percent in Argentina, Chile, Colombia, Costa Rica, Peru, and Uruguay in the 1980s. Within that category, the most important expenditures are for medicines, the costs of which have gradually increased partly because of overprescription, unnecessary diversification, sales promotions that cause users to demand specific brands, new discoveries that make existing stocks obsolete, etc.

• Lack of Integration Among Health Providers. The lack of integration, or at least coordination, among the various providers of health services (in particular the social insurance systems and the ministries of health) promotes duplication of physical plants and costly equipment as well as low percentages of hospital occupancy.

In the Latin American latecomer group and most of the intermediate group, expansion of effective health-care coverage under the current crisis is virtually impossible without integration or coordination between the two providers. Both providers have suffered under the crisis, but the ministries moreso than social insurance. Even in the remaining countries the control of (and hopefully reduction in) health-care costs necessitates efficient coordination. Finally, there is a need for better coordination and balance between preventive and curative medicine, as well as for a joint strategy to promote primary health care in the region. In the last three decades this problem has been discussed by regional and international organizations, as well as by associations and experts dealing with social security and public health, that have recommended coordination or integration of health services (PAHO 1981, 1987; Ugalde 1985; ILO/PAHO/CPISS 1986; Castellanos 1986; Mesa-Lago 1989a, 1992c; McGreevey 1990).

There are three levels of integration/coordination. The highest is represented by countries with unified national health systems. The intermediate level is made up of countries that have high coordination between the ministry of health and social insurance, with integration of certain services and a clear division of labor between the two institutions (Costa Rica is a good example). The lowest level is typical of countries that use standardized planning and normative systems in all institutions. In the 1970s there was a shift in preference from integration toward coordination and, since the early 1980s, toward a new approach that focuses on results (with the goal being universal coverage) rather than the method used to achieve them (Castellanos 1986).

In spite of the importance of this topic, few serious studies are available on concrete experiences of integration and coordination in LAC, except for the successful case of Costa Rica (Jaramillo Antillón and Miranda 1985). A recent study of Panama shows that integration caused an important reduction in urban-rural disparities in access to health care but failed to diminish the curative biases of the system or increase its efficiency (La Forgia 1990).

Since the 1980s an important process of rapprochement between the ILO and the World Health Organization (WHO) has taken place (and is reflected in each country's social insurance system and ministry of health); it has helped them coordinate their activities and promote a coherent strategy for health care, particularly at the primary level (ILO/ PAHO/CPISS 1986). However, in spite of some advances many problems remain: (1) although most countries have enacted legislation to establish national health systems (e.g., Mexico, Peru), effective progress has been slow, and coordination between the two major institutions in each country is nascent (with few exceptions) and continues to be a subject of debate; (2) the politics of coordination has not yet accomplished the incorporation of both institutions into the decisionmaking process and service delivery; and (3) there are resilient barriers to the process of coordination, such as separate clienteles, different financing means, and resistance from the two bureaucracies (Castellanos 1986). In a meeting of PAHO held in 1987 the existence of these problems was formally recognized, and it was acknowledged that despite a consensus on the benefits of coordination there is no unity concerning the proper methods to achieve that goal (PAHO 1987).

In 1990 the Pan American Health Organization (PAHO) appointed an advisory committee of social security and health experts (including a representative from ILO) to help deal with the issues of coordination/integration and expansion of population coverage. A document reviewed by that committee stated the need to accept the existence of multiple institutions of diverse origin and nature, and it stated the preference for functional rather than structural or administrative integration. Further, the document acknowledged both the potential of social *security* (not social *insurance*) and its advantages—vis-à-vis public assistance—in expanding health-care coverage to the population. Finally, it also stressed the need to define the responsibilities and areas of activity of the public and social security sectors, as well as the need to strengthen the political authority and coordinating role of each country's ministry of health. Noting significant financial constraints in the 1990s against reaching the target of health care for all, the document recommended a joint strategy based on three points: (1) social insurance would gradually evolve to become social security, with an expansion of coverage to currently excluded groups being a key element in such a transformation; (2) the individual ministries of health would maintain and increase their overall coordinating function; and (3) both types of institutions would retain their separate identities but promote functional integration on mutually agreeable terms (PAHO 1989).

• Hospital Inefficiency. Table 2.14 compares national averages of hospital occupancy and days of stay among 10 Latin American countries. Although figures are rough and not always comparable (e.g., they deal with different institutions), they show that hospital occupancy was 61 percent or below in three countries, below 71 percent in six, and above 80 percent in only two. Furthermore, with the exception of Costa Rica, those countries with the highest occupancy have abnormally high averages for days of stay. If the number of days of stay were reduced, the percentages of occupancy would decline as well. For instance, the occupancy percentage in Montevideo (81.8 percent) would have declined to 41 percent if the average number of days of stay had been cut from 13.3 to 6.6; in addition, outside of the capital city the occupancy averaged 51.2 percent with a still high average of 7.9 days of stay. It is true that tertiary (i.e., specialized) hospitals are concentrated in the capital city, and because some of the users travel long distances, they need more days at the hospital for diagnosis and post-surgery care. The average number of days of stay, however, is still too high by international standards.

National averages presented in Table 2.14 hide extreme variations among regions and individual hospitals. For instance, Ecuador's national occupancy average was 58 percent, but in 7 out of 20 provinces it was below 40 percent; and Peru's national average was 70 percent, but in 3 out of 8 regions it was below 50 percent. The low population coverage in these two countries makes such inefficiency even more serious. Low occupancy is usually the result of either excessive hospital capacity (often there are two hospitals—the ministry's and social insurance's—in the same location), poor hospital quality, or cultural barriers that impede proper use.

Another problem is that primary- and secondary-level services are often inadequately staffed and supplied; hence, the users, particularly of outpatient consultation, skip these levels and go directly to tertiary (specialized) hospitals, thereby increasing the workload of those hospitals and depleting resources of more complex services. Better integration, planning, allocation of resources, and education could overcome most of these problems.

In countries that have an indirect system of health care, contracts with private institutions lack proper control and have led to higher costs in services because of unnecessarily long hospital stays, unnecessary surgery or laboratory tests, overprescription of medicines, and charges for services that were not actually delivered (these problems have been documented in Brazil and Peru). Finally, irregularities in administration have also yielded higher costs. For instance, in 1986, 40 percent of the social insurance health services in the Dominican Republic were illegally provided to non-insured people with relatively high incomes and political connections (PAHO 1981, 1987; ILO/PAHO/CPISS 1986; Castellanos 1986; ILO 1988; Mesa-Lago 1992c).

High Administrative Expenditures and Other Managerial Deficiencies

High and rising administrative costs. Statistics on administrative costs and personnel in LAC are difficult to obtain and usually deficient. However, ILO data (1988, 1991a) clearly indicate that such costs (the regional average was

Table 2.14   Indicators of Hospital Efficiency for Social Insurance in Selected
Latin American Countries: 1980–1989

Countries	National Averages	
	% of Hospital Occupancy	Days of Stay
Argentina[a] (1980)	60.6	7.5–26.9[b]
Chile (1985)	75.3	8.5
Colombia (1984)	61.0	7.3
Costa Rica (1989)	78.9	6.2
Dominican Rep. (1985)	51.7	10.4
Ecuador (1981)	82.7	9.3
Mexico (1982)	67.0[c]	4.6[c]
Panama[d] (1984)	67.0	7.0
Peru (1985)	70.4	11.7
Uruguay[a] (1984)	81.8[e]	13.3[e]

Sources: Mesa-Lago 1992c, updated with CCSS 1989.
Notes: a. Public health sector.
b. Extreme variation among provinces.
c. IMSS data; the ISSSTE averages were 70% and 5.7.
d. Combined social insurance and public health.
e. Montevideo (excludes chronic patients); outside of Montevideo the averages were 51.2%
and 7.9.

18.5 percent of total expenditures in 1986) are considerably higher than those of developed countries in North America, Europe, and Asia (which average 2–4 percent) but slightly lower than those of developing countries in Africa (which averaged 22 percent). The size of and trends in the administrative share of social security may be influenced by several factors: age of the program, type of administrative organization, degree of population coverage, economies of scale, rate of urbanization, geographical obstacles, excessive personnel and overly high salaries, and other managerial inefficiencies.

Table 2.15 shows that the regional average share of administrative expenses slowly rose from 8.3 percent to 9.2 percent from 1965–1975 but jumped to 15.7 percent in 1980 and continued increasing (although at a slower pace) to 18.5 percent by 1986. In 1986 the administrative share ranged from 2–7.9 percent in Argentina, Costa Rica, Barbados, Panama, Jamaica, Uruguay, Brazil, and Chile; from 8–15.9 percent in Grenada, Guatemala, Trinidad and Tobago, Ecuador, Venezuela, and Honduras; from 16–29.9 percent in Mexico, Bolivia, Guyana, the Bahamas, the Dominican Republic, and El Salvador; and from 30–52 percent in Nicaragua, Dominica, St. Lucia, Colombia, Belize, and Peru. I have estimated higher shares than those shown in the table (Mesa-Lago 1987a, 1992b): for instance, 38 percent in Jamaica in 1965, 37 percent in 1970, 16 percent in

Table 2.15   Administrative Expenditures for Social Security in LAC: 1965–1986
(As Percentage of Total Expenditures)

	1965	1970	1975	1980[a]	1986
Argentina	•	•	•	4.2	2.3
Bahamas	•	•	•	31.6	23.2
Barbados	•	1.0[b]	1.9	6.4	5.2
Belize	•	•	•	7.8[c]	46.2
Bolivia	10.5[d]	9.7[e]	9.2	19.3	17.5
Brazil	10.0	6.9	12.3	4.7	6.4
Chile	13.1	7.6[b]	7.7	7.5	7.4
Colombia	4.4	6.1	7.1	12.4	42.2
Costa Rica	15.0	11.9	8.4	6.9	3.9
Dominica	•	•	•	54.7	32.0
Dominican Rep.	•	•	•	17.9[f]	24.0
Ecuador	14.4	10.7[e]	8.2[g]	28.0	11.9
El Salvador	5.4	13.6	19.0	15.0	25.0
Grenada	•	•	•	4.4[h]	9.0
Guatemala	6.9	6.3	6.0	11.7	10.9
Guyana	1.8	15.3[e]	17.0	24.7	18.1
Honduras	6.1	3.1	5.0[b]	15.3[c]	15.4
Jamaica	7.2	11.1	11.1	6.0	6.0
Mexico	11.9	11.2	11.4[g]	13.3	17.3
Nicaragua	9.1	8.4	10.0	11.6	30.3[h]
Panama	5.2	13.9[e]	13.6	5.4	5.5
Peru	•	•	•	9.9[c]	51.6
St. Lucia	•	•	•	54.1[c]	38.6
Trinidad & Tobago	•	•	3.6	13.8	11.8
Uruguay	8.6	•	8.2	7.7	6.0
Venezuela	2.6	14.8	6.1	14.0	14.9
Regional Average	8.3	9.4	9.2	15.7	18.5

Sources: ILO 1988, 1991a.
Notes: a. Data after 1978 exclude medical care provided by public health institutions.
b. 1971.
c. 1981.
d. 1961.
e. 1972.
f. 1984.
g. 1974.
h. 1983.
• Signifies data not available.

1980, and 9 percent in 1986. In addition, such data indicate that the share kept increasing in some countries up to 1988, e.g., 41 percent in the Dominican Republic and 13 percent in Ecuador.

The table does not suggest any clear relationship between the administrative burden and the age of the program, except that all the pioneer countries (those with the oldest programs) have the lowest percentages. In those countries where social security was introduced recently (as in the NLC), a high percentage of administrative expenditures could be partly explained by the necessary minimum of personnel, equipment, and physical plants to operate the system, combined with low initial benefit expenditures (particularly on pensions); as benefit expenditures increase the proportional cost of operation is greatly reduced. However, Table 2.15 shows significant variation among the NLC countries (e.g., 5 percent in Barbados and 46 percent in Belize), and this cannot be explained by the lengths of time the programs have been in operation. For instance, Trinidad and Tobago and Dominica launched their programs fairly close to the same time, but their shares of administrative expenditures are 12 percent and 32 percent, respectively. Therefore we have to search for other explanations.

In Latin American countries where there are multiple institutions (e.g., Bolivia, Colombia), the percentages for administrative expenditures tend to be higher than in countries that either began in a relatively unified manner or underwent unification and standardization (e.g., Argentina, Brazil, Chile, Costa Rica, Uruguay, and Panama). Usually administrative expenditures by privileged institutions are higher than those of general institutions; for instance, in Bolivia the petroleum institute spends six times per insured the amount spent by the general institute. Universal or high population coverage (in the pioneers, Costa Rica, and Panama) appears to be associated with small administrative shares, whereas the opposite is true in countries with low population coverage (e.g., the Dominican Republic, El Salvador, Colombia). Economies of scale may reduce costs, thus explaining the lower administrative expenditures in industrialized countries (as well as in LAC countries with the largest and unified programs). However, Denmark, Ireland, and Norway are small industrialized countries that have lower percentages for administrative expenditures than in all of LAC except Costa Rica. Countries with a high rate of urbanization (e.g., Argentina, Chile, Uruguay, Venezuela) usually have lower operational costs—because of a concentration of administrative offices and health-care facilities in large cities—than those with a large, dispersed rural population (e.g., Bolivia, Guyana, Peru). Some countries also face serious geographical barriers that increase administrative expenditures; for instance, the Bahamas are made up of numerous small islands that obstruct administrative centralization and increase transportation costs.

Excessive personnel and generous salaries. Probably the most important factor explaining high administrative costs in LAC is the presence of too many personnel who are not properly utilized and are generously remunerated. Personnel absorb the vast majority of administrative expenditures (e.g., 70 percent in Barbados). In the mid-1980s the ratio of employees per 1,000 insured ranged from 0.6–3.9 in Jamaica and Barbados; 4–9.9 in Venezuela, Nicaragua, Bolivia, Colombia, Guatemala, Costa Rica, and Mexico; 10–14.9 in Peru, Panama, and El Salvador; and over 20 in the Dominican Republic. In some countries the ratio is underestimated because personnel data exclude temporary employees, who could account for a sizable percentage of total employment. In addition, because population coverage data are often over-estimated, the ratio itself is underestimated. For instance, Peru's ratio of 8.1 per 1,000 in 1984 fell dramatically to 5.8 in 1985, but this was largely due to the increase in legal coverage of more than one million dependents, few of whom were actually covered. In 1988 the ratio (based on official figures of coverage) was 7.0, but when adjustments were made to eliminate two million who were not actually insured, the ratio increased to 10.5 and established a historical record.

In the late 1970s and the 1980s social security personnel rapidly in-creased in many countries: by 127 percent in the Bahamas from 1980–1985, 80 percent in Peru from 1985–1988, 44 percent in Ecuador from 1979–1983 (67 percent in nonmedical personnel from 1981–1987), 37 percent in Costa Rica from 1977–1982, and 30 percent in Colombia from 1975–1980. Such increases in personnel were not usually matched by sim-ilar increases in population coverage and/or services.

In many LAC countries social security institutions became major sources of employment to help alleviate high open unemployment. Per-sonnel were often hired without being tested or judged on merit; in a few NLC countries social security personnel were hired, promoted, and dis-missed by the central government for political reasons. In addition, per-sonnel skills needed to be upgraded in most countries. In some cases the employees did not actually work but collected their salaries; in others they did show up but wasted their time, came in late, left early, and were fre-quently absent. In Costa Rica the trade unions negotiated a cut of five hours in the weekly work schedule, and the workers were paid overtime to make up those reduced hours; for this reason alone the social security in-stitute accumulated a debt of U.S. $1.3 million. Employee strikes in de-mand for additional concessions from the administration were frequent (even among physicians). Turnover among the top personnel was com-mon: in Colombia from 1982–1986 the directors of the two major social insurance institutions changed three times and the minister of health four times; in Peru from 1985–1988 the director of social security changed four times (once per year). Each new director brings his or her own team, which entails replacing executive personnel who have never had enough time to learn and apply the policies in the first place.

In the 1980s personnel salaries and fringe benefits accounted for from one-half to three-fourths of administrative costs in several LAC countries. Social security employees are often the best paid in the public sector (their salaries are often indexed to inflation), and they enjoy labor conditions far superior to those of the insured. In Peru a collective agreement signed in 1986 granted automatic quarterly adjustment of salaries to match cost-of-living increases (such adjustments were far superior to the general salary adjustment); such indexation was enforced until mid-1988, significantly contributing to the grave financial crisis of social security there. Fringe benefits often include travel and housing allowances, free or subsidized meals, fellowships to study abroad, shops for consumer goods at subsidized prices, vacation centers, personal loans at low interest, and social security benefits more generous than those in the general system. For instance, in the Bahamas a special pension plan paid 80 percent of the regular salary to retired personnel in addition to the regular pension. In Ecuador 42 percent of the total remuneration was composed of 42 fringe benefits including five extra months of salary; an annual bonus; a store with goods at subsidized prices; health care for dependents (not available for the insured); subsidies for meals, housing, and transportation; and a private social club. In some countries the employees did not pay any contributions because their benefits were financed out of general social security revenue (e.g., for sickness/maternity in Costa Rica).

Adjustment programs introduced in the 1980s targeted this bureaucracy. Emergency plans reportedly cut personnel in several countries: by 36 percent in Argentina from 1980–1986, 10 percent in Costa Rica from 1982–1983, and 8 percent in Colombia from 1980–1984. In Peru a "rationalization of personnel" in 1988 was aimed at freezing new appointments, restricting overtime, and reducing travel and food costs. In Ecuador a 1989 plan called for the cancelation of vacant slots and suspension of new appointments. Uruguay enacted a law in 1990 providing incentives to social security employees to resign from their jobs. Detailed reports on the results of these plans are rarely available, so it is difficult to evaluate them. An exception is Costa Rica's emergency plan, which cut the administrative share of expenditures from 6.9 percent to 3.9 percent from 1980–1986 through the following measures: a freeze in all vacant positions and a halting of new appointments; virtual elimination of temporary replacements for those on vacation or leave; drastic reduction of overtime; enforcement of employee retirement by age 65; mandatory vacations to eliminate the double pay received by those who worked during vacation time; mandatory payment of the standard contribution to the sickness/maternity program for all employees; and reduction in salary replacement from 100 percent to 50 percent during the first four days of paid sick leave (ILO 1991a; Mesa-Lago and DeGeyndt 1987; Mesa-Lago 1988a, 1989b, 1991a, 1992c; CCSS 1989; BPS 1979–1991).

Other organizational and managerial deficiencies. The following organizational and managerial deficiencies are found in many LAC countries: multiple institutions, legal complexity, statistical inadequacies, deficiencies in registering contributors and ensuring their compliance, lack of coordination among departments, accounting flaws, cumbersome and protracted processing of benefits, and inefficient use of computer equipment (Mesa-Lago 1987a, 1988c, 1989b, 1991b, 1991c).

In the pioneer countries social security systems were initially characterized by multiple institutions—as many as 60 in some countries—each with its own programs, laws, sources of revenue, benefits, and entitlement conditions. Differences among those institutions were significant, and there was a lack of coordination among them. This situation had such adverse effects as legal and administrative complexity, unjustified inequalities, high administrative costs, the inability to create a single registry, difficulties in controlling evasion, and barriers against combining the times of service and contributions that were credited to an individual's pensions in various institutions. These problems were reduced in intermediate countries and virtually eliminated in the latecomers (particularly in the NLC) because one single institution in each country administers most programs and covers most insured groups. However, in Colombia there are 300 institutions with programs for pensions, sickness/maternity, and insured groups; Bolivia has 12 major institutions, 20 complementary funds, and 5 sickness/maternity programs; even in Costa Rica, where only 1 institution exists, there were 19 independent pension funds until recently. Such multiplicity was largely eliminated or reduced in the last three decades by a process of total or partial unification of institutions and increasing legal uniformity that occurred in pioneer and intermediate countries alike (e.g., in Argentina, Brazil, Chile, Cuba, Ecuador, Peru, Uruguay). But multiplicity remains the rule in Colombia; hundreds of social insurance health programs still operate in Argentina; and separate programs persist within Ecuador's unified system, with diverse contributions and benefits for various groups of insured. Another organizational flaw—already discussed—is the existence of multiple health providers (i.e., social insurance, ministry of health) with a lack of coordination among them that leads to duplications and gaps.

The social security systems in Latin America are normally characterized by a mosaic of laws, decrees, and other legal dispositions that are frequently amended and that casuistically attempt to regulate any conceivable case. Combined with the multiplicity of social security institutions, such a legalistic approach has created a juridical labyrinth. Codifications of social security have been attempted to solve this problem in some countries, but they have not always been successful. Even new unified programs have not escaped such a fate: in its first seven years the novel Chilean pension system, established in 1981, was the subject of 15 legal amendments and hundreds of administrative regulations. Such an intricate legal approach has negative consequences: the insured cannot understand their rights; the social insurance institutes, as well as the insured and the enterprises, are forced to contract lawyers; and what should be a relatively simple and short processing of benefits becomes a protracted, complex, and costly procedure.

Many social security institutions in LAC do not gather (or at least do not publish) accurate data on the following crucial aspects of their programs: (1) population coverage in terms of special groups (e.g., salaried workers, self-employed, or domestic servants; rural versus urban sectors) or for dependents (their number is normally estimated as a ratio of the active insured population); (2) evasion and payment delays, state debt, and real investment yields; (3) real pensions and other benefits (adjusted to inflation); (4) administrative costs, number of employees, and their salaries and fringe benefits; and (5) indicators of efficiency in hospital administration such as hospital occupancy, average days of stay, etc. Conversely, some data published do not have a specific purpose and clear utility or are unnecessarily detailed. In spite of some improvement in recent years, stemming from numerous international and regional meetings, many of these flaws persist. As an outcome of the 1980s crisis, as well as adjustment and emergency programs, some countries have either stopped publishing statistical yearbooks and annual reports or are years behind schedule. In other countries data have been cut down drastically, and the least useful figures are not always weeded out.

Registration is probably the Achilles' heel of most social security institutions. Some do not even know how many insured they have (e.g., Argentina, Peru) but roughly estimate them based on census and employment data. (I have also noted that the number of dependents is grossly estimated as a ratio of the number of active insured.) In other countries the number of insured registered is becoming increasingly inflated because those who die, withdraw from the labor force, or emigrate are not erased from the registry. As a result of such a problem Jamaica's 1987 mandatory actuarial review had to be postponed. Individual accounts are absent in the majority of countries, and in many countries manual processing is the rule. Another problem is the complex and cumbersome procedure for employers' registration and periodic reporting; it requires preparing several monthly forms and is a serious hindrance to medium and small enterprises. Because most countries lack an up-to-date list of delinquent employers, proper control of evasion and payment delays is impossible. Flat contribution sums, still used in a few NLC countries, make payment and control even more difficult (until recently Jamaica had both flat and percentage contributions that are now unified into just a percentage). Inspection is often weak, and because of adjustment programs some countries have reduced the number of inspectors. For instance, in 1987 the Bahamas reduced their number of inspectors from 16 to 5 despite the fact that from 20 to 36 were reportedly needed; in the early 1980s Colombia shut down its entire inspection department based on charges of corruption.

Lack of coordination among crucial departments creates duplication, delays, and inefficiency. Financing data are often divided among various departments (e.g., accounting, actuarial, budget, investment, and treasury) and either lack integration or are plagued with errors and contradictions. Budgets are commonly set by program (e.g., pension, sickness/maternity) rather than by function or budget category, and integration is again difficult or impossible. This problem is compounded by obscure transfers among programs. In other cases data are not disaggregated, so it is impossible to evaluate the financial status of each program. In some countries the accounting records do not clearly establish the links between contributions and benefit payments within a given program. In a few countries there have been no accounting records for relatively long periods (e.g, in Peru from 1968–1978). Rarely is there historical documentation on investment's real yields, overall and by instrument, so evaluating investment efficiency and policy formulation is difficult. Bidding procedures are cumbersome and legalistic; for instance, in Ecuador at the end of the 1980s the same procedure was used for the construction of a hospital and for buying aspirin. The lack of inventory control creates shortages and spoilage problems. External consultants are often hired to study accounting problems and formulate recommendations; these recommendations are then often ignored by an incoming administration that in turn hires new consultants to review the same problems.

The processing of benefits is extremely complex and takes a long time because of the predominant legalistic approach, the absence of individual accounts, and registry deficiencies. Thus the awarding of benefits usually requires judicial litigation wherein the claimants (i.e., the insured) must prove their rights through documentation (e.g., birth certificate, employer's certification of years of work), witnesses, etc. The average time for processing pensions in 1987–1989 was: 6–12 months or more in Jamaica; 8–12 months in Colombia (in the civil service fund it was 2–5 years); and as much as two years in Ecuador. The crisis of the 1980s prompted some countries to delay the awarding of pensions even more in an effort to reduce costs. Claimants' files in Jamaica are sent back and forth from local offices to central headquarters and go through five different checks; hence, about half of those entitled to pensions do not claim them. In 1987 in the Bahamas physicians had to check all claimants of disability benefits personally (previously such checks were done at random), a task made even more difficult by the large number of islands that make up that nation. In addition, the Bahamas have an administrative auditing process that is estimated to cost more than the resources it saves from fraud. In Ecuador monthly pension payments are largely handled manually, and the system is not fast enough to cancel payments to beneficiaries who have died or lost entitlement to benefits.

Inadequacies in health-care delivery lead to long queues for outpatient consultation and waiting periods for surgery. Physicians often give only half the amount of time they are expected to work; more hospital beds than necessary are occupied because of excessively long hospital stays; and outpatient consultation in hospitals is overcrowded, largely because of the inadequacy of primary-care service.

Computers, either owned or rented, are increasingly being used throughout LAC in an effort to cope with many of these administrative problems. They enable up-to-date registration, individual accounts, control of evasion and payment delays, and faster awarding and payment of benefits. At the end of the 1980s the computerization trend was present in both pioneers (e.g., modernization of obsolete and insufficient computer equipment in Uruguay) and latecomers (e.g., the Bahamas, Barbados, Jamaica). In Chile large private corporations that administer pensions use the most modern equipment and software; because they keep individual accounts up to date, the awarding of a pension takes only a couple of weeks. Some countries have introduced or are in the process of establishing a single coded ID for all contributors and their dependents, not only for social security purposes but for taxes and other financial functions.

There is no doubt that computerization can improve the administration of social security, but it demands highly skilled personnel, proper software, and maintenance to avoid underutilization, misuse, and breakage of equipment. In 1984 costly rented equipment in Ecuador was used once a month by the budget department, but calculations were normally done manually and then entered into the computer only for printing purposes. Computerization is not enough to solve problems that require follow-up actions; for example, up-to-date records of employers' payments should be supported by dynamic enforcement of collection among those who are delinquent, and I have shown that such action is rather weak in most of LAC. Overburdened courts are bottlenecked; in Colombia only a fraction of the claims are selected for trial by the labor courts.

Worsening Actuarial and Financial Disorder

The increasing burden of social security. The percentages of social security expenditures as part of GDP in LAC are the highest in the Third World and appear to be increasing. As Table 2.16 shows, based on ILO data (1988, 1991a) the regional average percentage for 28 LAC countries increased from 3.9 percent to 4.5 percent from 1965–1975 but declined to 3.3 percent by 1980. Such a decrease could have been caused by two statistical factors: (1) the table's data exclude expenditures for certain health services after 1978, and (2) the table's data from 1980 on include several NLC countries that have very low percentages. In any case the regional percentage of expenditures as a percentage of GDP steadily increased from 3.3 percent in 1980 to 3.7 percent in 1983 and 3.9 percent in 1986. Other sources estimate higher percentages than those shown in the table, e.g., 7 percent in Colombia in 1984 and 11.2 percent in Uruguay in 1986 (Mesa-Lago 1991b). Between 1980 and 1986, 15 countries increased their percentages, three were stagnant, and eight decreased. In 1983 seven countries had their highest percentages ever on record, and in 1986 nine countries reached a zenith.

The systems of the pioneer countries—which have the oldest programs, broadest population coverage, and most liberal benefits—exhibited

the highest expenditures as a percentage of GDP in 1986: 14.7 percent in
Cuba, 13.1 percent in Chile, 9.6 percent in Uruguay, and 6.1 percent in
Argentina. (Two intermediate countries that have universal or very high
coverage also exhibited high percentages: 7.3 percent in Costa Rica and
8.3 percent in Panama, but Brazil—a pioneer—had only 5 percent.) The
percentages of Cuba, Chile, and Uruguay were similar to those of industrialized countries such as Japan, Australia, the United States, and the former USSR. Countries in the intermediate group (excluding Costa Rica and
Panama) had expenditures that ranged from 1.3–5.2 percent. The expenditures of the latecomer countries ranged from 0.5–2.8 percent (except in
Barbados, which faced high costs for unemployment insurance). These
lower percentages are explained by the newness of their programs and
meagerness of their benefits, plus very low population coverage among
the Latin American countries and the exclusion of health-care costs
among the NLC countries.

Steady increases in administrative costs and medical expenditures
have contributed to the overall rising trend in the burden of social security. The high percentages in several LAC countries raise the questions of
whether developing countries can afford to divert so many resources from
investment and what the costs of that burden are in terms of economic
growth. Furthermore, high percentages in countries with low population
coverage are an indicator of inequality in coverage. In spite of the importance of these questions, so far no serious investigations have been conducted to answer them.

Reasons for increasing deficits.   Increasing social security expenditures and
declining revenues in LAC have had adverse effects on actuarial and financial equilibrium. As explained earlier, real revenues shrank in the 1980s
because of declines in population coverage, real wages, and investment
yields, combined with increases in unemployment, informal employment,
tax evasion, and state debt. Causes for the increase in expenditures are discussed later in this section. Despite high and rising payroll contributions,
particularly in the pioneers, many countries faced financial disequilibrium in
the 1980s; actuarial imbalances should be worse, although accurate data are
not available from many countries.

Table 2.17 presents estimates of the annual financial surplus or deficit
for social security systems in 27 LAC countries from 1978–1986. The estimates exclude state contributions as such (although they include the state
contributions as employer) because such contributions are subsidies or
transfers (Mackenzie 1988). In 1978, 20 percent of the countries suffered
a deficit, but as the 1980s crisis unfolded the situation deteriorated, and
at its worst point (1983–1984) 31 percent of the countries had deficits.
Following the recuperation of 1985–1986 there was an improvement,
and by 1986 only 20 percent of the systems faced deficits. If only the
Latin American countries had been considered in these calculations, the

Table 2.16   Social Security System Expenditures as Percentage of GDP
in LAC: 1965–1986

Countries	1965	1975	1980	1983	1986
Argentina	•	6.8	9.3	7.3	6.1
Bahamas	•	•	0.5	1.1	1.4
Barbados	•	4.9	2.2	3.7	4.9
Belize	•	•	1.1[a]	1.6	0.6
Bolivia	3.6[b]	3.1	2.9	2.1	5.2
Brazil	4.3	5.7	4.8	5.7	5.0
Chile	12.1	11.0	10.7	14.3	13.1
Colombia	1.1	3.1	2.8	2.2	2.0
Costa Rica	2.3	5.1	7.1	6.1	7.3
Cuba	8.3	9.7	11.7	11.5	14.7
Dominica	•	•	0.8	0.9	1.4
Dominican Rep.	2.7	2.4	0.7	0.5[c]	0.5
Ecuador	3.2	3.0	2.9	3.6	3.0
El Salvador	2.2	3.3	1.7	1.7	1.1
Grenada	•	•	1.7	1.8	1.7
Guatemala	2.0	2.0	1.2	1.0	0.8
Guyana	4.3	1.9	1.3	1.8	2.8
Honduras	1.0	•	0.8	0.9	1.0
Jamaica	2.7	3.2	1.4	1.5	1.3
Mexico	2.6	3.1	2.7	2.6	2.7
Nicaragua	2.1	2.8	2.3	1.1	•
Panama	6.0	7.5	5.9	7.7	8.3
Peru	2.5	3.1	2.2	1.9	1.6
St. Lucia	•	•	0.5	0.6	0.8
Suriname	•	•	2.1	4.6	•
Trinidad & Tobago	2.8	2.4	0.7	2.4	2.2
Uruguay	9.6	10.7	8.2	11.0	9.6
Venezuela	3.1	3.9	1.3	1.5	1.3
Regional Average	3.9	4.5	3.3	3.7	3.9

Sources: ILO 1988, 1991a.
Notes: a. 1981.
b. 1961.
c. 1984.
• Signifies data not available.

proportion of those with deficits would be much higher because the NLC
countries generate surpluses.

In the year 1984, at the trough of the crisis, all pioneer countries suffered deficits (in Chile,[6] Cuba, and Uruguay it ranged from -4.8 percent to
-6.7 percent of GDP). More than one-third of the intermediate countries
also had deficits, though the rest enjoyed surpluses. The highest surpluses
were in Costa Rica (2.4 percent) and Ecuador (2.5 percent); the former
was therefore able to universalize coverage and successfully confront the
crisis. All the latecomer countries generated surpluses, but the amounts
were much higher in the NLC group (an average of 2.2 percent of GDP)
than in the Latin American group (an average of 0.4 percent).

Table 2.17 Surpluses or Deficits of Social Security Systems as Percentage of GDP in LAC: 1978–1986[a]

	1978	1979	1980	1981	1982	1983	1984	1985	1986
Argentina	0.3	-0.0	-0.4	-3.0	-2.2	-2.3	-1.3	-0.1	-0.7
Bahamas	•	•	1.6	2.1	1.3	1.6	1.4	1.9	1.8
Barbados	0.4	0.5	0.5	0.3	2.0	2.5	1.6	1.6	0.4
Belize	•	•	•	0.5	1.1	1.6	2.3	2.1	2.0
Bolivia	0.0	0.2	0.0	0.7	0.6	0.1	-1.4	0.2	•
Brazil	•	•	•	-0.3	0.0	-0.4	-0.6	0.1	0.2
Chile	-1.7	-2.0	-2.0	-2.3	-7.7	-5.7	-6.7	-4.2	-3.9
Colombia	-0.2	-0.1	0.0	-0.2	-0.6	-0.2	0.3	0.3	0.4
Costa Rica	1.4	1.2	1.0	0.8	0.8	2.5	2.4	2.6	1.9
Cuba	•	•	•	-6.2	-6.4	-6.4	-6.5	-7.1	-8.5
Dominica	•	•	2.3	•	•	2.4	2.4	2.8	2.6
Domincan Rep.	•	•	•	•	•	•	0.1	0.0	0.0
Ecuador	1.8	2.1	1.7	1.3	1.5	1.3	2.5	3.3	3.5
El Salvador	0.6	0.6	0.4	0.6	0.8	0.8	0.2	0.3	0.4
Grenada	•	•	•	-0.1	•	1.2	2.3	2.7	2.6
Guatemala	0.4	0.5	0.4	0.4	0.3	0.3	0.4	0.3	0.5
Guyana	•	•	4.8	•	•	7.5	7.3	7.0	6.1
Honduras	•	•	•	0.3	0.1	0.2	0.8	0.9	1.1
Jamaica	0.3	0.3	0.3	0.7	1.0	0.6	0.2	0.3	0.3
Mexico	•	•	0.4	0.4	0.5	0.1	0.1	0.3	0.2
Nicaragua	0.0	0.5	0.9	0.7	0.6	0.8	•	•	•
Panama	1.0	1.7	1.9	2.7	3.1	2.4	1.1	0.9	1.1
Peru	•	•	•	0.4	0.0	-0.1	-0.1	-0.2	0.2
St. Lucia	•	•	•	1.9	•	1.2	1.8	2.2	2.6
Trinidad & Tobago	0.3	•	0.2	0.0	0.0	-0.5	0.2	0.3	-0.3
Uruguay	-0.5	-0.3	-0.8	-3.7	-5.8	-4.3	-4.8	-2.4	-2.2
Venezuela	0.4	0.2	0.3	0.2	0.2	0.0	-0.1	-0.1	0.0

Sources: MacKenzie 1988 and Mesa-Lago 1991b, updated with ILO 1991a.
Notes: a. Excludes contribution of state as such (not as employer); positive value signifies surplus, negative value signifies deficit.
• Signifies data not available.

Among the pioneers, expenditures have increased at a faster rate than revenue. On the expenditure side, the reasons for this problem are (1) the universal extension of coverage; (2) excessively liberal legislation concerning benefits; (3) morbidity and pathology profiles typical of developed countries; (4) pension schemes that have matured; (5) increasing numbers of pensioners who are living longer than was expected in both the original legislation and the old actuarial estimates, and who are thus receiving pensions and health-care benefits for longer periods; and (6) adjustments to pensions and other benefits in line with changes in the cost of living. Revenue in the pioneer countries is becoming proportionately lower for the following reasons: (1) coverage cannot be extended any further (and if it were it would be to bring in lower-income groups, which would worsen the disequilibrium); (2) the number of active contributors is steadily dropping in comparison with the growing number of beneficiaries; (3) there is a high level of employer tax evasion and payment delays, particularly in countries with high and sustained inflation; (4) the states often fail to meet their financial obligations, leading to the accumulation of very large debts; (5) the contribution burden of social security is very heavy, and it is very difficult—politically and economically—to increase either wage contributions or taxes; and (6) with the exception of Chile the pioneer countries lack substantial reserves and thus do not generate investment revenue.

Some of the intermediate countries share the above features with the pioneers, whereas others are closer to the latecomers. But the general financial situation is aggravated by the following factors: (1) in practically all countries the sickness/maternity programs have suffered steady deficits that have been financed by transfers from the pension programs; (2) in all countries there are special programs in the public sector that show deficits and are subsidized by either the states or the general institutes; and (3) at least two of these countries have suffered a liquidity crisis, and the rest either face actuarial deficits or have not conducted actuarial balances for a long period.

The latecomer countries enjoy the best situation because their expenditures are lower (for reasons explained earlier) and their revenues can still expand with increasing population coverage (in the Latin American group) and rising contributions (in both groups). Furthermore, investment performance in the NLC has generally been better than in Latin America.

Scattered data available on the sickness/maternity programs of several countries indicate that their disequilibrium is worse than that of social security as a whole. The reason is that the pension programs usually generate surpluses that compensate and help reduce—through loans or transfers—the deficits faced by the sickness/maternity programs. The following information *includes* the state contribution as a third party: in Mexico the sickness/maternity program has annually ended in deficit since its creation in 1943, except for three years; in Panama there has been a steady deficit since 1975 that reached U.S. $196 million by 1986; in Peru there has been a deficit since 1977 (the cumulative deficit reached U.S. $162 million by 1985); in Ecuador there was a steady deficit from 1980–1988 (a cumulative deficit of U.S. $35 million by 1987); in Costa Rica the cumulative deficit for 1977–1981 was U.S. $44 million (although it became a surplus in the second half of the 1980s); in Uruguay the cumulative deficit for 1982–1986 was U.S. $17 million; in Bolivia there was an annual deficit from 1982–1986, except for one year; and in Colombia the cumulative deficit for 1981–1985 was U.S. $13 million. Deficits in sickness/maternity programs were traditionally covered with loans from the pension programs, but the former could neither amortize the debts nor pay interest and thus contributed to the decapitalization of the pension funds. As pension programs matured and their expenditures increased, the surpluses shrank and deficits appeared in these programs as well, thus forcing a halt in transfers to the sickness/maternity programs, which in turn found themselves in trouble.

Following the recuperation in the second half of the 1980s, all but four countries improved the financial status of their systems. However, four pioneers still confronted deficits in 1986, and because restructuring is expanding in the region, the situation might deteriorate again in some countries, at least temporarily. Furthermore, systems that currently generate surpluses may eventually be afflicted by the same problems suffered by the pioneers unless they introduce substantial reforms (Mesa-Lago 1991b, 1992c).

The Social Security Crisis
and the Need to Change the System

Although they are the most advanced in the developing world, LAC's social security systems, particularly their social insurance systems, can do little in most of the region in their current forms to alleviate the social costs induced by the regional economic crisis and the process of adjustment/restructuring. Only a few of the most developed countries in LAC have universal coverage plus an adequate combination of social insurance and public assistance to provide the minimum protection in terms of health care and income maintenance for the poor and other vulnerable groups. But even in those few countries social security is afflicted by financial difficulties that have been aggravated by the crisis, thereby making it more difficult to provide coverage.

In the great majority of LAC, social insurance is geared toward protecting the urban formal sector of the labor force and possibly the modern rural sector as well. The urban informal and rural traditional sectors, which together account for the majority of the labor force in many of those countries, are often legally excluded from coverage. The self-employed, peasants, domestic servants, microenterprise employees, seasonal and temporary workers, and the unemployed are therefore either legally unprotected or practically out of the system. The economic crisis, adjustment, and restructuring worsened the situation as poverty, the informal sector, and unemployment grew; coverage of the formal sector shrank; the few nonconventional programs protecting rural populations stagnated or suffered reversals; public social services were cut; and the quantity and quality of social security benefits declined. The economic recovery of the late 1980s and early 1990s has somewhat improved that dismal picture, but such improvement is not universal in the region. Furthermore, social costs should worsen as more LAC countries go through the process of restructuring during the rest of the 1990s.

Unemployment insurance/assistance is available in only one-fifth of the LAC countries, and it normally covers only a minority of the labor force, imposes tough entitlement conditions, and pays meager benefits. In two countries with fairly liberal unemployment insurance schemes the increase in the number of jobless workers in the 1980s led to significant increases in program costs. Furthermore, the nature of unemployment in LAC is different than that in the industrialized world: it is a chronic, massive, structural, and long-term phenomenon rather than a cyclical or frictional and short-term problem. The expansion of unemployment programs in LAC not only would be financially unfeasible but would be geared to the formal-sector minority and would deplete resources needed to help the uncovered majority of the labor force and generate more jobs.

The financing methods of social security are part of the problem. Payroll contributions, the main source of revenue, are very high and exhibit an increasing trend. In two pioneer countries the total contribution is about 50 percent of the payroll, but at least their systems cover virtually the entire population. The situation is worse for several Latin American countries in the intermediate and latecomer groups that endure relatively high contribution percentages (e.g., 21 percent) but have less than one-fifth of their populations covered. About two-thirds of the contributions are legally supposed to be paid by the employers and the state, and only one-third by the insured. In countries with very low coverage it appears that most of the population, who are out of the system, contribute to financing the covered minority via increased consumer prices (to make up for the employers' contributions) and regressive taxes. Noncompliance is a serious and growing problem; evasion and payment delays have become worse. The state debt to the system is not paid, and its real value has steadily shrunk. Another important source of revenue, investment (particularly of pension funds), has been harmed by inefficient policies and very low or negative yields that have led to a gradual decapitalization of the funds. The economic crisis and reform have had negative effects on social security revenues in terms of a decline in real wages and contributions, an increase in noncompliance, and a deterioration of investment yields. Escalating inflation has been a major culprit because it has provided incentives for employers to retain their payroll contributions, deposit them in banks that offer higher interest rates than the fines for *mora*, and pay later with devalued currency. Most investment funds are placed in instruments that are not indexed to inflation; hence, the real value of the reserves has rapidly shrunk, and real yields have become increasingly negative.

Social security benefits in LAC are the most advanced within the developing world, and some of the pioneer countries' benefits used to approximate those of industrialized countries. In general, the most liberal benefits and entitlement conditions are found in the pioneer group, and the strictest are in the latecomer group. Very low ages of retirement (particularly in conjunction with high life expectancy), seniority pensions (based on years of service, regardless of age), generous salary-replacement rates, adjustment of pensions to the cost of living, and liberal medical benefits have all contributed to skyrocketing expenditures that are not matched by comparable revenue increases. The bad example of the pioneers was followed by some countries in the intermediate and latecomer groups, where such an approach contrasted with the lack of coverage for the majority of their populations. The economic crisis and reform have had a negative impact on the real value and quality of benefits: inflation led to adjustments in personnel salaries and pensions to match increases in the cost of living, and it also increased the costs of imported drugs and medical equipment. But the financial crisis faced by social security programs eventually forced cuts in real benefits and the quality of health care. Therefore, even those protected have suffered from a deterioration of benefits.

Health-care costs rapidly increased, partly because of external factors (i.e., inflation, demographics—such as aging populations) but also because of internal factors: the overwhelming predominance of costly curative medicine over preventive medicine and PHC; the lack of integration and coordination among major providers (particularly social insurance systems and ministries of health); the expansion of social insurance coverage (in some countries) to lower-income groups with a higher incidence of disease and tendency to use the services more often; the increasing costs of medical personnel and supplies; the generosity of benefits and entitlement conditions; and inefficiencies in hospital administration.

Administrative expenditures for social security in LAC are probably the highest in the world and show a rising trend: the average administrative share of total social security expenditures increased from 8 percent to 18 percent from 1965–1986, in contrast to averages of 2–4 percent in industrialized countries. The major reason for this phenomenon is the large number of personnel who are paid relatively high salaries and are entitled to generous fringe benefits that are superior to those received by the average insured. Other causes of high administrative costs include multiple institutions, geographic obstacles to reaching parts of the population, legal complexity, flaws in registration, lack of coordination among departments, accounting deficiencies, and complex and protracted processing of benefits. The economic crisis and reform, combined with the financial difficulties suffered by social security, are forcing a trimming of the bureaucracy as well as an improvement in administrative efficiency.

The cost of social security in LAC is quite high: it averaged 4 percent of GDP in 1986 (the latest year for which data are available) but ranged from 10–15 percent in three pioneer countries (similar to the percentages of Japan, the United States, and the former USSR). In 1983–1984, at the worst point of the economic crisis, 31 percent of the 27 LAC countries considered suffered financial deficits in social security; the situation had improved by 1985–1986, but 20 percent of the systems still showed deficits. This assessment is based on rough macroeconomic estimates, but more detailed and accurate studies conducted in several Latin American countries from 1986–1992 clearly show a rapid financial deterioration of their systems, particularly among the pioneers but also among some countries in the other two groups. Actuarial deficits are probably universal and worsening. The pioneers (with the exception of Chile) have shifted from partial capitalization methods to pay-as-you-go approaches and are heavily subsidized by the state. Systems that currently generate financial surpluses may eventually be afflicted by the same problems suffered by the pioneers unless they introduce substantial changes.

The pressure to reform social security in LAC reached unparalleled heights at the beginning of the 1990s. The next chapter is devoted to studying the countries that have already introduced or are in the process of implementing reforms, and to discussing the nature of such changes and their effects on the alleviation of social costs.

3

Changing Social Security:
Case Studies of Reform, Privatization,
and Universalization

Trends and Types of Reform

In the pioneer countries partial social security reforms that were introduced in the 1960s and 1970s did not tackle the fundamental problems faced by their systems, and attempts to introduce profound reforms failed in the 1980s. An exception was Chile, which launched a radical reform (privatization) at the beginning of the 1980s. The Chilean model did not have a significant influence in Latin America until the 1990s because it was associated with the military government of Pinochet. When the new, democratic Chilean government endorsed the previous social security reform, however, the reform became politically acceptable in the region. Adjustment and restructuring economic policies advocated by international lending agencies pushed for the Chilean model of privatization. And governments, crushed by the heavy cost of debt service and external pressure, became open to social security reform. In the 1990s, therefore, a series of reforms began to unfold in the region, most of them considering some degree of privatization.

Toward the end of the 1980s about 90 percent of the benefit expenditures for social insurance and family allowances in 24 Latin American and Caribbean countries went to pensions (54 percent) and sickness/maternity (36 percent), obviously the two most important social security schemes in the region. As the pension schemes matured in the pioneer countries, they required higher proportions of total benefit expenditures, e.g., an average of 76 percent, compared with an average of 28 percent among latecomer countries such as the Dominican Republic, Venezuela, and those of Central America. Although the problems concerning health care should not be underestimated, the social security crisis is largely an outcome of disequilibrium in the pension schemes, a problem that in the future will affect more and more countries. Even worse, the sickness/maternity schemes have usually received transfers from the pension schemes, so financial problems in the latter will close a major source of funding to the former, and both types of programs may go bankrupt.

Because of these problems it is not surprising that most social security reforms in Latin America (and the most radical reforms) focus on the pension schemes. This chapter offers a general view of all types of ongoing reforms in the region, in terms of both pensions and health care. Case studies of reform are discussed in the following sections.

Pensions

Four general types of pension reform are evolving in Latin America: (1) *reformed public schemes*, wherein the current public scheme continues but is substantially modified; (2) *substitutive private schemes*, wherein the public scheme is closed and supplanted by a fully funded private scheme; (3) *mixed schemes* that involve a combination of a reformed public scheme and a fully funded scheme that could be either public, private, or a combination of both; and (4) *supplementary pension schemes* that assume many forms and complement, but do not replace, reformed public schemes of the first and third types. In all cases there might be a public assistance, noncontributory pension for the elderly dispossessed who are not covered by social security.

Reformed public schemes. The best example of a reformed public scheme is found in Costa Rica, which in the 1980s and early 1990s introduced reforms in its general social security institute (CCSS) to stabilize its pension scheme, including (1) increases in the ages of early retirement; (2) an increase in the overall payroll contribution and the introduction of scaled years of contribution to discourage early retirement (so that the lower the age, the more years of contribution required, and vice versa); (3) control measures to reduce evasion and payment delays, as well as agreements with the state to pay past debts; and (4) adjustment and other efficient policies to cut administrative expenditures. In addition, a 1992 law "closed" several independent pension schemes for civil servants, who enjoyed unjustified privileges, and incorporated these schemes into the CCSS.

Mexico and Brazil have so far maintained public pension schemes without major structural reforms. In Mexico the general social security institute (IMSS) increased the payroll contributions, and a new compulsory supplementary pension scheme was introduced in 1992. In Brazil a constitutional reform, scheduled to take place in 1993, is expected to eliminate or at least restrict the seniority pension and perhaps incorporate privileged independent pensions into the general public scheme; a supplementary pension scheme is also a possibility. The cases of Costa Rica and Mexico are analyzed later in this chapter, as is Jamaica's unreformed public scheme.

Substitutive private schemes. Chile is the pioneer and model of privatization, not only in Latin America but probably in the world. In substitutive private schemes the old public scheme (often based on a pay-as-you-go approach and suffering a deficit) is "closed" (i.e., new affiliations are not allowed) and is replaced by a new mandatory, private, fully funded scheme administered by private corporations (Administradoras de Fondos de Pensiones, AFPs). Those insured in the public scheme are given the option to stay in or move to an AFP within a given period of time. Conditions in the public scheme are standardized and tightened, and the scheme itself disappears when all its potential beneficiaries have died. Only those insured contribute to the new system (in both the public and private schemes); the employers' contributions are eliminated, and the state finances all ensuing deficit related to the reform.

After implementing a modified Chilean-style reform in 1991, Peru enacted a law in 1992 that follows the Chilean model. There have been no other reforms of this type implemented in Latin America, but in Colombia a legal draft submitted to the congress in 1992 followed this approach; the draft, however, was withdrawn and is currently under discussion. The cases of Chile, Peru, and Colombia will also be analyzed later in this chapter.

Mixed schemes. Legal drafts submitted in 1992 to the congressional bodies of Argentina and Uruguay are examples of the mixed-scheme approach. In both cases the public scheme continues but is reformed; in Argentina the tightening of entitlement conditions and benefits is more drastic than in Uruguay. In both countries the public scheme provides a basic pension. In Argentina the supplementary scheme basically follows the Chilean model; but in Uruguay it is voluntary, can be administered by public and private nonprofit institutions, and has varying benefits and types of financing. (In Peru and Colombia there were, respectively, a decree-law and projects in an effort to follow the mixed approach before their governments decided to shift to the substitutive private scheme.) The cases of Argentina and Uruguay are also studied later in this chapter.

A theoretical variant of the mixed approach has been proposed by ILO officials but has not yet been considered by any country: the public scheme guarantees a minimum pension; a collective, partially funded scheme (instead of individual, fully funded ones) retains employers' contributions and pays an earnings-related pension; an optional supplementary scheme (of a nonspecified nature) pays another supplement; and a public assistance pension is available for the noninsured who lack resources (Gillion and Bonilla 1992).

Reforms are currently being studied in Bolivia, Ecuador, Guatemala, and Venezuela, but it is still too early to predict what models they will apply (Abril Ojeda 1991; Uthoff and Szalachman 1991; CIEN 1992; Mesa-Lago 1992b).

Supplementary pension schemes. Supplementary pension schemes (SPSs) have been under discussion and in operation in Europe for the last 25 years, but they are incipient in Latin America and were not analyzed at a regional meeting until 1989. The supplementary pension complements the pension of the general public scheme, usually because the latter is basic or minimal and uniform; hence, its level is very low and does not provide adequate protection. The purpose of the supplement is therefore to raise the combined pension to maintain the standard of living that the pensioner had prior to retirement. But in Latin America most of the few existing SPSs do not match that purpose; instead they complement general-scheme pensions that are not basic and uniform but rather related to both the insured's previous incomes and their periods of affiliation and contribution. However, as pensions of the general scheme in many LAC countries were eroded by inflation during the crisis they offered a more basic or minimum level, a situation that has raised the demand for SPSs. These SPSs can assume a variety of forms: mandatory or voluntary; established by law, collective agreements, or enterprises; managed by social security institutions, private corporations (nonprofit or for-profit), or both; and financed by the insured, the employer, or both (Castro-Gutiérrez 1990).

At least four Latin American countries have SPSs: Ecuador, Guatemala, Mexico, and Uruguay. In addition, there are projects under consideration in Argentina, Colombia, and other countries. In Ecuador SPSs are of voluntary affiliation, regulated by law, exclusively administered by the general social security institute (IESS) through contracts with individuals or groups of insured, and financed by both employer's and insured's contributions. In 1990 there were only three SPSs in Ecuador (for public teachers and communication and printing workers) that offered early retirement and an additional pension over the general one. In Guatemala SPSs are voluntary; regulated by law; administered by private, nonprofit associations or enterprises (authorized and supervised by the general institute—IGSS); and financed by both employers and insured. In 1990 there were eight SPSs (for employees in several banks, for autonomous institutions, one for each municipality and each university, and for a port enterprise) that offered old-age pensions (with earlier retirement and an additional pension) and disability/survivors pensions. In Mexico there were 1,160 SPSs in 1990 that covered almost one million workers; SPSs are regulated by law but assume a wide variety of forms (Castro-Gutiérrez 1990). In 1992 a law established mandatory SPSs for all workers covered by the major social security institute of the private sector (IMSS); federal civil servants are expected to be entitled to SPSs soon. Employers mandatorily contribute 2 percent of the payroll (the insured can add voluntary contributions); this amount is collected through the banking system responsible for opening and maintaining individual accounts for the insured. All funds, however, must be deposited in the Bank of Mexico (in the account of the IMSS), which invests them in treasury bills. The sums in the individual accounts are adjusted to the price index and exempted from taxes, and they must earn a real interest rate no lower than 2 percent yearly. The insured will have access to the accumulated funds upon reaching 65 years of age or becoming entitled to an IMSS pension; the fund may then be paid in a lump sum or used to buy a life annuity from an insurance company. The law also allows an individual fund to be transferred to a private investment corporation to increase its yield (Soto Pérez 1992). In addition to the SPSs regulated by law, there are many more in Latin America established by collective agreements or by enterprise plans. (SPSs in Uruguay are discussed later in this chapter.)

Health Care

Health care in Latin America is provided by three sectors. The public sector is overseen by the country's ministry of public health, which normally covers the lowest income groups of the population. The social insurance sector (the sickness/maternity scheme) usually covers middle-income groups. These two sectors combined cover the great majority of the population and continue to be the largest in the region. The private sector is the smallest; it usually covers high- and upper middle-income groups but is rapidly expanding in many countries. It comprises nonprofit institutions (or NGOs, such as religious and charitable organizations, development institutes, and community organizations) and for-profit providers (such as prepaid plans; private hospitals, clinics, and medical personnel; and traditional medical practitioners) (Mesa-Lago 1992c).

So far there are no examples in the region of full privatization of health-care services. Three types of health-care reforms are taking place: (1) continuations of the public social insurance system but with marginal privatization or collaboration with the private sector; (2) partial substitutive private schemes; and (3) supplementary private schemes.

Public-private collaboration and marginal privatization. In Costa Rica the public and social insurance (CCSS) sectors have integrated their health-care facilities and services since the 1970s: all hospitals are operated by the CCSS, and the ministry of public health offers preventive medicine and primary health care for marginal urban and rural groups. The CCSS has reduced health-care costs, increased its efficiency, and improved the quality of its services through five collaborative programs with the private sector. So far, however, the joint private-sector programs are available to no more than one-fifth of the insured in the CCSS.

Under the influence of Costa Rica, in the late 1980s Colombia's major social security institute (ISS) signed agreements with cooperatives but without the same positive results. A law enacted in 1991 empowered

the ministry of public health and the ISS to sign contracts with private institutions and provided incentives to promote integration of public and
private health services. A full reform of social security (combining pensions and health care) was passed in 1993.

In Jamaica the public sector (i.e., the ministry of health) legally covers
the entire population because social insurance lacks a sickness/maternity
scheme. Since the late 1980s there has been an increasing use of private facilities to reduce costs and improve the quality of the ministry's nonmedical services. In addition, more than one-fourth of the doctors in the public
sector are now private practitioners. The ministry signs contracts with private providers and oversees their services. Privatization of hospitals and
selected preventive and curative services was scheduled to start in 1989 but
was halted by the change in government that year. The cases of Costa Rica,
Jamaica, and Colombia will be analyzed later in this chapter.

Partial substitutive private schemes. In 1981 Chile reformed its health-care
system allowing the insured to select between the public social insurance
scheme (FONASA) or private HMOs (known in Chile as ISAPREs) of their
choice. The payroll contribution of 7 percent is paid to either FONASA or
the ISAPRE; those insured by an ISAPRE have to add a copayment to
finance the package of benefits offered, which must be better than that in the
public sector but does not offer preventive, maternity, and emergency services (hence, it is indirectly subsidized by the public scheme). In 1991, 72
percent of the population was covered by FONASA, 19 percent by ISAPREs,
5 percent by the armed forces, and 4 percent was not covered; it is projected
that in 1996, 29 percent will be covered by ISAPREs. As coverage by the
ISAPREs has grown, the lower-income groups have been left in the public
scheme and are increasingly deprived of the contributions of higher-income
groups; hence, public services have deteriorated, and emergency services
faced a crisis at the end of 1992. Those insured in ISAPREs can either pay
to the provider and get an agreed-upon percentage reimbursed by the
ISAPRE; buy vouchers from the ISAPRE to pay the provider, who gets reimbursed by the ISAPRE; or receive direct services from an ISAPRE that has
the necessary facilities. The number of ISAPREs rapidly increased to 34 by
the end of 1991 (more than twice the number of AFPs); the six largest
ISAPREs cover close to three-fourths of the beneficiaries. There seems to be
more competition among ISAPREs than among AFPs; the costs of administration and sales in ISAPREs declined from 40.5 percent to 18.9 percent of
total expenditures from 1981–1991 but are still quite high. A superintendency of ISAPREs supervises the private sector. In spite of its rapid expansion,
the private health sector in Chile covers only about one-fifth of the population (Iglesias and Acuña 1991; CIEDESS 1992; Gillion and Bonilla 1992).

A law enacted in Peru in November 1991 that followed the Chilean
model introduced a private health system; the insured can stay in the

social security institute (IPSS) or transfer to the HMOs (known in Peru as OSSs), which offer different health packages. However, the Peruvian system adds an element of solidarity lacking in the Chilean one: the entire employer's contribution and part of the insured's contribution is kept at the IPSS. The rest of the insured's compulsory contribution (as well as any additional voluntary contribution) is transferred to the OSS of the individual's choice, which freely charges additional fees to the individual for its services too. The IPSS can subcontract with an OSS for the provision of emergency and high-tech medical services. A superintendency of OSSs regulates and supervises the private system. However, by the end of 1992 the new system had not yet been regulated, so it was not operative ("Crean el Sistema . . ." 1991; López González and Céspedes Garay 1992).

Supplementary private schemes. In a small but increasing number of Latin American countries HMOs are expanding their coverage among the noninsured. In the Dominican Republic, where social security covers only about 4 percent of the population and health services are inadequate, HMOs (known as *igualas*) are not only incorporating the noninsured but also offering better supplementary services for the few insured. For a monthly premium *igualas* provide comprehensive health care to about 7 percent of the population, some of whom are covered by social security but do not use its services. Employers of large and midsize enterprises finance 75 percent of the total premium, but 145,000 microenterprises that employ a total of 400,000 workers cannot afford that level of payment. Recently there have been negotiations between associations of these microenterprises (which are willing to enroll members and collect fees) and the *igualas*, which are studying a low-cost package—based on a large group of insured—to provide primary health care and related services to potential members (Mesa-Lago 1992c).

Costa Rica:
A Reformed Public Scheme with Universal Coverage

The Achievement of Universalization

The Costa Rican social insurance fund (CCSS) was established in 1941 and began to operate sickness/maternity and pension programs in 1943. Its coverage was initially limited to urban salaried workers, who were mainly in the capital city and provincial capitals: in 1960 only 15.4 percent of the total population (25 percent of the EAP) was insured. In 1961 and 1971 two laws ordered the CCSS to achieve universalization in one decade; in the 1970s mandatory coverage was thus granted to domestic servants and employees of microenterprises (even those with one employee), and voluntary coverage became available for the self-employed, seasonal workers, unpaid family workers, and employers. Social assistance (i.e., non-contributory) coverage became mandatory for health care (except for cash benefits) and pensions to indigents, i.e., the dispossessed or those who have earnings lower than 75 percent of the minimum agricultural wage; these pensions were conditioned to a means test. Pensioners under either contributory or noncontributory programs were entitled to health care, as were the dependent families of all the groups protected by the CCSS.

In 1973 all hospitals of the ministry of health (MH) were transferred to the CCSS; the ministry's functions were limited to preventive medicine, and the CCSS focused on curative medicine (in the future the CCSS would become involved with prevention as well). The MH was also entrusted with the task of expanding primary health care (PHC) to the most remote, dispersed rural population as well as to urban marginal groups. The MH's rural health program began in 1973, and its urban community program started in 1976; both targeted the poor and the low-income population. The social development and family-allowances program was established in 1974, funded as part of the MH's programs for health care for the poor and prevention. In 1979 a national health system was legally formalized, with a clearer division of functions between the CCSS and the MH; since the 1980s a process of integrating these two institutions has been taking place (Jaramillo Antillón and Miranda 1985; Mesa-Lago 1989c; Quirós Coronado 1991).

Total population coverage for health care increased to 38.4 percent in 1970 and peaked at 84.4 percent in 1979. Because of the economic crisis the coverage declined to 77 percent in 1981; however, although the number of insured in the contributory program decreased, that of covered indigents increased. Since 1984 the percentage of coverage has been rising again, and by 1989 it reached the historical record of 85.4 percent. The remaining 14.6 percent of the population—which is not covered by the CCSS—is said to have enough resources to buy its own protection; therefore virtually the entire population is covered in terms of health care. (Coverage of the EAP by pensions was only 47.3 percent in 1988, although indigents are entitled to a separate social assistance pension.) Even if some of the poor—mainly in remote, rural, isolated areas—are not covered by CCSS curative medicine, practically all of them are reached by the MH's preventive and PHC services. In 1987 the combined MH coverage in urban and rural areas was 53 percent of the total population, thus overlapping with the CCSS coverage. Health-care services target other vulnerable groups such as pregnant women and infants: in 1987, 90.7 percent of all births in the country took place at CCSS facilities, and 85 percent of all children were immunized against the most common contagious diseases. These programs have contributed to the impressive health standards of that nation: infant mortality declined from 76 to 13.7 per 1,000 from 1960–1990, and life expectancy increased from 63 years to 75.8 years in the same period (CCSS 1988, 1989; Mesa Lago 1989c, 1992c).

Factors Facilitating Universalization

One important question is how Costa Rica, with a relatively young program as well as fewer resources and lower per-capita income than other countries, has been able to accomplish the elusive task of universalization. The following general factors provide an explanation: (1) Costa Rica is a relatively small country with no significant topographical barriers, a very good communication system, and a culturally integrated population with one of the highest literacy rates in the region; (2) it has enjoyed political stability and pluralistic democracy for more than three decades, and it has no radical differences between the two major political parties and no armed forces (and so does not have defense expenditures); (3) it has the smallest informal sector in the region (with the probable exception of Cuba), the second highest percentage of salaried workers in the labor force (i.e., the second smallest combined sector of self-employed, domestic servants, and unpaid family workers), and one of the lowest rates of poverty; and (4) it has a rural sector that, in spite of being one of the five largest in LAC, is relatively prosperous and does not exhibit significant inequalities in income relative to the urban sector.

However, these facilitating factors should not diminish the importance of a steady national political commitment to social security expansion. Important policy instruments used by Costa Rica have been (1) a basic public assistance program integrated with social insurance; (2) fair integration between the CCSS and MH health services; (3) mandatory coverage of domestic servants and microenterprises; (4) voluntary coverage of self-employed, with a low percentage contribution assigned for sickness/maternity—an effective average of 5.8 percent, compared with 5.5 percent paid by salaried workers (conversely, the respective contributions for pensions are 7.25 percent and 2.5 percent, a fact that explains the low coverage of the self-employed in that program); (5) coverage extension agreements between the CCSS and cooperatives, unions, and associations of the self-employed, peasants, and similar groups; and (6) easy access to health care, even for those who lack proper credentials as either insured or indigent (services are provided, and the user is then asked to obtain the proper certification) (Mesa-Lago 1992c).

Another important policy element is financing: the three major programs that have facilitated the extension of coverage beyond the salaried labor force receive strong state support, are based on solidarity transfers, or operate under a combination of both. The health-care program for indigents is entirely paid for by the state; it was financed at a cost of U.S. $20 million in 1988: 74.6 percent from direct state transfers, 18.5 percent from lottery revenue, and 6.9 percent from earmarked hospital stamps. The public assistance pension program for indigents is financed by a 5 percent payroll tax paid by employers plus 20 percent of the sales tax revenue (reduced to 15 percent in the mid-1980s). The health-care program for self-employed and seasonal workers below a certain income is partly financed by the state; in 1988 that group contributed an average of 6.6 percent of their earnings, and the state was expected to contribute the remaining 5.65 percent to complete a total statutory contribution of 12.25 percent (López Castaño and Tobón Bernal 1990).

The Financial Situation

The possibility of maintaining universal coverage in the future, with benefits that are reasonable in terms of real amount and quality, will largely be dependent on the economic capacity of the state to continue its financial support. This will in turn depend on overall economic performance. In the past the state debt to the system (a result of not meeting all its financial obligations) reached dangerous proportions and contributed to serious financial difficulties faced by the CCSS. From 1975–1981 the sickness/maternity program faced a growing financial deficit that peaked at 22 percent of expenditures in 1981. One major reason for the deficit was that the state's failure to fulfill its obligations amounted to 24 percent of the program's expenditures. Although in the rest of the 1980s the government signed debt payment agreements and better fulfilled its financial commitments to the CCSS, state transfers to all three major programs discussed above were still partly delayed (e.g., 31 percent of the sales tax revenue due the CCSS was collected but not paid by the state in 1988). In addition, the state payroll contribution was reduced from 2 percent to 0.75 percent, and the proportion of the sales tax going to the public assistance pension program was cut from 20 percent to 15 percent. The CCSS fought back and had the contribution percentages raised and expenditures reduced through adjustment policies. In spite of these positive steps, however, the real average monthly pension for indigents declined 60 percent from 1979–1988, from U.S. $58 to U.S. $22 (public health expenditures per capita in constant *colones* declined by more than one-half from 1980–1989). CCSS adjustment policies have managed to turn the deficit faced by the sickness/maternity program into a healthy surplus since 1982; this surplus peaked at 26 percent of expenditures in 1987. However, increased personnel salaries largely absorbed that surplus and reduced it to 3 percent in 1990; these salary increases were granted despite the fact that in 1987 the average salary of CCSS personnel was the highest in the nation and was twice as high as the average salary of all the insured. A major catalyst of disequilibrium in the pension program is the liberal entitlement conditions that, combined with maturation of the program, forced the use of the reserves to pay part of the pensions from 1987–1989. Furthermore, state transfers to social security are highly skewed in favor of the special independent pension programs for certain civil servants (these workers are covered by 19 programs outside of the CCSS). In 1987,

42 percent of the total cost of pensions went to the 20 percent of the total number of pensioners who are in those special independent programs, while the remaining 58 percent went to the other 80 percent of CCSS pensioners including both the contributory and non-contributory programs. The state transfer to all pensions was equal to 1.5 percent of GDP, and 68 percent of it went to the civil servants (Abel-Smith and Creese 1988; Mesa-Lago 1988b; CCSS 1988, 1989; López Castaño and Tobón Bernal 1990; Cartin Carranza 1991; Miranda 1991; Quirós Coronado 1991).

Reforms to Reduce Costs and Increase Efficiency

Important reforms introduced in the 1980s and 1990s aim at further reducing costs in both the pension and sickness/maternity programs. In 1991 the minimum ages for early retirement were increased from 55 to 60.5 for females and from 57 to 62.5 for males; in addition, the required contributions were set so as to discourage retirement at an early age: the lower the age, the higher the contribution (CCSS 1990). The costly pension program for civil servants was reformed by a 1992 law. All new appointees to civil service jobs are automatically incorporated into the CCSS and their entitlement conditions standardized: normal retirement is at age 60 for 30 years of contribution or age 65 for 20, and the base salary is calculated as the average of the best two years and adjusted in the same way as wages. Contributions are 7 percent by the insured and 7 percent by the employer (i.e., the state) but can be raised to 9 percent each if actuarially required. Those insured by the old programs retain their entitlement conditions and benefits.

The CCSS has been trying to reduce health-care costs, increase efficiency, and improve the quality of services by increasingly relying on the private sector and decentralizing its services. Five programs have been launched: enterprise physicians (EP), mixed medicine (MM), capitation, local health systems (SILOS), and contracts with private pharmacies.

The first two programs began in 1982–1983 when the CCSS signed agreements with the private sector to provide ambulatory medical services. In the EP program 766 enterprises hire and pay a doctor and provide him or her with an office and a nurse, and the CCSS supplies laboratory and diagnostic services and drugs. Under the MM program the insured selects a physician (from those enrolled in the program) and pays for his or her services, and the CCSS provides support services and drugs. Both programs combined served 17 percent of the population covered by CCSS in 1989 (two-thirds of those served are in EP and one-third in MM); the annual number of consultations per capita averaged 3.6 (higher in EP than in MM), slightly higher than the CCSS average of 3.1, but average expenditures per capita for EP and MM were about one-fourth of the per-capita costs for the entire CCSS (Quirós Coronado 1991; Mesa-Lago 1992c).

In 1986 a well-known health-care expert recommended the British system of capitation for the first level of care: the insured is able to register with a doctor of his of her choice, and the doctor is paid on a capitation basis, i.e., a monthly payment for each patient registered. The first pilot program covered 20,000 insured, but the frequency of consultation was the same as in the CCSS, costs were 15 percent higher, and the use of drugs was also higher. However, users of the new system indicated a higher degree of satisfaction (90 percent) than those using CCSS direct services (65 percent). In a second test the program was modified (participating physicians received a brief training course) and applied to three additional communities with reportedly better results: declines in consultation frequency, costs, and use of drugs (Abel-Smith and Creese 1988; Miranda 1991).

The SILOS program, which began at the end of the 1980s, consists of an integrated health-care program that is managed by a cooperative or self-managed organization through a contract with the CCSS and the ministry of health. The first experiment was launched in 1988 with a cooperative organized in a neighborhood of the capital city that has 50,000 inhabitants. The cooperative now has 173 health professionals who buy co-op shares. The CCSS transferred a fully equipped clinic to the co-op (at a cost of U.S. $1.5 million) for the period of the contract; the CCSS also pays a monthly sum per user, and the MH pays a monthly lump sum. The co-op provides users with PHC services, curative medicine, drugs, and milk to pregnant women and undernourished children. The population (both insured and indigents) freely selects a physician from the cooperative; the co-op is responsible for all its personnel, must maintain the building and equipment properly (it is to be returned to the CCSS in good shape at the end of the contract), and buys all needed supplies and inputs. In 1990 the cost of outpatient consultation in the co-op was about half of that in the CCSS. In the same year a second agreement with another co-op was signed to cover 55,000 people, and it has reportedly had similarly good results (Quirós Coronado 1991; Miranda 1991; Mesa-Lago 1992c).

Finally, in 1990 the CCSS began signing contracts with private pharmacies to reduce delays in drug deliveries to users and eliminate long queues at the CCSS. Costs of operation under the new system are said to be about half those at the CCSS.

Other measures proposed to reduce costs or increase revenues are (1) a recovery of charges from the noninsured who are capable of paying for CCSS services by improving the system of control; (2) an introduction of user fees for curative care and drugs (this measure has been rejected by both political parties and unions); (3) payment of inspectors on a commission rather than salary basis; and (4) further integration of the CCSS and MH to eliminate current overlapping, particularly in the provision of preventive services (Abel-Smith and Creese 1988).

Mexico: A Public Scheme Extended to Rural Areas

The Evolution of the Rural Solidarity Program

In 1954 the Mexican institute of social insurance (IMSS) slowly began to extend its population coverage to rural areas to include salaried workers (permanent, seasonal, or temporary) in agricultural enterprises and credit societies, as well as workers on sugar, tobacco, and sisal plantations, member of *ejidos*, and so forth. In spite of the progress made, by 1972 only 13 percent of the total insured were rural (compared with 40 percent of the total population). In 1973 IMSS launched a welfare program of social solidarity—the first to depart significantly from the conventional model of social insurance—to expand health-care coverage for both marginal urban and dispersed rural populations, though the focus was on the latter. The covered rural population received basic health services for free in exchange for 10 days of community work a year.

In 1976, at the height of the oil boom, a national institute to coordinate aid for marginal zones (COPLAMAR) was established, and in 1979 it developed an agreement with the IMSS to extend primary health care to marginalized rural zones. The rationale for this action was that, despite the good done by social insurances, they "contributed to the creation of a minority covered against all risks, side-by-side with a majority excluded from all protection, [hence] there is a need to enforce the redistributive function of social security beyond the classic scope of social insurance" (IMSS 1983, 15). The rural areas in which to establish IMSS-COPLAMAR health services were selected on the basis of four criteria: (1) 19 indicators of marginality (e.g., poverty incidence, high proportion of non-insured, lack of health facilities, concentration of Indian population); (2) knowledge of local conditions; (3) existence of minimum facilities (e.g., roads, electricity); and (4) population size: 500–2,500 inhabitants for clinics and 5,000–10,000 inhabitants for hospitals.

By 1985, at the peak of its evolution, IMSS-COPLAMAR had built 3,246 rural clinics and 65 rural hospitals and covered 14.5 million rural inhabitants in 24 states of Mexico, equivalent to 57 percent of the rural population (87 percent of all Indian groups) and 30 percent of all the IMSS-protected population. The population covered by IMSS-COPLAMAR was in great need of health care: it was poor (69 percent worked on subsistence agriculture); it had some of the nation's highest rates of infant mortality, death by contagious and parasitic diseases, illiteracy, and lack of piped water and waste disposal systems; it was 30–40 percent Indian; and 96 percent of it was in villages or small towns with less than 2,500 inhabitants.

When Miguel de la Madrid became president, the economic crisis was at its worst, and an adjustment program was soon introduced: priority was given to servicing the external debt, the state deficit had to be reduced, and social programs became a target. Decentralization of federal services to the states was rationalized on the premise that the states could handle them more efficiently and cheaply. In 1983 COPLAMAR was disbanded (although the IMSS retained control of its health program), but from 1985–1988 between 22 and 29 percent of its facilities and population were transferred to the health ministries of the states. By the end of 1988 the IMSS retained 2,323 clinics and 51 hospitals for 10 million people in 17 states (the poorest and most rural), and the states received 290 clinics and 14 hospitals for four million people. The IMSS ceased providing the 40 percent of the funding it gave to those facilities that were transferred to the states. The states themselves became responsible for the financing; this reportedly led to cuts in and deterioration of the transferred services.

In 1989 the decentralization process was halted by President Salinas, and the 70 percent segment of the program retained by the IMSS resumed its growth. In 1990 it was renamed Solidarity (and thereafter IMSS-S); it operated 3,079 clinics and 53 hospitals and covered about 11.3 million rural people, or 31 percent of the total population protected by the IMSS. In contrast, the IMSS's regular insurance program for rural workers covered only 1.8 million people, or 5.3 percent of the total insured.

Organization of the Rural Solidarity Program

The IMSS-S covers the head of the household, his or her spouse or companion, and dependent children and parents. About half of those covered are females, and about half are less than 15 years old; mothers and children are primary users of clinic services. Beneficiaries are entitled to health-care services at the first level in IMSS-S clinics, at the second level in the program hospitals, and at the third level in specialized hospitals of the secretariat of health (SS) but not in IMSS-S hospitals. The percentage distributions of the tended population by level are 85 percent, 12 percent, and 3 percent, respectively. Clinics and hospitals are open 24 hours a day. The specific services provided by all three levels (free of charge) are detection and control of chronic diseases; prevention and immunization of contagious diseases; curative medical/hospital care at the three levels; medicines; family planning; health education; and promotion of or guidance on environmental health, sanitation, nutrition, and housing improvement. Beneficiaries are expected to contribute such forms of community work as health-care assistance, sewage and garbage disposal, home improvement, pest control, and construction of water and drainage systems (although service is rarely denied to those who refuse to work).

Because all the IMSS-S clinics are the same throughout Mexico, the unique model is criticized for not being adapted to diverse local conditions. Services provided by the clinics include primary health care, outpatient consultation, mother/infant care, minor surgeries, medicines (from a basic list), and community services. The clinics are staffed with one *pasante* (a medical student in the last year of school who has to give one year of social service) or a recently graduated physician (also hired for one year), and two clinic assistants. At the beginning, the program basically relied on *pasantes*, but by 1986, 72 percent were contract doctors, resulting in higher costs. There are heavy demands on each doctor's time and skills, and the doctors normally try to avoid posts in the most isolated communities (when a doctor cannot be hired, a rural health technician—trained in six months—performs the job). The doctor's brief time of service, combined with language and cultural differences, usually prevents him or her from establishing close contact with the population. Clinic assistants are mostly young women recruited from the community who have completed primary school and are bilingual in Spanish and the local Indian language. Because of their age and low level of formal education, they have little autonomy and their role is limited.

Hospitals have between 10 and 70 beds, serve 40 clinics, and provide both primary health care to the inhabitants of the immediate area and secondary health care for patients referred from a surrounding area of approximately 200,000 inhabitants. They are staffed with physicians, *pasantes*, and other professionals as well as assistants; they offer emergency services, outpatient consultation, diagnostic services, dental care, medicines, and hospitalization. A surgeon heads a staff of residents in family medicine, pediatrics, obstetrics and gynecology, general surgery, internal medicine, and anesthesiology.

Community participation is good at the local level but poor or nil at state and federal levels. Locally there are volunteers, assistants, and a health committee. Volunteers oversee the health needs of 10 families each, help in the clinic, and learn basic nursing skills. Assistants provide rudimentary health services in outreach communities, for which they receive a token salary that is insufficient and thus contributes to a high dropout rate. The health committee maintains the clinic, transports supplies, assesses community needs, and helps deliver services. Clinic personnel are encouraged to plant medicinal herb gardens and exchange information and patients with traditional medicine practitioners, but competition and friction often exist. Relationships with midwives are better: in many communities, midwives deliver most babies and send high-risk patients to the clinic personnel; the clinics train midwives and allocate medical supplies to them to promote family planning and safe births. In 1989 there were 6,348 midwives and 4,202 traditional doctors cooperating with the IMSS-S.

The original social solidarity program of 1973–1978 was financed (in terms of construction, equipment, and operational costs) 60 percent by the federal government and 40 percent by the IMSS. When IMSS-COPLAMAR was established in 1979, the federal government agreed to pay all costs (capital and current) of the new program, and the social solidarity program continued with the same level of financing. Indirect support to COPLAMAR by the IMSS and later the IMSS-S (e.g., services such as planning and supervision, use of administrative facilities and equipment, training, and consultation) has been estimated by IMSS to be as high as 50 percent of total program costs, but this figure is probably inflated. Current financing to the IMSS-S is the same as it was to IMSS-COPLAMAR.

Efficiency and Impact on Health Standards

The IMSS-S stresses low-cost medical services, partly by emphasizing prevention and clinic-based services that satisfy 85 percent of the demand and are much cheaper than hospital services. The program's 1986 budget was 45.5 percent for curative services and 27.9 percent for prevention; the latter was far above the share of any other health institution in the nation (e.g., the SS spent 17.4 percent on prevention, the IMSS spent 2.3 percent, and the average for the whole health sector was 5 percent). Furthermore, prevention has been given increasing attention in recent years. Hospital efficiency shows an increasing trend. The rate of hospital occupancy gradually rose from 42 percent in 1980 to 67 percent in 1982 and 83 percent in 1985–1986; the average number of days of stay decreased from 4.0 in 1983 to 3.3 for 1986–1989. Although the IMSS has not provided data on hospital occupancy since 1981, its average number of days of stay in 1989 was 4.4, 33 percent higher than that of the IMSS-S. However, the poorest and most indigenous states are reported to have the lowest hospital occupancy rates: in 1986 Oaxaca's rate was 61 percent, largely because of transportation difficulties and cultural barriers to using institutional services. IMSS-S officials claim that its expenditures per capita (U.S. $7 in 1989) are the lowest of any health-care program in the nation. In 1987 the ratios of per-capita expenditures of other programs relative to the IMSS-S program were as follows: 5.8 times higher for the SS, 8.2 times higher for the civil servant institute (ISSSTE), 9.2 times higher for the IMSS, and 24 times higher for the petroleum workers institute (PEMEX). Even considering that the cost of IMSS institutional (indirect) support is not included in these calculations, the IMSS-S still appears to be the least expensive program in Mexico.

Evaluating the impact of IMSS-S on rural population health standards is difficult because (1) little information is available on the services transferred to the states, which makes comparisons before and after 1985 difficult; (2) because of the economic crisis, the IMSS-S budget was cut (per-capita expenditures were halved from 1982–1986), leading to reductions in personnel and supplies; and (3) the program success rate varies significantly among communities depending on geographic accessibility, previous living standards, ethnicity, local authority support, and the presence of skilled personnel. The unprecedented commitment of federal funds and IMSS resources permitted the program to develop a health service infrastructure in most remote rural areas of Mexico within a short time span and to succeed in delivering free institutional health care to the rural poor, who had practically no protection before. The formidable task of constructing, maintaining, and supplying clinics, even in geographically isolated areas, has generally been successful. There may have been a decline in population coverage and services from 1986–1988 (when the decentralization process took place), but later there was an increase in both population coverage and facilities, at least in the two-thirds of the program retained by IMSS.

Comparable data on IMSS and IMSS-S service and personnel rates show that the population covered by the former (i.e., the insured) receives much more services per capita than the latter; e.g., in 1986 the population covered by the IMSS received coverage for 1,357 times more consultations, 3,225 times more child deliveries, 3,350 times more surgery, and 26,650 more X-rays. Nevertheless, immunization rates are similar within both populations, and the rural poor receive other badly needed prevention services and disease treatments not available to the urban-IMSS insured population. Most services rates (per 10,000 people covered) increased substantially between 1980–1982 and 1986: from 50–370 percent in prevention and sanitation services, 50–100 percent in treatment of prioritized diseases, and 16–100 percent in all hospital services (though rates of clinical services declined). Morbidity rates for 1983–1989 need to be interpreted with caution but indicate significant declines from 1983–1986 in practically all transmittable diseases (by 11–65 percent, according to different estimates), such as influenza, enteritis, acute tonsillitis, amebiasis, etc. (only scabies rates increased). Rates of immunopreventable diseases also declined (by 29–83 percent) for polio, pertussis, meningitis, tetanus, measles, and tuberculosis (though human rabies and typhoid rates increased). Although the decline in such rates cannot be assumed to be an exclusive result of IMSS-S prevention and sanitation services, these services have played a positive role in reducing rural morbidity. More recent data, whose accuracy could not be checked, report that by 1988 polio had been virtually eradicated and that from 1985–1989 the following declines occurred: malnutrition went from 35 percent to 23 percent, child dehydration due to diarrhea from 12.6 percent to 5.8 percent, and child mortality from 8.5 percent to 6 percent (Mesa-Lago 1992c; Sherraden 1989).

Current Problems and Needed Assessments

Although there is little room for doubt on the good performance of the IMSS-S, some problems remain and new ones have appeared: (1) declines in rates of all clinic services such as outpatient consultation, prescriptions, and minor surgery; (2) inadequate coverage of the mother/infant group (in 1989 only 52 percent of pregnant women and 45 percent of deliveries were treated institutionally or by qualified midwives); (3) a reduction in budgetary allocations that contributed to a 55 percent decline in per-capita expenditures from 1982–1986 (this could also have been the result of increasing efficiency); (4) delays of state payments to the IMSS-S in 1987 that forced the IMSS to divert funds from other programs (this problem was corrected in 1988); (5) a reduction in the number of *pasantes* and in the ratio of nursing personnel to physicians (both of which have increased costs); and (6) insufficient participation of the covered population in health-care activities.

To further improve its performance, the IMSS-S program should have first priority in the allocation of federal funds, and some changes should be introduced: (1) prevention, sanitation, and the use of local paramedic personnel should be further emphasized over curative medicine and physicians; (2) the single health model should become more diversified to take into account specific features and needs of the villages; (3) community participation through health committees should be strengthened; (4) physicians should be trained before being assigned and should spend at least two or three years in a rural post to be able to learn from the community and be accepted by it (in order to attract more physicians, they should be sensitized to the national importance of this program while in medical school and have proper material incentives offered to them); (5) administrative procedures should be simplified to increase the time personnel devote to health functions; (6) qualified clinic assistants must be given more responsibility and training to perform more important tasks, and the number and roles of health volunteers should be expanded and their stipends raised; and (7) community work, done in exchange for health services, should be specified and tailored to community needs, resources, and interests (IMSS 1983, 1988, 1990a, 1991b; IMSS-COPLAMAR 1987a, 1987b, 1987c, 1988a, 1988b; IMSS-Solidaridad 1991; Velázquez 1989, 1990, 1991; Sherraden 1989; Mesa-Lago 1992c).

Jamaica: A Universal Public Scheme
with Marginal Privatization in Health Care

Prior to gaining independence, Jamaica had social insurance and social assistance old-age pensions for sugar workers, a general social assistance program, and a national public health program. After Jamaica became independent in 1965, the National Insurance Act (the first in the NLC) introduced social insurance pensions and grants. The National Insurance Scheme (NIS) began to function in 1966, covering all the employed labor force in the private and public sectors (including the armed forces, though civil servants have a special program) as well as sugar workers. Mandatory coverage of the self-employed and farmers, as well as a voluntary program for the rest of the labor force, were added in 1968. A compulsory employment injury program (for all the employed) and a maternity allowance program for domestic workers were introduced in 1970 and 1979, respectively. A public assistance program (PAP) manages several programs for the noninsured dispossessed. The Ministry of Labor, Welfare, and Sports (MLWS) is responsible for the NIS and the PAP, but the two programs are completely separated. The Ministry of Health (MH) is responsible for all public health-care services, both preventive and curative at all levels, through 375 health centers and 24 hospitals throughout the island. There is an extended system of private health insurance (Blue Cross/Blue Shield) as well as private health services, including six hospitals, but the hospitals serve a very small percentage of the population (Mesa-Lago 1987a). This section analyzes the NIS, PAP, and MH programs separately.

Social Insurance

The NIS provides (1) pensions for old age, disability, and survivors; (2) grants (lump sums) for the insured who do not qualify for pensions but have made a minimum number of contributions; (3) funeral grants; (4) employment injury benefits including medical care, temporary disability payments, and permanent disability pensions; and (5) a special program for sugar workers. The NIS does not provide sickness and maternity paid leaves (except for maternity leaves for domestic servants), family allowances, or unemployment compensation (MLWS 1990b).

The rate of open unemployment reached 27 percent of the labor force in 1982 (unofficial figures were as high as 30 percent), but as the economy experienced a modest recovery, the unemployment rate steadily declined to 15.7 percent in 1990. Still, this is a very high rate, and there has been discussion on whether unemployment insurance should be introduced. From 1980–1989 government officials argued that—with unemployment a massive, chronic phenomenon in Jamaica—it was financially unfeasible to introduce unemployment insurance; scarce resources should instead be used to create new, productive jobs, and the jobless should modestly be helped with public assistance. Employers oppose an unemployment program largely because it would increase payroll contributions, but union leaders are in favor of one. The political leadership in power since 1989 has proposed in their plan for 1990–1994 the creation of unemployment insurance with the following arrangement: those employed with 26 weekly contributions would be eligible (after a 14-day waiting period) for compensation equal to 60–75 percent of the insured wage for 13 weeks. The current five-year plan also proposes (1) a reduction in the male age of retirement from 65 to 60 years of age, to match the female age of retirement; (2) the introduction of a paid sick leave equal to 75 percent of the insured wage; (3) extension of employment injury benefits to the self-employed, farmers, domestic servants, and the armed forces; and (4) improvement of current benefits available to the disabled, widows, and other survivors. The plan, however, does not consider an increase in contributions to support these new programs (MLWS 1990a). An actuarial firm that was consulted on those changes opposed the reduction in the male age of retirement and recommended instead that the age for females be increased to 65 (Coke 1990).

Statistics on NIS population coverage significantly overestimate registration of the insured because of duplication (i.e., people registered more than once) and the continued inclusion of those who have emigrated or withdrawn from the scheme (although the retired and dead are now deleted from registration). In 1985 the number of those registered for pensions and grants was slightly higher than the labor force; registration for employment injury was slightly smaller because the self-employed are not entitled to such benefits. When registration figures were adjusted to account for the distortions, the proportion of the labor force insured was 93 percent. But if the number of active contributors was used instead, coverage of the labor force declined to 57.6 percent. Data on registration (adjusted or not) or active contributors are not available after 1985. The number of self-employed in 1987 was 352,900 (one-third of the labor force), but only 19,000 were registered (5.3 percent), and among them only 8,400 were active contributors (2.4 percent). In 1982, 17 percent of the population in the pensionable age bracket was receiving pensions; the proportion increased to 23 percent in 1990, but the vast majority was still not covered. Noncompliance is a serious problem: in 1987, 44 percent of the registered employers (including 23 percent of public-sector employers) were in arrears, and that figure excludes evasion. Reasons for this problem include excessive paperwork for registration, payments, and reporting; very low benefits and cumbersome, protracted procedures to claim them; lack of an up-to-date list of those who are noncompliant; and inefficient prosecution of delinquent employers. A process of computerization, initiated in 1987 and expanded under the 1990–1994 plan, is expected to clean up the registration data and provide a solid base for estimating coverage and fighting evasion and payment delays. Other improvement measures are the conditioning of import permits to an employer's compliance and a collaboration between the NIS and the Internal Revenue Department (Mesa-Lago 1987a, 1990c; MLWS 1990a; PIJ 1990; SIJ 1990a).

In addition to the above-mentioned difficulties in extending coverage to the self-employed and controlling noncompliance, the NIS confronts several problems: (1) low levels of benefits and contributions; (2) inadequate personnel skills and long delays in the processing of benefits;

(3) poor investment performance; and (4) a lack of regular actuarial evaluations.

The level of NIS benefits is extremely low, partly because of a notoriously insufficient flat-rate pension and a wage-related pension limited by a low ceiling on contributions. From 1980–1987 inflation reduced the average real insurance pension by 14 percent; measured in U.S. dollars the monthly pension declined by $38.50 to $14.60. In mid-1987 NIS monetary benefits were raised by 100 percent to 150 percent, and new increases (ranging from 20–60 percent) took place in 1990. In 1990 the average real insurance pension was almost 50 percent above the 1980 level but was no higher than the 1983 level, and it equaled U.S. $29.50 monthly (Mesa-Lago 1987a, updated with PIJ 1988–1991; conversions in U.S. dollars based on IDB 1991). The NIS lacks a structural mechanism to adjust its benefits to match inflation, and the 1990–1994 plan has proposed either to adjust such benefits automatically to 75 percent of the national minimum wage or to adjust benefits and contributions (as well as their ceiling) every other year (MLWS 1990a).

Civil servants (within NIS) enjoy superior benefits and more liberal entitlement conditions than the rest of the insured: males can retire at age 60 (instead of 65), and with 33 years of service, retirement is possible at 55 for both sexes; double pensions are allowed, and pensioners below a certain age may continue to work; and paid sick leave and BC/BS coverage (half paid by the state) are provided. Because of these exceptional benefits, in 1989, 26.5 percent of all social security expenditures went to civil servants, even though they accounted for only 7 percent of the labor force (ILO 1991c; SIJ 1990b). Benefits and entitlement conditions for civil servants should be standardized to match the rest of those insured under NIS to provide more resources for the meager NIS benefits.

Initially, NIS contributions were of two types: a flat rate (for those earning below J $12 weekly) and an additional wage-related rate (for those earning from J $12 to J $150 weekly). The NIS flat contribution rates were not increased for 24 years (from the inception of the scheme in 1966 until 1990), and although the contribution ceiling was raised, it was still very low. In the meantime the cost of living jumped by 1,300 percent, which largely explains the low level of NIS benefits. In 1990 contributions were modified as follows: (1) the rate for most salaried employees was standardized to 2.5 percent for employers and 2.5 percent for employees; (2) the flat rates for salaried employees in domestic service and the armed forces were increased almost seven times (now J $1 weekly each for the employer and the employee); in addition, the same percentage rates noted in (1) were applied to earnings between J $12 and J $290 weekly; (3) the flat rate for the self-employed and voluntarily insured was set at J $2 weekly plus 5 percent of earnings between J $12 and J $290 weekly; and (4) the wage ceiling was increased almost two-fold from

J \$7,800 to J \$15,080 yearly. These measures should have raised the contribution revenue considerably in 1991 (MLWS 1990a, 1990b, 1990c).

NIS administrative expenditures as a percentage of total expenditures declined from 38 percent to 10 percent from 1978–1990. If the newness of the NIS scheme is taken into account this proportion appears to be low. However, the NIS does not provide sickness/maternity benefits, its contributions are collected by the government, and its pensions are paid by the post offices. Administrative expenses are not disaggregated, so it is impossible to determine which are the key items. The number of NIS employees per 1,000 insured (with adjusted registration figures) was 0.4 in 1985, or 0.6 based on active contributors; both ratios are probably the lowest in LAC. Not only is the NIS staff small, but it has a great need to upgrade its skills. The 1990–1994 plan proposes to expand and train NIS personnel. The major administrative problems faced by the NIS are a high level of evasion and noncompliance, a poor record of making financial reports and disseminating information, and an excessively lengthy and complicated processing of benefits. In 1986, out of 99,000 potential pensioners only 48,000 claimed benefits, allegedly because of a lack of information, cumbersome procedures, and the low level of benefits. Post offices are unable to pay pensions promptly: they often run out of cash, and pensioners usually have to stay in line for hours to collect their pensions. Computerization is expected to help simplify and expedite benefit processing, and there is a plan to replace post offices with workers' savings and loan banks, where the insured could also open savings accounts (Mesa-Lago 1987a; PIJ 1988–1991; MLWS 1990a).

Investment returns generated a share of NIS revenue that increased from 29 percent to 53 percent from 1977–1990. However, the annual real investment yield from 1979–1990 was positive only in three years and averaged -7.3 percent, so the real reserves declined by 7 percent in the same period. Reasons for the negative yield were a high rate of inflation (an annual average of 17 percent); concentration of investment in government stocks (99 percent of the portfolio in 1985) that paid a lower yield than commercial banks; and control of investment by the Ministry of Finance, which, at least from 1983–1987, retained accrued interest and did not invest significant sums. Since 1988 some measures have been taken to correct that situation. The portfolio has been diversified, and in 1990 the proportion in government stocks had declined to 63.2 percent; the rest was invested in loans (15.4 percent), treasury bills (10.4 percent), certificates of deposit (4.6 percent), and stock market shares (3 percent). Aided by a decline in inflation, in 1987 and 1988 the yield became positive (about 6 percent), but a sharp increase in inflation in 1989 and 1990 turned the yield negative again (-6 percent). In 1990 an Investment Office was established at the MLWS to work in close cooperation with the NIS to improve investment performance and further diversify the portfolio. If inflation is abated, the new policy may prove to be effective.

It is impossible to assess the actuarial stability of the NIS pension fund because there has not been a thorough actuarial evaluation since 1977. Although legally such an evaluation has to be done every five years, the 1981/82 and 1986/87 reviews were postponed because of inadequate data on the insured and on finances. An interim actuarial report done by a consulting firm in 1985 advised that in order to augment benefits it was necessary to increase the contributions (benefits were raised in 1987— more than advised by the actuary—and 1990, but contributions were not raised until 1990). The interim report argued that the investment yield had to be increased dramatically to compensate for the increase in benefits, but such an increase has not occurred. I have noted that the 1990–1994 plan recommends the creation of new programs, an expansion of benefits, and a liberalization of entitlement conditions without providing the necessary increase in revenue, and that a 1990 actuarial report advised against such an expansion. So far none of the proposed modifications has been implemented. The NIS generated a financial surplus in each year of the 1979–1990 period, but as a percentage of revenue the surplus declined from 80 percent to 47 percent, and in real terms the surplus was halved in the same period; the real reserves declined by 7 percent in that period. The current five-year plan expects that the computerization process will generate the needed data to conduct regular actuarial evaluations (Mesa-Lago 1987a, updated with PIJ 1988–1990; Coke 1990; PIJ 1990a).

Public Assistance

The PAP administers six programs for the dispossessed: (1) old-age disability pensions for about 30,000 who do not qualify for NIS pensions and grants and who pass a means test; (2) food stamps for the poor, elderly, pregnant and lactating women, and children under five, helping 354,000 people; (3) outdoor aid to 18,000 totally destitute and 1,613 elderly people in infirmaries; (4) aid to the dispossessed aged that consists of meals, clothing, occupational therapy, and transportation; (5) retraining for the disabled to enable them to get jobs; (6) financial aid, shelters, beds, clothing, and furniture for more than 2,000 affected by natural disasters; and (7) in 1988 an employment antipoverty program to provide jobs and income to 12,600 rural poor. In 1985 all these programs helped about half a million people, or about 20 percent of the total population. The PAP has complemented the NIS and helped move Jamaica toward a universal system of social security. Furthermore, the separation of these two programs (and the wide gap in benefits between them) has allowed some of the problems faced in the Bahamas and Barbados to be avoided. Still, the PAP is afflicted by several problems: (1) its budget is insufficient and is often depleted by mid-year, and the quality of its services has deteriorated; (2) the level of the assistance pension in 1985 was only U.S. $4.20 monthly, and although it increased to about U.S. $6.50 in 1990 it was still grossly insufficient; (3) a considerable number of beneficiaries of the food stamp program receive multiple benefits or are not really in need, though periodic revisions have cut their numbers considerably (e.g., from 366,480 to 291,883 from 1987–1988 and from 438,778 to 207,517 from 1989–1990); (4) the stamps have low purchasing power, they are often delivered late, and their mix of food items is inflexible (Mesa-Lago 1987a; PIJ 1988–1991; MLWS 1990a).

The 1990–1994 plan has proposed several measures to cope with some of the problems explained above: (1) an annual review of public assistance cases to verify needs as well as to review and standardize the eligibility criteria in order to plug loopholes, eliminate multiple benefits, and increase the level of support to those really in need; (2) a limitation of food stamps to only children under five and pregnant/lactating mothers; those in need who are excluded from this program will receive small loans to develop businesses of their own; (3) delivery of food stamps by mail and increased flexibility in the mix of food items; (4) a gradual increase in the real benefit level; and (5) computerization of the program to help eliminate fraud and expedite the delivery of stamps and the overall processing of benefits (MLWS 1990a; PIJ 1990a).

Public Health

Legally the entire population should be covered by the public health system, but since the mid-1970s the system has deteriorated—a situation aggravated by the economic crisis of the 1980s. All the dispossessed have free access to the system (including drugs), conditioned to a means test administered by the PAP food stamp program. PHC, tests for diagnosing communicable diseases, and prenatal care are provided free to the entire population. User fees are charged for secondary and tertiary levels of care, although the charges are quite low. Public hospitals have private wards or private beds that charge higher fees. About 95 percent of the total number of hospital beds are in the public sector, as are 50 percent of the physicians. An increasing number of people use private facilities, particularly hospital services.

The numbers of physicians per 10,000 inhabitants and hospital beds per 1,000 decreased by 50 percent from 1970–1988: from 3.8 to 1.6 and from 4.1 to 2.2, respectively. But hospital occupancy increased from 53 percent to 79 percent in that period (though it declined again to 67 percent in 1990), and the average number of days of stay fell from 11 to 7.6. In the same period the infant mortality rate decreased from 32.2 to 27 per thousand, and life expectancy at birth rose from 68.5 to 71. However, a slowdown in the improvement of these indicators has been clear since the second half of the 1970s. The proportion of pregnant women who received prenatal care increased from 83 percent to 88.8 percent from

1984–1987 but declined to 67.8 percent in 1990. Conversely, there were steady increases from 1984–1990 in the proportions of mothers who received postnatal care (from 53 percent to 67.8 percent); infants who received care (47 percent to 69.8 percent); and children younger than one who were immunized—e.g., for DPT from 56.9 percent to 85.7 percent, for polio 55.7 percent to 86 percent, and for measles 16.1 percent to 64.8 percent. In spite of these efforts epidemics of measles, typhoid, and dengue significantly increased the incidence of these diseases. Diarrheal diseases and malnutrition are leading causes of death in children under five: in 1985 only 59 percent of children below 60 months were of normal nutritional status (PIJ 1987–1990; SIJ 1990a, 1990b; PAHO 1990).

Since the mid-1970s the public health sector has been afflicted by several problems that explain its mixed performance. The per-capita annual health expenditure in constant prices declined from J $75.06 to J $46.50 from 1982–1988, and public health expenditures as a proportion of total health expenditures decreased from 68 percent to 55 percent from 1982–1986 (whereas the share of private expenditures rose from 32 percent to 45 percent). A scarcity of personnel has become a major problem; the percentages of unfilled vacancies for nurses, pharmacists, and doctors may be as high as 50 percent. Salaries lagging behind the cost of living have resulted in a massive emigration of medical personnel. The physical plant and equipment have gradually deteriorated because of a lack of maintenance and replacement; health centers are underutilized (use of their outpatient services declined 23 percent from 1984–1986) because of a lack of doctors and physicians and a poor supply of drugs; and there is a long waiting time for inpatient care. Wide devastation caused by Hurricane Gilbert aggravated many of these problems. The deterioration of the public health system has forced the poor to use private services. A survey conducted in the late 1980s showed that 42 percent of the poorest two-fifths of the population used private care, but only 1.2 percent of that group had health insurance (Abel-Smith and Creese 1988; Government of Jamaica 1988; SIJ 1989; PIJ 1988–1991).

External aid has provided some relief, for instance, a new central public health laboratory built with European Economic Community (EEC) aid and the restoration and re-equipment of health-care facilities with USAID and IDB help. Targeting the poor and the mother/infant group has been another positive step, but the fundamental flaws of the system cannot be corrected with these policies. Four major alternatives have been explored: compulsory health insurance, user fees, extension of voluntary private insurance, and privatization of services. The creation of a sickness/maternity program within the NIS was recommended by some technical reports, but in 1988 the government rejected the proposal because it considered the idea of increasing payroll contributions to be unacceptable. Some sectors of the population also felt that the NIS should improve its current benefits before adding new programs. The current 1990–1994 plan does not contemplate compulsory health insurance.

User fees for hospital services were frozen from 1968–1984 and then increased somewhat, but they still remain very low; the poor (as certified by the PAP) are exempted from paying the fees. In 1986 the hospitals that collect the fees were allowed to retain 50 percent of the revenue (to improve services), and that proportion was increased to 75 percent in 1990. The 1990–1994 plan recommends that the amount of the fees approximate the real cost of providing the services.

Voluntary insurance with an indemnity type of policy (e.g., BC/BS) has rapidly expanded in Jamaica, but it has some disadvantages: it excludes high-risk groups and major medical risks, and it requires substantial copayments that make the services unaffordable by the low-income insured. HMO models can provide fuller coverage at lower costs, but the copayments still are high for the lowest income groups (including most of the self-employed). Sick funds or friendly society contracts, of the type operated in Europe or some Latin American countries prior to the introduction of compulsory insurance, could provide basic coverage (with referrals to public hospitals) and do so rapidly and at lower costs than BC/BS and HMOs.

Finally, there has been an increasing use of private services to reduce costs and improve the quality of public nonmedical services, but plans for a full privatization of medical services have been halted. Hospital divestiture of nonmedical services began in 1987 in three areas: housekeeping, janitorial, and portering; catering; and laundry. The first group of services was contracted out in 1987 with the private sector, through formal bidding, for the three public hospitals in Kingston. The results have been positive: costs have been cut in half, quality has improved, and staff morale has risen. Catering and laundry services for the same hospitals began in 1988; in addition, there was a plan to contract out hospital equipment services. The MH oversees and evaluates contracted services. According to a high-level MH official, at the end of 1991 the privatization of nonmedical services was not yet complete but was progressing. The 1990–1994 plan recommended the participation of private practitioners for providing services at public facilities (to ease the personnel shortage), and by the end of 1991 more than one-fourth of the doctors in the public sector were private practitioners. Privatization of medical services, mainly in terms of hospitals but also for selected preventive and curative services, was scheduled to start in 1989. Three models were going to be tested: (1) one hospital fully operated by a private contractor during a five-year period with an option for extension; (2) one hospital managed by a private group for a three-year renewable contract, with the MH assuming the financial risk; and (3) one hospital managed and controlled by a private corporation, with the government holding the majority of shares. The change in administration in 1989 halted the privatization of medical services, and by the end of 1991 the situation remained unchanged (Abel-Smith and Creese 1988; Lewis 1988; SIJ 1990a; MLWS 1990a).

Chile: Pioneer and Model of Privatization

General Characteristics of the Reform

Together with Uruguay, Chile is a pioneer in the introduction of social insurance in LAC. At the beginning of the 1970s the Chilean social security system was one of the two most advanced in the Western hemisphere: it covered all contingencies, reached virtually the entire population (through the combination of contributory and noncontributory schemes), and offered generous benefits. But it was extremely fragmented and legally complex and stratified (it comprised 100 independent pension programs plus many others covering different contingencies); it also lacked effective coordination, allowed unjustified privileges and significant inequalities, constituted a heavy economic burden (the payroll tax was 65 percent, and in 1971 total expenditures reached the historical continental record of 17 percent of GDP), suffered financial and actuarial disequilibrium, and required substantial state subsidies (29 percent of total social security revenues). Interest groups blocked the urgently needed system reforms recommended under successive administrations (Mesa-Lago 1978, 1989c; Piñera 1991; Cheyre Valenzuela 1991; Iglesias and Acuña 1991; Santamaría 1992).

In 1973 the long Chilean democratic tradition was interrupted, and the new authoritarian regime destabilized or banned trade unions, professional associations, and political parties. The weakening of the pressure groups and empowering of the state, combined with social pressure, contributed to the reform of social security. Legislation enacted in 1979 eliminated the most blatant inequalities, such as seniority pensions and the *perseguidora* (a pension for high-ranking civil servants that was continually adjusted to equal the current salary of the post formerly occupied by the privileged pensioner), and standardized some entitlement conditions; e.g., retirement ages were uniformly set at 65/60 for males/females. A gradual process of unifying the old system took place in the 1970s and 1980s. Pension schemes were divided into three groups: (1) blue-collar, private white-collar, and railroad workers; (2) municipal and race-track workers; and (3) merchant-marine workers. Civil servant and banking schemes remained independent temporarily, and the military and police schemes were completely excluded from the reform. An institute of social insurance standardization (INP) was appointed to manage the unified schemes, develop methods to standardize them, and administer a special fund (financed by the state) to cover the growing deficit. In 1988, 17 funds merged in the INP, which incorporated the remaining civilian pension schemes by the end of the decade. The old superintendency of social security continues to supervise the old system and to collect and publish data on the entire social security system.

A new pension scheme with uniform entitlement conditions and regulations was introduced in 1980 and began to operate in May 1981. Based on the "social market" ideology, the new scheme has the following characteristics: (1) it assigns to the state a subsidiary role in social security, entrusting the operation of the new scheme to freely competing private pension fund administrative corporations (AFPs or *sociedades anónimas*) that are strictly regulated, supervised, and audited by a new superintendency (SAFP), and with a series of state guarantees; (2) it establishes a compulsory saving/pension program (for old age, plus disability and survivors coverage through separate private insurance companies); (3) it is financed by the insured workers alone (the employers continued paying some contributions for other contingencies until 1988, when the state became the only financier of all those programs except employment injury); (4) the insured's contributions are credited to individual accounts, and all funds are invested by the AFP in different instruments; investment returns are proportionally credited to the account of the insured, who is also entitled to open a voluntary savings account; and (5) at the time of retirement the insured can choose from among various old-age pension options. There is a debate on whether the new scheme is truly private. Two ILO officials claim that the scheme does not really have a clear private-public dichotomy because it downplays the important role of the state in providing substantial subsidies and guarantees (Gillion and Bonilla 1992).

Those insured in the old pension scheme were allowed to exercise some of their acquired rights (e.g., seniority pensions) only during a transition period but to keep other rights permanently. In addition, they were given a five-year period (which expired in May 1986) to stay in the old scheme or move into the new one. A strong incentive to move was a significant reduction in the insured's payroll contribution in the new system, combined with a publicity campaign criticizing the flaws of the old scheme and exalting the virtues of the new one. By the end of 1982, 1.6 million insured (half the labor force and close to 70 percent of all the insured) had moved to the new scheme. Since 1983 all salaried new entrants in the labor force are obligated to join the new scheme. The old scheme is expected to last for about 40–50 years. In the following analysis I refer to the old and new pension schemes as public and private, respectively (Baeza and Manubens 1988; Arellano 1989; Ferrara 1989; Mesa-Lago 1989c; Castro Jiménez 1990; Borzutzky 1991; Piñera 1991; Iglesias and Acuña 1992; CIEDESS 1992).

Population Coverage

According to the law all salaried workers, including agricultural workers, domestic servants, and employees of microenterprises, are compulsorily covered in the private scheme, whereas the self-employed can join voluntarily. Those insured who do not meet the needed requirements for a regular pension are entitled to a minimum pension with state support. Pensioners and their dependent families are eligible for health care. The noninsured, including the unemployed, unpaid family workers, and the noncovered self-employed, are entitled to a public assistance pension paid by the state.

The proportion of the labor force covered by the public scheme steadily increased and peaked at 76 percent in 1973; it declined to about 62 percent in 1980. Once the two schemes were combined (but excluding the military and the police), coverage continued decreasing to a trough of 57 percent in 1982 (in the midst of the economic crisis) and steadily rose thereafter to 79 percent in 1988 and close to 86 percent in 1991. (The percentage of coverage based on the number of registered insured is considerably higher than that based on the number of contributing insured—see the next subsection.) Reasons for the decline in coverage were the sharp increase in unemployment, expansion of the informal sector, and evasion, plus statistical corrections made to the registry to eliminate or reduce double counting of the insured. The upswing in coverage resulted mostly from an economic recuperation and a decrease in unemployment during the second half of the 1980s. In August 1991, 90 percent of the insured were registered in the private scheme; the number of insured in the private scheme increased almost three-fold from 1981–1991, whereas the number of insured in the public scheme declined by more than one-half. About 60 percent of those in the private scheme are below 35 years of age, but the public scheme mostly covers people close to retirement. In 1987 about 97 percent of the population aged 60 and older received some type of public assistance pension (SAFP 1981–1992; SSS 1982–1992; Mesa-Lago 1987b, 1988a, 1989c; Cheyre Valenzuela 1991; Iglesias and Acuña 1991; Arrau 1992; CIEDESS 1992).

A labor survey conducted in 1988 showed that 19.5 percent of the labor force was not covered by social security, but that percentage varied in different occupational groups: 16 percent among salaried workers, 36 percent among domestic servants, 58 percent among employees of enterprises with less than five workers (but only 8 percent in enterprises with more than 50 workers), 71 percent among the self-employed, and 92 percent among unpaid family workers. Most of the noncovered population consists of the self-employed: the majority of those insured are professionals with relatively high incomes, but the bulk of the informal self-employed are not affiliated. In 1991 only 3 percent of those registered were self-employed, and it was estimated that two-thirds of the registered self-employed were not covered. Reasons given for such low coverage are: (1) voluntary affiliation (the official explanation for the lack of mandatory coverage is the difficulty in controlling it) combined with poor information about rights and poor foresight among these workers; (2) the low and unstable income of this group; (3) the high percentage of contribution (however, both the self-employed's percentage contributions and benefits are equal to those for salaried workers); and (4) the disincentive for affiliation created by available, free, public assistance alternatives, such as pensions, health care, and family subsidies. To become insured, the self-employed have to join all social security programs, and one-half of the contribution (i.e., 10 percent of earnings) goes to the old-age pension scheme. Some suggestions to increase protection of this group are to allow coverage for sickness/maternity and disability/survivors to be separate from old-age pensions and to create a special pension program tailored to the self-employed's needs and capacities to pay. The new democratic government has not tackled this problem, although in 1991 it was considering a special program for 250,000 low-paid seasonal workers who pick and pack fruit exports. Optional incorporation of the military and police into the new system has also recently been suggested (SAFP 1981–1992; Mesa-Lago 1987b, 1988a, 1989c, 1990; Arellano 1989; Marcel and Arenas 1991).

Compliance

The creators of the private scheme thought that it would reduce evasion and payment delays and thus increase the number of effective contributors. The rationale was that the workers would register and pay their contributions (which would be safe and grow into a sizable sum) and employers would not have to pay contributions and so would have no incentive to underreport salaries (Piñera 1991; CIEDESS 1992; Santamaría 1992). But that hope has not materialized because of a lack of adequate controls, a high contribution for the insured, high inflation that created an incentive for employers to delay the transfer of salary deductions, difficulties in incorporating the self-employed, and cheaper alternatives in public assistance.

The proportion of those registered in the public scheme who pay their contribution increased steadily from 68 percent to 86 percent from 1980–1987, as they came closer to the retirement age. Conversely, in the private scheme the proportion decreased from a peak of 76 percent in 1983 to 70 percent in 1987 and further to 61 percent or 53 percent in 1990 (based on different calculations) and 52 percent in 1991. This private-scheme behavior, which is contrary to what was expected given the economic crisis and subsequent recuperation, might have been caused by flaws in the SAFP data on affiliation (e.g., pensioners who remain registered as active), by actual increases in evasion and payment delays (in 1991 the obligations of employers who deducted their workers' contributions but did not transfer them to the scheme amounted to U.S. $200 million), or by a combination of both. It appears that those insured who have low incomes delay payment to reduce contributions in order to get a minimum pension. At the end of 1988, 56 percent of the labor force was registered and contributing, 24 percent was registered and not contributing, and close to 20 percent was not covered. A good portion of the noncontributors were temporary workers and unemployed, and others had withdrawn from the labor force. Among the noncontributors, 50 percent had not paid for one year or less and 34 percent for more than one year. The proportion of contributors among the registered self-employed was 40 percent in 1991, considerably lower than the 53 percent among salaried workers. When the number of contributors instead of the number registered is used, the proportion of the labor force covered is cut by about one-half: in 1990, 79 percent were registered and 42 percent were contributing, and in 1991 the proportions were 86 percent and 44 percent, respectively (these figures exclude contributors in the public system; when these are added, coverage increased to 51 percent in 1991—without the armed forces). In addition, there is significant underreporting of earnings: the gap between insurable earnings and actual contributions expanded from 1982–1990, reaching about 20 percent in 1990, when one-fourth of the contributors paid based on earnings equal to or lower than the minimum wage, largely because they were interested only in the minimum pension (SAFP 1981–1992; SSS 1982–1992; Iglesias and Acuña 1991; Arrau 1992; CIEDESS 1992).

Compliance in the private scheme could be improved by using a single universal identification for all financial transactions, unifying the collection of contributions, promptly correcting the registry to account for labor force withdrawals and pensioners, promptly detecting late payers through computerized records, increasing the level of reporting by those insured whose employers fail to transfer contributions, and more effectively prosecuting delinquent employers. But some of these measures are not easily implemented; for instance, the insured are expected to check the AFP's quarterly reports of their individual accounts (*cartolas*) regularly and detect if employers are not transferring their contributions, but many don't do so, and others cannot understand the report. The AFPs can prosecute delinquent employers, but many fail to do so because they fear that the employer will encourage his or her employees to shift to another AFP. The employer must complete as many monthly forms as the social security institutions that cover the employees; hence, large enterprises have to complete dozens of forms, but the problem is even worse for mid-sized enterprises without computer facilities. A unified, fully computerized collection system with a single form for reporting would speed up payments, reduce employer costs, and strengthen control of evasion and payment delays. Both at the beginning and toward the end of the 1980s there were several projects to accomplish that task. But the SAFP and the largest AFPs opposed such a change for the following reasons: fear that a powerful state agency could use information against the AFPs; loss of the competitive edge that the largest AFPs have gained by having a national network of collecting branches; potential damages that the collecting agency could incur via computational errors and the resulting legal issues concerning responsibility for such errors; opposition to the investment of all collected funds by the agency; and questions on who (i.e., the AFP, the employer, or the state) would pay for the collecting agency. At the end of 1988 a comprehensive project tackled many of these issues, but it was not implemented (SAFP 1981–1992; Mesa-Lago 1987b, 1988a; Marcel and Arenas 1991).

Benefits and Entitlement Conditions

Entitlement conditions and regulations for pensions are uniform in the private scheme. The old-age pension requires 20 years of contribution and a minimum age of 65 for males and 60 for females. Early retirement is allowed when the individual insured's accumulated fund can finance a pension higher than 50 percent of his or her average earnings in the last 10 years and is equal to at least 110 percent of the minimum old-age pension. The old-age pension fund consists of the insured's net contributions (after deducting commissions to the AFP), a state recognition bond,[7] the corresponding investment returns, and possibly the money from a savings account.

The insured has three options at the time of retirement: (1) a life annuity from a private insurance company, calculated on the basis of the insured's sex, age, and number of beneficiaries; the company becomes the owner of the accumulated pension fund (which is transferred from the AFP) and guarantees a fixed monthly pension for the insured and his or her survivors (but there is no right of inheritance for what is left of the fund in the absence of survivors entitled to the pension); the insured's decision for this option is irrevocable; (2) a programmed pension paid directly by the AFP, annually calculated (and hence fluctuating) based on the size and yield of the fund, life expectancy changes, and the number of the insured's beneficiaries; the insured retains ownership of the fund (which can be inherited) and can change his or her decision at any time; (3) a programmed pension for a number of years and a life annuity later.

The AFP must provide all the needed information (including facts about the different insurance companies) for the insured to make a decision, but reportedly 90 percent of the insured do not understand the complexities involved and so hire experts who charge fees ranging from 3–5 percent of the total value of the accumulated fund (Gillion and Bonilla 1992). Furthermore, the AFP is never responsible if the insured's decision results in an insufficient length or amount of the pension.

Disability and survivors pensions are paid not by the AFP but by the insurance company contracted for that purpose. A total disability pension (for loss of at least two-thirds of work capacity) pays 70 percent of the average earnings of the last 10 years to those younger than the standard retirement age, and a partial disability pension (for loss of at least one-half of work capacity) pays 50 percent. Survivor pensions are paid to widows or disabled widowers, children below age 18 (or 24 if a student, any age if an invalid), and parents if there are no other beneficiaries.

A minimum pension is guaranteed by the state if the insured's accumulated fund is not sufficient to finance that amount and if other requirements for old age or disability are met. Insured unemployed and part-time workers are entitled to disability/survivors coverage and the minimum pension for one year after dismissal if they have accumulated six months of contributions in the previous year. A public assistance pension is paid by the state to all the noninsured and those insured not entitled to minimum pensions.

The entire social security system is denominated in terms of a separate monetary currency called *Unidad de Fomento* (UF) whose value is adjusted monthly for inflation so that currency units maintain a constant value. All benefits (including pensions), individual accounts, and investment returns are expressed in terms of UF. A comparison of the average level of pensions in the public and private schemes showed that by 1991 private-scheme pensions were 43 percent higher for old age (U.S. $149 monthly pension in private scheme), 100 percent higher for disability (U.S. $206), and 46 percent higher for survivors (U.S. $92). But the validity of this comparison has been questioned on the grounds that in that year there were fewer than 100,000 pensioners in the private scheme but close to one million in the public scheme. Although no data are available, the level of pensions for the armed forces is probably higher than for the average pension in the private scheme; in 1980 the military pension was four times higher than the average general pension. And pensions for insured females are considerably lower than those for males because females have a lower retirement age and live longer. The minimum monthly pension appears insufficient to meet basic needs; it was U.S. $75 in 1991, equivalent to 22 percent of the average national wage, and it has been estimated that about half of the insured will receive a minimum pension. The public assistance pension is considerably lower (U.S. $36 in 1992); furthermore, the number of such pensions is limited to 300,000, there is a long waiting list, and the means test is reportedly very strict. Except for the presence of a minimum pension the private scheme does not apply the solidarity principle of social security, and even this minimum pension is financed with a state contribution outside of the pension scheme (Mesa-Lago 1988a; Arellano 1989; Ferrara 1989; SAFP 1991–1992; Gillion and Bonilla 1992).

Estimates of the future levels of average private pensions, based on simulation exercises, make use of too many assumptions; hence, results vary widely depending on whether the assumptions are optimistic or pessimistic. Based on a 5 percent interest rate—which is judged conservative in view of the average yield of 14 percent for 1981–1991—a Chilean research institution has calculated a pension salary-replacement rate of 80–86 percent for males and 53–56 percent for females (CIEDESS 1992). The ILO, using a 3 percent interest rate—which is considered by the authors to be high—has in turn projected a 44 percent replacement rate for males (Gillion and Bonilla 1992). It is based on a full rate contribution, but if the actual percentage of contributors among the registered is used the replacement rate declines to 30 percent.

Processing of the pensions has been greatly simplified and made much faster in the private scheme. An application form can be mailed or presented to any AFP, and the individual accounts facilitate the process. According to one source the first pension check is usually received within 15 to 30 days after the application is submitted, but another source gives an average period of three months. Since 1990 a preliminary pension has been paid 10 days after the application is filed and has been readjusted later. In 1988 a system of voluntary savings accounts, handled by the AFPs, was introduced, and total savings had increased three-fold by 1991 (Mesa-Lago 1988a; Arellano 1989; Ferrara 1989; Iglesias and Acuña 1991; Margozzini 1991).

Insured Contributions and Commissions

In both the public and private pension schemes only the insured contribute, but the state finances the deficit of the public scheme and contributes to the private scheme as well (as discussed in detail below). The employer's contribution for pensions was abolished in 1980, and other employers' contributions (for unemployment compensation and family allowances) were eliminated in 1988 and totally absorbed by the state, except for employment injury. The insured percentage contribution for pensions is uniform in the private scheme (although there are still differences in the public scheme): 10 percent for old age plus an additional 2.5–3.7 percent (varying among AFPs), of which 0.85–1.7 percent pays the premium for disability and survivors coverage to be provided by an insurance company and the remaining 1.75–2.84 percent provides a commission to the AFP. There is a voluntary additional contribution of 10 percent to increase the basic old-age pension, available for salaried workers but not for the self-employed. The total compulsory contributions to pensions range from 12.5–13.7 percent. In addition, the insured pay 7 percent for sickness/

maternity for a mandatory total of 19.5–20.7 percent in the private scheme and 25.6–27.7 percent in the public scheme. The lower contribution in the private scheme was initially justified by its allegedly more efficient administration, but it was largely the result of the 1979 reform that eliminated costly benefits and tightened entitlement conditions. These savings were not passed on to the insured in the public scheme in order to provide an incentive for transferring to the private scheme (Arellano 1989; Mesa-Lago 1989c; SAFP 1992).

The insured must pay to the AFP freely set commissions, usually of two types: a fixed sum (deducted from the 10 percent contribution for old-age pensions) and a variable percentage (deducted from the contribution to disability/survivors coverage). Until 1987 there was a third commission consisting of a percentage of the balance in the individual account. In that same year the variable-percentage commission (until then hidden within the payment for the disability/survivors premium) was made transparent, i.e., the AFP must now separate it from the premium. It was noted above that the commission represented about 70 percent of the total payment made by the insured (the other 30 percent going to pay the premium). Because of the large number of insured in the AFPs, insurance companies reduced the disability/survivors premium; however, the resulting economies of scale were not transferred to the insured but rather absorbed by the AFP. The 1987 reform therefore put pressure on the AFPs to cut down the percentage commission (Mesa-Lago 1987b, 1988a).

The fixed commission has a regressive effect because it is proportionally higher among the lower-income insured (thereby reducing both their net contributions for old-age pensions and their investment returns). For instance, in 1987 the commission represented an 18 percent reduction in the deposit of an insured individual in the 10,000-pesos-per-month bracket but only a 0.9 percent reduction for someone in the 100,000-peso bracket. For the same reason the investment yield for the lowest income bracket averaged 7.6 percent from 1981–1987, compared with 11.34 percent for the 60,000-peso bracket. Because of such regression the fixed commission was the subject of strong criticism in the 1980s from both domestic and foreign experts who suggested alternative approaches; however, the smaller AFPs opposed such a change (because they have more lower-income insured and the fixed commission generated most of their revenue), and the government also resisted the modification.

The elimination of the commission on the balances of individual accounts, the clearer distinction between commissions and insurance premiums, and public criticism of the fixed commission have led to declines in the levels of both the specific and combined commissions. In current pesos the fixed monthly commission reached a peak of 695 in 1983 and declined to 250 in 1991 (four AFPs do not charge this type of commission); in constant pesos the commission declined by three-fourths. The average percentage commission peaked at 3.6 percent in 1983 and declined to 3.1 percent in 1991. The total combined commission decreased from 4.5 percent to 3.6 percent from 1983–1990. Costs of the combined commission for an insured with an average salary increased from 8.3 percent in 1981 to 12.3 percent in 1983 and declined thereafter to 9 percent in 1991. As the fixed commission declined, both in absolute level and as a share of the combined commission (from 54 percent to 10 percent from 1982–1991), its regressive effect also diminished, although this effect has not been completely eliminated. Despite wide criticism of the fixed commission by experts who now have prominent positions in the new democratic government, it has not been abolished, apparently because of technical difficulties. Finally, differences in the combined commissions charged by the various AFPs have gradually shrunk—allegedly as a result of increased competition among them; this is discussed in more detail in a later section (SAFP 1983–1992; Mesa-Lago 1987b, 1988a; Arellano 1989; Bonilla García 1991; Cheyre Valenzuela 1991; Marcel and Arenas 1991; Arrau 1992; CIEDESS 1992).

Investment

The combined pension funds of all AFPs increased by two-fold every two or three years from 1981–1991; in 1991 they reached U.S. $10 billion, equal to 34.5 percent of GDP and half of the external debt (CIEDESS 1992; SAFP 1992). It is projected that under favorable conditions the funds will reach 50 percent of GDP in the year 2000 and 100 percent in 2025. The real annual investment yield was as follows: 12.7 percent (1981), 26.5 percent (1982), 22.7 percent (1983), 2.9 percent (1984), 13.4 percent (1985), 12.0 percent (1986), 6.4 percent (1987), 4.8 percent (1988), 6.7 percent (1989), 17.7 percent (1990), and 28.6 percent (1991). The average annual real yield for 1981–1991 was 14 percent, the highest in Latin America and the Caribbean. The yield steadily surpassed (except for 1981) the real commercial bank interest for short- and long-term deposits, but many claim that such high yields will not be sustainable in the future.

There has been a gradual diversification of the portfolio, particularly after laws in 1985, 1989, and 1990 expanded the range of instruments. The central bank determines the ceilings for investment in particular instruments; in 1991 they were as follows: 45 percent (reduced from 50 percent) for state securities; 80 percent for mortgage bills; 30–50 percent for fixed bank deposits; 30 percent for public and private bonds; 10–30 percent for shares; and 1–10 percent for foreign instruments. In 1983, after the crisis and the subsequent state intervention in several banks and enterprises to prevent widespread bankruptcy, 97 percent of investment was in debt instruments (e.g., 44.5 percent in state securities, 50.7 percent in mortgage bills) and 72 percent was in state instruments. This was considered to be dangerous, so a 1985 law allowed investment in shares and private bonds, and a 1990 law did the same for foreign instruments. In 1983 the portfolio distribution was as follows: 44 percent in state securities, 51 percent in mortgage bills, 3 percent in bank deposits and bonds, 2 percent in enterprise bonds, and nothing in shares. By 1991 the portfolio was much more diversified: 38 percent in state securities, 14 percent in mortgage bills, 13 percent in bank deposits and bonds, and 24 percent in enterprise shares. Therefore only 38 percent of the portfolio was in state instruments and 65 percent in debt instruments (Mesa-Lago 1991a; Iglesias and Acuña 1991; SAFP 1983–1992).

The creators of the private scheme initially believed that it would help significantly develop the domestic capital market (Piñera 1991); although the market has indeed grown, the huge accumulation of pension funds has not met the original expectations. Only in 1991 did the proportion of investment in private-enterprise shares and bonds exceed one-third of the total. It is argued that the high yields of the 1980s reflected a similar performance in other stock and bond markets throughout the world as they recovered from the decline suffered in the second half of the 1970s and the start of the 1980s; the slowdown in Chilean pension fund yields from 1987–1989 thus reflected a similar downward world trend. The very high Chilean yields of 1990–1991 are then explained by the high demand for these types of instruments (particularly shares) and the relatively few that are eligible for AFP investment. (A commission for risk classification ranks the suitability of stocks for AFP investment according to their degrees of risk; since the late 1980s there have been several private corporations in operation that informally classify stocks and thus can challenge the official ranking.) Other concerns voiced by experts are (1) AFPs can invest jointly or separately in one single enterprise, thereby influencing the value of that enterprise's shares; (2) insurance companies that are shareholders in an AFP can also invest in shares; and (3) the high book value of an AFP investment is not necessarily the market value of the instrument, e.g., investment in state securities (Mesa-Lago 1988a; Bonilla García 1991; Gillion and Bonilla 1992).

An opposite viewpoint is that the pension funds have significantly contributed toward increasing domestic and foreign confidence in the Santiago stock market and have stimulated the growth of insurance companies. In addition, the funds have played a principal role in debt-equity swaps, thus reducing the external debt and promoting foreign investment. It is also argued that the Chilean model proves that the existence of a mature domestic capital market is not an essential prerequisite for pension privatization (Cheyre Valenzuela 1991; Iglesias and Acuña 1991; Santamaría 1992).

Another important question is whether enough alternatives for investment of the pension funds will be available in the near future. If the total value of the fund grows to equal 50 percent of GDP by the year 2000, it might foster higher rates of investment (provided there are enough opportunities) and economic growth. Conversely, if capital supply exceeds demand, the rates of return might decline and/or capital outflows increase. One view is that opportunities for investment were dramatically expanded in the 1980s by the government privatization program but that now, when the process is virtually completed, there are fewer opportunities. The public sector cannot continue emission of public securities at the same pace, there are obvious limitations to the expansion of enterprise shares and bonds, and investment in personal/mortgage loans and housing construction is considered too risky. Recently investment in real estate has been allowed in the form of shares of mutual funds. The 1990 authorization to invest in foreign instruments (with a ceiling increasing from 1 percent to 10 percent from 1991–1996) has been seen by some as a way out from the constraints of the domestic capital market. A study by the Centro de Estudios Públicos argues that if 10 percent had been invested in public bonds of developed countries in 1990 and 1991, there would have been an increase in the yield of 0.5 percentage points, or 1.2 points if the investment had been in shares from Japan, the United States, and England. But another group opposes the export of domestic savings (Arrau 1991; Marcel and Arenas 1991; Margozzini 1991; Mesa-Lago 1991a).

Finally, there is the issue of the impact of the private pension funds on national savings and investment. The original argument of the founders of the scheme was that the replacement of the pay-as-you-go system by a fully funded pension scheme would increase capital accumulation (Piñera 1991). A divergent viewpoint was that in order to have such a positive effect the AFPs' savings had to be greater than the public deficit generated by the reform (Arellano 1989). Recent analyses of the relationship conducted by experts with different views concur that there is no conclusive evidence that private pensions have generated higher national savings. For instance, in 1989–90 the increase in national savings was induced by external savings and in 1991 by private savings outside of the AFPs (Arrau 1992; CIEDESS 1992; Gillion and Bonilla 1992; Santamaría 1992).

The Burden of the Pension Deficit and State Subsidies

The cost of social security in Chile was the highest in Latin America and the Caribbean, with the possible exception of Cuba in the second half of the 1980s. Social security expenditures as a percentage of GDP steadily increased in the 1960s, peaked at 17.5 percent in 1971 (a historic record in the Western hemisphere), declined to 9.3 percent in 1975, steadily rose again to 15.6 percent in 1982 (in the midst of the crisis), and decreased to 13.1 percent in 1986. Two-thirds of the expenditures were for all the pension programs. The active/passive ratio (number of active workers contributing per pensioner) steadily declined from 10.6 in 1960 to 4.4 in 1970, 2.2 in 1980, and 1.9 in 1988. The decrease in the share of social security expenditures as a part of GDP from 1982–1986 and the slowdown in the decline of the active/passive ratio in the 1980s are both results of the social security reform, in particular the increase in ages of retirement (Mesa-Lago 1988a, 1989c, 1991b).

The state contributes to the private pension scheme in two ways: (1) paying recognition bonds, which are estimated to account for one-half to three-fourths of the capital of those retiring until the end of this century, or an average of nine years' worth of pension funds (paid by the state all at once instead of spread throughout the retirement period as in the public scheme); and (2) making up the difference to provide minimum pensions for those who lack sufficient funds in an AFP (it is estimated that at the end of the 1990s the annual cost of this program will be U.S. $60 million). In addition, the state has to finance the deficit of the public pension scheme (civilian and armed forces), public assistance pensions, unemployment compensation, family allowances, and health care for indigents. Therefore, to secure a sound private pension scheme, the state has made a financial commitment for huge long-run or permanent contributions to the entire social security system (Arellano 1989; Bonilla García 1991).

If all the revenues and expenditures of the social security system are taken into account, the system appears to have generated a surplus in the 1980s. However, when the state subsidy (excluding the contribution of the state as an employer) is subtracted, the surplus turns into a deficit that increased from 1.7 percent in 1980 to a peak of 8.2 percent in 1982 and then slowed down to 5 percent for 1989–1990. Within the pension system, in 1988 the private scheme had 84 percent of the total number of active contributors and only 4 percent of the total number of pensioners; hence, it generated a substantial surplus. But the public sector (i.e., civilian, armed forces, and public assistance pensions) had only 16 percent of the active contributors and 96 percent of the pensioners, so it ended in a huge deficit that increased from 2.2 percent of GDP in 1981 to 6.3 percent in 1986 (87 percent of expenditures were subsidized by the state). The composition of the public pension deficit in 1986 was as follows: 57.8 percent civilian pensions, 33.5 percent armed forces pensions, and 8.7 percent public assistance pensions (Mesa-Lago 1988a, 1991b).

Unfortunately there are no consolidated data to estimate the balance of the entire social security system. Experts provide different estimates of the state subsidy (as a percentage of GDP) required to cover the cost of the deficits in various sectors: (1) the deficit in the old pension system was 3.5 percent in 1981 and 3.2 percent in 1991 (CIEDESS 1992); (2) the state subsidy to the private system was 6 percent in 1990 (Gillion and Bonilla 1992); (3) the deficit related to the pension reform (the operational deficit plus the cost of recognition bonds) was 1.2 percent in 1981 and 4.8 percent in 1991; when armed forces pensions and other state-supported schemes (e.g., public assistance pensions) are added the deficit increases to 4.1 percent in 1981 and 5 percent in 1991 (Arrau 1992); and (4) the deficit of the entire social security system (without specifics) was 7.4 percent in 1984 and 4.1 percent in 1991 (Santamaría 1992). The lack of coherence of these figures and imprecision of exactly what they cover points to the dearth of accurate global data. But it is clear that the state's commitment to the pension scheme has reduced public funds for such other programs as health care for the lowest income groups.

The deficit in the public pension sector will last for another 25 years; it is estimated that it will peak in the mid-1990s and slow down thereafter; contributions will stop in 2038, and the last pensions will be paid in 2050. The deficit induced by the recognition bonds will keep growing until 2007 and then slow down; some estimates place this deficit at twice as high as the initial calculations. The combined deficit for the public assistance and minimum pensions will be permanent and will exhibit an increasing trend. The total pension deficit will peak in the year 2000 and by 2016 will equal 2.2 percent of GDP (down from 6.3 percent in 1986), but other estimates give higher figures because of underestimates of the cost of the recognition bonds and the public assistance and minimum pensions.

It is unclear how the state will finance the pension deficit: with taxes, public debt, a reduction in consumption, or a combination of all three. Some simulation studies have analyzed the various alternatives and their potential effects. Financing the deficit with public debt will place the burden on future generations and the young to the benefit the current generation and the old; financing with taxes will place the burden on the current generation. The first alternative has so far been predominant; it has been estimated that if all the deficit is financed through public debt, the debt will increase from 25 percent to 67 percent of GDP in 30 years and later stabilize at 56 percent (Arrau 1992).

There is a dearth of actuarial studies and even a lack of financial data for the entire public and private pension system. The same is true of global simulation exercises based on total contributions, investment returns, state subsidies, and expenditures. These data and studies are badly needed to determine the future equilibrium of the system and assess the state's economic capacity to subsidize it.

Administration

The creators of the private pension scheme assumed that its market elements (i.e., free entry and exit, competition, flexible selection of AFPs by the insured), combined with state supervision and minimum guarantees, would ensure its efficiency and result in expanded population coverage, reduced evasion and payment delays, an increased number of AFPs, decreased administrative costs and commissions, and maximized investment yields (Piñera 1991). I have noted that some of these goals have not been met (i.e., coverage, compliance), whereas others have (i.e., investment yields, commissions). In this section I analyze whether the system is truly competitive and discuss its effects on administrative efficiency and the role of the state in establishing minimum guarantees.

The number of AFPs was practically stagnant in the first decade of the scheme. Initially there were 12 AFPs, and by 1991 there were 13. Of these 13, 10 had been there since the scheme's inception, one was the result of a merger of two of the original AFPs, and two were created in the second half of the 1980s. In 1992 two new AFPs entered the market, and one more had been authorized. Two AFPs are managed by unions/professional associations, and nine have been controlled by the largest economic conglomerates that grew in the 1970s during the privatization process. During the 1982 crisis two of these conglomerates went bankrupt, and their assets were temporarily administered by the state; they were reprivatized later and sold to foreign corporations under the debt-equity swap program. Currently the four largest AFPs are largely controlled by foreign corporations. There is a high degree of concentration in the AFPs: the largest three combined covered 60 percent of all the insured in 1981, and this proportion increased to almost 68 percent in 1991; the proportion in the largest two declined from 53 percent to 50 percent in the same period (Mesa-Lago 1988a, 1989c; SAFP 1992; CIEDESS 1992).

Data on the AFPs' operational costs are fragmentary and contradictory. One analyst estimates that the costs per insured in constant pesos were halved from 1982–1986. Another claims that in 1989, 25 percent of the total revenue from contributions went to operational costs. In 1981 there were 3,500 employees in the public scheme, which was considered the single largest public institution in Chile; the number of employees in the private scheme was 8,000 in 1990. The private scheme now has 10 percent more personnel than the public scheme had prior to the reform. About 30 percent of AFP personnel are salespeople (see below), and the share of publicity expenditures is very high; these types of expenditures were not needed in the old system. Because of a lack of data and inconsistent estimates of the overall number of insured and pensioners, it is practically impossible to measure and compare efficiency in the two schemes, but one expert concludes that overall costs of the entire system are almost twice as high as before because there are two schemes in operation.

During most of the 1980s the three AFPs with the largest numbers of insured charged the highest fixed and percentage commissions, but by 1991 they had the lowest percentage commissions, and two of them also had the lowest fixed commissions. From 1981–1991 the average investment yield of those three AFPs was below the overall average yield. Therefore, at least in the 1980s, the insured's selections of AFPs were not made on the basis of lower commissions and higher yields; hence, competition did not seem to be working. The selections were apparently made based on the tactics of salespeople and the publicity displayed by the largest AFPs. Although there is no limit on the number of times an insured can change AFPs, in practice it can reasonably be done three times a year and at no cost to the insured. In 1990, 17 percent of all contributors shifted AFPs, and 90 percent of those changes were managed by salespeople who work on commission. The insured—particularly the elderly and females—usually ignore the differences among AFPs in terms of commissions and yields and so are easy prey for the salespeople. The change is not always beneficial. Insurance company sales personnel can also harm the insured. Information provided by the AFPs on commissions and yields were poor until the end of the 1980s, when such information became more widely available; e.g., the percentage commission is now listed separately from the insurance premium, real instead of nominal yields are published, and a simplified explanation of the quarterly report is provided. But a very substantial amount of the AFPs' costs still goes to publicity and very little or none is used to educate the public effectively on how to make a wise decision based on the real advantages of specific AFPs (though in 1987 the association of AFPs initiated educational campaigns) (Mesa-Lago 1988a, 1989c; Iglesias and Acuña 1991; CIEDESS 1992).

The state has established a series of guarantees (particularly after the bankruptcies of 1982) to make the private scheme as sound as possible. These measures have largely achieved their goal, but a few of them have raised significant barriers that prevent the entry of new AFPs. The most important guarantees are (1) the SAFP regulates, supervises, and audits the private scheme; (2) AFPs can neither be involved in any business other than pensions nor offer other benefits (except for voluntary savings account services and funeral grants); (3) the pension fund is separated from the AFP's own assets; in case of bankruptcy the SAFP manages the fund until it is transferred to another AFP; (4) each AFP has to provide an initial amount of capital that varies depending on its number of insured: from 5,000 UF for less than 5,000 insured, to 20,000 UF for 10,000 or more insured (to facilitate entry, the initial amount of capital has been reduced, and the largest AFPs have been authorized to subcontract such services as the collection of contributions, charges to individual accounts, and the investment of funds to smaller AFPs); (5) the AFPs are responsible for an average monthly yield over the last 12 months of no less than the lesser of the following: the average yield of all funds minus two percentage points, or 50 percent of the average yield of all funds; (6) all AFPs must establish a "reserve of yield fluctuation" to cover any gap in the required yield; (7) in addition, a second reserve (*encaje*) equal to 1 percent of the value of the pension fund is required;[8] (8) if both reserves are insufficient to match the required minimum yield the state is obliged to finance the difference; (9) 90 percent of the investment instruments must be deposited in the central bank; (10) there are ceilings fixed to investments in each instrument, and shares are officially classified according to risks; and (11) the AFP must send quarterly reports of the individual accounts to its affiliates and provide them with other specific information (Bustamante Jeraldo 1991; Marcel and Arenas 1991; Margozzini 1991).

Overall Evaluation

The social security reform and the private pension scheme have brought advantages and disadvantages for the three major participants. The insured workers have benefitted from lower payroll contributions, a higher level of benefits (so far), freedom of choice concerning AFPs and retirement plans, the recognition of previous contributions, eligibility for a minimum pension, a sounder pension program with state guarantees, high investment yields, and faster and simpler processing of pensions. Disadvantages are the decline in coverage (when coverage is estimated based on active contributors), the payment of commissions to the AFPs, poor information concerning what percentage of contributions goes to commissions (at least until recently), restrictions against using the accumulated fund until the time of retirement (e.g., to invest in a small business, buy a house, etc.), lack of knowledge on crucial issues and decisions, and the elimination of the employer's contribution. The latter has been advantageous for employers, whose only disadvantage is the considerable paperwork involved in the monthly reporting and transferring of their workers' contributions. The state seems to have mostly disadvantages (through subsidies to the whole system) and few advantages, most of which are not clearly demonstrated; e.g., avoidance of the potentially negative impact of an employers' payroll tax on employment, some beneficial effects on the capital market (although not as much as originally expected), and the eventual termination of the troublesome public scheme. Society as a whole has profited from the elimination of unjustified costly privileges (although not all have been terminated) but will have to confront the heavy cost of state obligations in the future. The outcomes of the schemes are extremely sensitive to the interest rate, level of compliance, and general economic conditions. The state may be required to meet various guarantees at once, and some risks may occur simultaneously, e.g., high unemployment and inflation combined with low real rates of return. There is no evidence that the capitalization system has generated higher national savings.

The social security reform and the introduction of the private pension scheme have had two opposite effects on income distribution. Probable progressive effects are (1) the elimination of seniority pensions and *perseguidoras* and the standardization of retirement ages and pension adjustments (which reduced payments to the relatively high-income insured); (2) the introduction of the minimum pension and expansion of public assistance pensions (which help the relatively low-income insured and poor noninsured, respectively, although the levels are quite low, particularly for the public assistance pension); and (3) a possible halt of price transfers to noninsured consumers resulting from the termination of the employers' contribution (the effects would be different if there was a negative impact on employment or a transfer of costs only to workers). Probable regressive (or neutral) effects are (1) a private pension scheme based on a strict correspondence between premiums and benefits and a virtual exclusion of solidarity; (2) declines in population coverage and no significant progress in coverage of such low-income groups as the self-employed and other informal workers; (3) preservation of some inequalities in entitlement conditions and benefits in the public scheme and particularly in the armed forces schemes; (4) lower pensions for women because of a lower age of retirement and longer life expectancy; and (5) the regressive impact of the fixed commission. It has also been argued that the private scheme favors high- and low-income insured (because of proportionally higher investment yields on behalf of the former and minimum pensions for the latter), whereas it discriminates against the middle-income insured (through the regressive effect of the fixed commission).

Prior to the 1990 elections the opposition cautiously accepted the social security reform and the private scheme but was critical of various aspects: the lack of solidarity and participation of the insured in the administration; the poor coverage of important sectors of the population, such as the self-employed; the low minimum pensions; the regressiveness of the fixed commission; the need for more AFPs; the foreign ownership of AFPs; and the investment of funds in foreign instruments. The new democratic government has not introduced any substantial changes in the system, but it has focused on tax reform to improve redistribution; it has also increased minimum pensions and is planning to extend population coverage.

Several lessons can be learned from the Chilean experience. One is that the cost of the transition must be very carefully evaluated. The maintenance of part of the old entitlement, the recognition bonds, and the minimum pensions are humane elements of the reform, but they are extremely costly; hence, they must be balanced with an accurate assessment of the future burden on society and the costs of alternative public programs for lower-income groups. Another lesson is that the presence of a market and private administrators does not necessarily ensure competition, control evasion and payment delays, and promote other efficiency improvements. Huge collective savings have not led to a corresponding expansion of the domestic capital market, either. Finally, the exclusion of part of the population (e.g., the armed forces) from the reform and the maintenance of its privileged entitlement conditions and benefits, though perhaps initially unavoidable for political reasons, can eventually become a salient inequality that must be eradicated (Mesa-Lago 1989c; Castro Jiménez 1990; Borzutzky 1991; Marcel and Arenas 1991; Gillion and Bonilla 1992).

Peru: Moving Closer to the Chilean Model

The social security system of Peru is administered by the Peruvian institute of social security (IPSS). Its pension fund has suffered a dramatic decapitalization in real terms (particularly in the 1980s) because of negative real investment yields (from -21 percent to -29 percent from 1981–1987); a significant state debt (U.S. $194 million, which virtually vanished because of very high inflation rates and a lack of debt indexation); considerable employers' evasion and payment delays (33 percent for evasion alone); and huge administrative costs (52 percent of total expenditures in 1986, largely because of adjustment of personnel salaries to inflation). Additional problems are low population coverage (one-third of the labor force and one-fifth of the population), a sharp decline in the real value of pensions, excessively long and bureaucratic procedures to solicit these pensions, a lack of actuarial studies for a long period, and overall inefficiency and waste. Obviously there was a need for reform, but the debate focused on the proper type: improvement of the public scheme, privatization, or a mixed approach. Important differences between the Peruvian system and that of Chile prior to their reforms were that Peru had one central social insurance agency (instead of multiple funds), considerably lower population coverage, and a worse financial and administrative situation (Mesa-Lago 1989c, 1990, 1991a, 1991b, 1992c; Marcos Rueda 1992).

In November 1991—within the general economic framework of an adjustment and restructuring program—a decree-law was enacted by the executive that introduced a private pension scheme almost identical to Chile's. It was scheduled to begin operation on July 28, 1992, and although its title referred to "supplementary private pensions," it was really an alternative to the public pension scheme because the insured in that scheme could freely transfer to AFPs that would provide better conditions and benefits than the IPSS. However, there were some differences with respect to the Chilean model: (1) because of constitutional regulations the public scheme in Peru (through the IPSS) could not be terminated, so the law granted all workers (including future participants) the right to choose affiliation in the public or private schemes; (2) entitlement conditions in the public scheme remained unchanged, and they are more liberal than in the private scheme (e.g., 60/55 versus 65/60 for male/female ages of retirement); (3) there was no minimum pension guaranteed by the state in the decree-law; (4) the employer's contribution was to be reduced from 6 percent to 1 percent, and the insured's was to be increased from 3 percent to 8 percent (plus additional voluntary contributions and commissions); overall contributions in the public scheme were apparently not changed; and (5) based on the solidarity principle the entire employer's contribution and part of the insured's was to be transferred to the public scheme ("Créase el Sistema . . ." 1991; Marcos Rueda 1992). Incentives provided to move to the private scheme were the financial crisis faced by the public scheme, the potential for a financially sounder private scheme with higher pensions, and the lower contributions charged to employers (who could try to influence their employees to move). Incentives to stay in the public scheme were significantly lower contributions for the insured and more liberal entitlement conditions.

The 1992 coup led by President Fujimore and the suspension of the political constitution paved the way to move the Peruvian pension reform closer to its Chilean counterpart. A draft of a new decree-law and its regulations, published in the official gazette on July 16, 1992, abrogated the 1991 decree-law (just before it was to be enforced) and introduced some changes. Inclusion in the private scheme (AFPs) was to become mandatory to all those not previously insured in the IPSS, who retained the right to move to the private system. All new entrants into the labor force or those who lost affiliation with the IPSS had to enter the private scheme; therefore, as in the Chilean case, the public scheme was to be closed (Anteproyecto . . ." 1992). But the final law, enacted in December 1992, shifted again to the model of the 1991 law. Those insured in the IPSS have the right to stay in or move to the private scheme; if they switch, they still can return to the IPSS within a two-year period after the enactment of the law. If they stay in the IPSS, their contributions and those of their employers remain unchanged, and the insured retain all rights under the public scheme. Affiliation to the private scheme is voluntary for new entrants into the labor force, who can choose to enter either the public scheme or an AFP. Therefore the public scheme is not closed. A summary of the new features of the private scheme under the 1992 law follows.

Contributions of the insured have been further increased to make them equal to the Chilean model: a mandatory 10 percent for old-age pensions plus another contribution (freely set by the AFPs) for disability and survivors, as well as a voluntary additional contribution for the old-age pension with a maximum of 20 percent (twice that of Chile). In addition, there is a compulsory 1 percent contribution by the insured (formerly imposed on the employer by the 1991 decree-law) to be transferred—as part of a solidarity approach—to the IPSS to defray the cost of public assistance to the disabled and elderly who are destitute. Therefore the insured contribution is probably higher than in Chile. Mandatory contributions for employers have been eliminated, and only voluntary ones are left. As in the case of Chile, salaries of the insured who move from the public scheme to the private one are to be increased by 10 percent (representing a transferral of the eliminated employer's contribution), then by another 3 percent.

There are a few differences with the Chilean model. A maximum of 60,000 new *soles* is placed on the recognition bond, a ceiling that does not exist in Chile (at the end of 1992 the ceiling was equal to U.S. $40,000, which was quite high for Peru, but the new *sol* was declining). The bond is indexed for inflation but does not earn interest. It is granted only to those registered in the IPSS who had six months of contributions immediately before the enactment of the law plus a minimum of four years of contributions in the last 10 years; the number of years accounted for by the bond increases with the age of the insured up to a maximum of 19 years. The minimum capital needed for an AFP to enter the market is only 500,000 *soles* (equal to U.S. $400,000 at the end of 1992)—compared with a theoretical minimum of U.S. $100,000 in Chile—but no less than U.S. $2 million in practice. Finally, the maximum allowable investment percentages for particular instruments also differ, e.g., 60 percent for state securities (compared with 45 percent in Chile) and 5 percent in foreign instruments (versus 10 percent in Chile) ("Sistema Privado . . ." 1992).

Incentives to move to the new system are now greater: not only would the insured get a substantial salary increase, but employers put pressure on their employees to shift in order to take advantage of lower contributions. (If the insured move to the private scheme and then return to the IPSS, all salary increments are eliminated.) There is also a government-sponsored campaign encouraging people to move to the AFP and help minimize the role of the IPSS. The IPSS's financial situation has worsened: there are 300,000 pensioners who are expected to be paid a total of U.S. $35 million monthly in pensions, but it is not clear where the money will come from. Procedures for starting new pensions have been halted, there is no attempt to control compliance, and the personnel are being pressured to resign (López González and Céspedes Garay 1992). A new office of pension standardization that began to function in January 1993 has absorbed the IPSS pension scheme. Under these conditions an overwhelming majority of those insured by the IPSS will likely move into the new system.

The new Peruvian model reduces the cost of the transition by eliminating the minimum pension and placing limits (and not paying interest) on the recognition bonds. But Peru has always been below the Chilean level of development, and Peru's economy is currently in chaos (compared with the Chilean economic boom of 1980). Furthermore, population coverage in Chile prior to the reform approximated universality, but in Peru more than two-thirds of the labor force is not insured and about half is informal (in addition, there is a very large population of peasants outside the national market); hence, expansion of coverage will be extremely difficult. Finally, in a country with much more poverty and more lower-income groups than Chile, a state commitment to subsidize the transition (even if at somewhat lower costs) would deplete resources from basic services for those most in need.

Colombia: Mixed or Private Scheme?

At the beginning of the 1990s there was a general consensus in Colombia that the social security system was facing a crisis and needed a drastic reform. The new constitution of 1991 ratified the state responsibility and guiding role in social security but allowed the private sector to participate as a provider of benefits. A lively debate has ensued on the roles of the state and the private sector, but by November 1991 concrete reforms had not been introduced yet.

The Social Security Crisis

Colombia's social security system is one of the most fragmented in LAC. In 1990 there were 1,040 institutions: 12 at the national level, four managed by universities, and 1,024 managed by departments, districts, and municipalities. Only 20.9 percent of the total population was covered, ranking Colombia thirteenth among all Latin America. About 70 percent of those covered are under the social insurance institute for private workers (ISS), and 5 percent are under the main social insurance institute covering civil servants (CAJANAL). Practically all those insured are urban salaried workers, but about half of those expected to be registered are evaders; and the ISS has had difficulties in expanding coverage beyond the formal sector (only 14 percent of all the municipalities of Colombia were tied to the ISS in 1989). In 1988, 57 percent of all urban employment was composed of microenterprises (owners and employees), informal self-employed, domestic servants, and unpaid family workers. Coverage among the latter three groups was minimal: 8.3 percent, 14.5 percent, and 8.2 percent, respectively, and part of such coverage was by private insurance. Legislation enacted in 1988–1989 offered ISS coverage to domestic servants (mandatory) and self-employed (voluntary), but only a small fraction of both groups has registered, particularly among the latter. In 1990, 21 percent of the population was covered in terms of health care by social insurance and similar institutions and 12 percent by the private sector; the remaining 67 percent was legally under the charge of the public national health system (SNS), but only 39 percent actually had access to it, thus leaving 27 percent of the population unprotected (Mesa-Lago and De Geyndt 1987; López and Tobón 1990; ISS 1990; Jaime 1991).

Although the total payroll contributions to the ISS are the ninth highest in Latin America, they are grossly insufficient to finance the system. ISS contributions range from 15.5–20.5 percent, compared to 13 percent in CAJANAL and 5–20 percent in other funds. (In addition, there is a 4 percent contribution for family allowances.) The lowest rates are in the public sector, where the insured do not contribute to either the pension or the health program (both of which are financed by the government); in

1989 the state financed 67 percent of CAJANAL expenditures. Employer evasion and payment delays to the ISS were estimated to be U.S. $305 million in 1985, and the state debt (as an employer and a third party) was U.S. $370 million in 1988. The percentage of ISS annual revenue allocated to financial investment steadily declined from 27 percent to 7.3 percent from 1975–1989, and the value of the reserves in constant pesos decreased by two-thirds from 1975–1985 (ISS reserves can be invested only in state instruments). Initially the total payroll contribution for ISS pensions was set at 6.5 percent (3 percent by the employer, 1.5 percent the insured, and 1.5 percent the state as a third party), but the state contribution was later eliminated; in 1985 the total contribution was increased to 6.5 percent (4.33 percent by the employer and 2.17 percent by the insured). Theoretically, the ISS is based on scaled premiums, but the necessary required increases in contributions were not implemented; thus, in practice it is on a pay-as-you-go method. The required level of contribution to put the system back on partial capitalization would be 18 percent for 1991–1995, rising to 21 percent for 1996–2000; even financing the system with pay-as-you-go would require an increase of the current 6.5 percent contribution to 8 percent in the current five-year period and to 10.7 percent in the next. The ISS's actuarial deficit in 1988 was estimated to be U.S. $2,000 million, and the deficit was U.S. $1,138 million for CAJANAL. The latter does not have reserves or even a financing method, and with its generous benefits and entitlement conditions it would require at least a two-fold increase in its current level of contribution. The ISS did not conduct any formal actuarial reviews in the 1980s, although one was planned for 1991 (López Montaño et al. 1991b; DNP 1991; López Castaño and Martínez 1991).

Benefits for the insured in the public sector (particularly selected civil servants, the judiciary, congressional representatives, and the armed forces) are very generous and entitlement conditions quite liberal. The retirement age in CAJANAL is 10 years lower than in the ISS (which is in turn quite low: 60/55 for males/females), and in some other public funds retirement is possible with only 10–20 years of service regardless of age. In 1988 the average CAJANAL pension was 70 percent higher than that in the ISS. The annual allocation of health expenditures per capita in 1989 was also quite unequal: U.S. $15 for the SNS, $66 for the ISS, and $134 for CAJANAL. I have noted that the state heavily subsidizes the latter (Mesa-Lago and De Geyndt 1987; Departamento Nacional de Planificacion 1990; Jaime González 1991). Administrative expenditures as a percentage of total social security expenditures increased from 4.4 percent to 42.2 percent from 1965–1986, ranking Colombia's percentage among the three highest in LAC.

One viewpoint about the crisis is that it can be solved, within the current social security system, through a series of reforms. Another viewpoint, however, is that the crisis cannot be solved without the participation of the private sector.

The Role of the Private Sector in a New System

The 1991 constitution devotes two articles to the regulation of social security and health care. Article 48 states that social security is a public service of a mandatory nature; to be provided under state direction, coordination, and control; and adherent to the principles of universality, solidarity, and efficiency. The state will guarantee the right to social security to all inhabitants and, with private participation, progressively expand population coverage of those services determined by law. Social security can be provided by public or private institutions according to law. Other articles guarantee the right to social security of vulnerable groups of the population such as pregnant women, children, senior citizens, the disabled, and indigents (the state's responsibility in this protection is specifically mentioned).

Article 47 states that environmental sanitation and health care are public services under the charge of the state and guaranteed to the entire population. The state tasks are to organize, direct, and regulate those services according to the same three principles of social security mentioned above. In addition, the state will set the policies for the provision of health services by private institutions and will supervise and control them. Health services must be decentralized by levels of care and with community participation. Basic services will be mandatory and free for all citizens, and children below one year of age are entitled to free care in all health institutions that receive state funds.

The new constitutional rules concerning the private sector have led to a lively debate in Colombian society, the enactment of legislation, and several proposals. This issue is discussed in the following two subsections on health and pensions.

Private services in health care. Prior to the 1991 constitution there was a modest but growing role of the private sector in the extension of coverage. For instance, 34 percent of the informal self-employed were protected by private health insurance, the importance of which (in relation to the total population covered by health care) increased from 8.3 percent to 9.2 percent from 1984–1988. Under the influence of the Costa Rican model the ISS also signed agreements with cooperatives for the provision of health-care services. And in 1990 the ISS contracted with private health services at an annual cost of U.S. $90 million, but reportedly the quality of these services was not better than those provided by the ISS. To improve that quality and efficiency the ISS must closely supervise and control the private providers (López Castaño and Tobón Bernal 1990; Jaime González 1991; López Montaño et al. 1991b).

The SNS was reorganized by a law enacted in 1991 that established that the ministry of health (MH) will regulate the operation of private corporations, institutions, and foundations that provide health services and that can contract with public health institutions. For that purpose private organizations must register and supply the required documentation; in addition, those receiving public funds in dealings with the ISS, the MH, and the public sector must sign a contract and provide a plan concerning the use of such funds and the costs and quality of the services to be supplied. The law also authorizes association between public and private institutions and the allocation of public resources to them. The ISS, the family-allowances program, and similar institutions can contract with private organizations to provide health services to the noninsured. Finally, the law introduces stimuli to encourage the functional integration of health services, e.g., by giving priority to contracts with public institutions, as well as grants, training, maintenance functions, and government projects (Castelblanco de Castro 1991).

A recent document reviews the potential alternatives that the constitution allows and, after discarding both the completely public and completely free-market extremes as unconstitutional, identifies three options: (1) mandatory affiliation to private insurance combined with a state subsidy to protect the indigents (this option is basically viewed as unacceptable because of the lack of solidarity within the private sector and among risks and income groups); (2) mandatory insurance protection for all workers, to be paid for by their employers (this alternative is considered nonviable because the majority of the labor force is not salaried); and (3) compulsory social insurance health coverage with private participation (judged to be the most viable option). The latter would be based on a pool of all public health facilities and resources (from the SNS, ISS, CAJANAL, other funds, family allowances, etc.) to expand health-care coverage to the entire population. The integrated health system would be financed with current social insurance contributions from employers and the insured, state grants to cover the cost of protecting the poor, and a transfer of 25 percent from family-allowances revenue. The system would provide integral health services at the three levels of care, with emphasis on the secondary and tertiary levels because they are considered the most expensive (although it is acknowledged that 80 percent of care is met at the primary level). The resulting system is expected to avoid any deficit, although only very elementary financial calculations are provided in the document. The administration would be decentralized and placed under the charge of municipal health funds that receive the revenue and contract with public and private institutions and medical professionals. These institutions and individuals are expected to compete among themselves to reduce costs, whereas the central government sets minimum standards, impedes the formation of oligopolies, and supervises and controls the system. Tariffs set by a national agency would have to be accepted by all participants. The population covered would be free to select the providers (Restrepo et al. 1991).

Private pensions. There were three different positions concerning how to conduct the reform of the pension scheme: (1) maintain the current public scheme but with stricter entitlement conditions and higher contributions; (2) develop a mixed scheme that combines a drastically reformed public pension scheme with a supplementary scheme, mostly of a private nature (voluntary or mandatory); and (3) entirely replace the public scheme with a fully funded private one.

The first position argued that the actuarial deficits faced by the ISS and CAJANAL were so huge that the creation of a Chilean-style fully funded private pension scheme was impossible. It would cost 30 percent of public expenditures for about 45 years to finance three things: (1) the obligations to the current pensioners (plus those who had acquired rights); (2) the guaranteed transfer of contributions (paid in the past to the current public system) to the new private system; and (3) the cost of a minimum pension within the new system to those who do not qualify for a full pension. Furthermore, economic and political differences between Chile and Colombia would make the application of the former's model very difficult in the latter. Colombia has many more poor people, informal workers, and noninsured people than Chile, and access by that marginal population to a private scheme would be impossible. In addition, passing a Chilean-style reform would be much more difficult politically in Colombia. Proponents of this position therefore proposed to solve the crisis within the current social security system through a series of reforms, such as: (1) unification of the private and public pension funds and standardization of entitlement conditions and benefits; (2) extension of population coverage with state support to finance the incorporation of urban informal and rural sectors; (3) a gradual increase in the age of retirement from 60/55 (55 for both sexes in CAJANAL) to 65/60, as well as increase in payroll contributions and the required number of weeks of contribution, to put the system on sound financial ground (these conditions should be made uniform among all covered groups); (4) aggressive pursuit of payment evaders and late payers through improved computerization, inspection, and prosecution techniques; (5) reduction of administrative costs with higher efficiency; and (6) periodic actuarial studies (Jaime González 1991; López Montaño 1992a).

The second position endorsed a mixed scheme, arguing that total privatization was not allowed by the constitution (Cárdenas 1992). Three alternative proposals were elaborated in 1990 and 1991 by experts: Ulpiano Ayala, Hernando Zulueta (together with FEDESARROLLO), and an actuarial firm (JLB Actuarios). All of them agreed that the current scheme could not be fixed on a fully funded or partially funded basis but that it could be financed by a pay-as-you-go approach provided that current entitlement conditions were significantly tightened and contributions moderately increased. All three proposals maintained the current pensioners' rights; provided a basic (reduced) pension for future pensioners ranging from one-half to three times the minimum legal salary; attempted to reduce costs by increasing the retirement age for future pensions from 60/55 to 65/60, as well as the number of weeks of contribution and the number of years used to compute the base salary; and offered a supplementary pension program, mainly through private providers.

The differences between the three proposals were as follows: (1) only JLB arranged for a transitional period and a gradual increase in the age of retirement and other conditions; the other two proposals involved abrupt change; (2) Ayala maintained that the current payroll contribution could finance the obligations toward current pensioners, the reformed basic pensions, and the supplementary pension program; the other two proposals required an increase in payroll contributions (only to finance the current and future pensions) plus an additional payroll contribution to finance the supplementary pensions; (3) Ayala believed that state subsidies were not necessary, whereas the other two agreed with that proposition for the ISS but not for public funds (they thought the state should help finance the deficits of its own employees' pensions); (4) there were different arrangements concerning the minimum salaries to be paid by the supplementary programs and their combination of compulsory and voluntary components; and (5) all three proposals endorsed a private administration of the supplementary pension scheme (except in the case of JLB's compulsory variation). All three proposals recommended the incorporation of public pension funds within the reformed ISS system but with much tighter entitlement conditions and increased contributions plus effective payment of state subsidies.

The proposals were all evaluated using a simulation technique, with the following results: Ayala's proposal was considered financially nonviable (the proposed payroll contributions were grossly insufficient to support the old and new programs), and it was politically nonviable because of its sharp cut in the basic pension and its abrupt nature. Zulueta's proposal was thought to be financially viable and more politically viable than Ayala's because it provided for a much higher basic pension. JLB's proposal was considered to be viable both financially and politically—politically because of the inclusion of a transition period and a reasonable basic pension. Contributions to the fully funded supplementary pensions were expected to be high, although specific rates were not provided (except for an insufficient one in Ayala's proposal) (López and Martínez 1991; López Castaño 1992).

The third position contended that the second position (i.e., the mixed approach) would retain the flaws of the public system, that the fiscal burden would continue, and that the supplementary funds would be very small and thus inadequate as a channel for savings and investment. Thus a fully funded capitalization scheme should be developed. Although some proponents of this approach said that it did not have to be tantamount to privatization, most supporters advocated the Chilean model. Interestingly, Zulueta, who first endorsed the mixed approach, switched to the third position in 1992 (Zulueta 1992).

The Government Chooses the Third Option: Privatization

The second position described above appeared to be the most popular in 1991 and was eventually endorsed by the director of the ISS, but the neo-conservative group that supported the privatization approach (composed of individuals from the ministry of finance, the national planning direction, and the bank of the republic) grew stronger and ultimately prevailed. In the spring of 1992 President César Gaviria decided to separate the reforms for pensions and health care, and in September he submitted a legal draft to the congress that basically followed the Chilean pension reform model, an action that prompted the resignation of the director of the ISS, who strongly criticized the legal draft. The features of the new system that diverged from those of Chile are described below.

The draft closed the ISS and the public-fund pension schemes and replaced them with a new private pension scheme involving programs known as SAFPs. All salaried workers (in the private and public sectors) entering the labor force for the first time had mandatory coverage by the private scheme; voluntary coverage was offered to nonsalaried workers. Those insured by the ISS and public pension funds who were younger than 55 (for males) or 50 (for females) were given the option to move to the private scheme. The insured above those ages were to remain in the old schemes unless they decided to continue their contributions until age 65, in which case they had the option to join the new scheme. The military and the police were excluded from the new system. The entitlement conditions and benefits of the ISS program were substantially tightened, but the draft introduced no changes to CAJANAL and other public funds except for integrating them into a new fund for national public pensions. The old schemes were projected to be terminated in about 40 years.

The new private scheme was to provide pensions for old age (directly under control of the SAFPs) and disability/survivors (under coverage by private insurance companies). The conditions for old age in the draft were 65 years of age for both sexes plus 30 years of contribution (these were tougher than the Chilean scheme, which requires five fewer years of age for women and 10 fewer years of contribution for both sexes). A recognition bond would be paid by the state at time of retirement to account for the years of contribution to the old system; this bond would be indexed to inflation and would earn an undetermined interest rate; there would be a minimum pension guaranteed by the state for those who lacked the needed requirements. ISS conditions were toughened: the age of retirement was gradually increased over eight years from 60/55 (for males/females) to 65 for both sexes; the number of years of contribution was expanded from 10 or 20 years to 30 years; the salary base, which used to be the last two years, was increased to 10 years and adjusted to inflation; the maximum pension was set equal to the lesser of 90 percent of the insured's salary at the time of retirement or 15 times the minimum legal salary; and all pensions were to be adjusted to the cost of living. The privileged conditions of public funds were left untouched by the draft. The draft also introduced a public assistance pension (to start in 1994) for those age 70 and above living under conditions of extreme poverty, which provides up to one-half of the minimum-wage salary.

The combined insured/employer payroll for pensions in the ISS was 6.5 percent (4.3 percent from the employer and 2.2 percent from the insured) but was less for public funds. This contribution was raised to 8 percent (5.3 percent the employer and 2.7 percent the insured) a few weeks before the legal draft was submitted to congress. The draft established a uniform overall contribution of 13.5 percent for both the old system (including private and public sectors) and the new private scheme: 10 percent to be paid by the employer and 3.5 percent by the insured. In the new scheme all the employers' contributions would go to the insured's individual accounts for old-age pensions; a portion of the insured's contributions would finance the premiums for disability/survivors insurance, with the rest being retained by the SAFPs as a commission. Contrary to the Chilean model, therefore, the Columbian draft did not eliminate the employer's contribution but increased it by 132 percent; it did not reduce the insured's contribution in the private scheme but increased it by 60 percent. The state was to finance the operational deficit of the old system; the recognition bonds, the minimum pensions, and other guarantees in the new system; and the public assistance pension for the dispossessed.

The administration of the private pension scheme was to be performed by Chilean-style SAFPs, including private fiduciary and savings associations, as well as by public financial entities. In addition to the commission included in the insured's 3.5 percent contributions, the SAFP could charge a percentage commission. Changes to different SAFPs by the insured were limited to two per year, publicity was to be regulated by the state, and a maximum of 45 percent for SAFP investment in state securities was set (MTSS 1992).

Criticism of the Government Proposal

The legal draft became the target of criticism by some members of the congress and state agencies (e.g., the national comptroller) as well as research institutions and experts. (The following summary is based on

Contraloría 1992; López Castaño 1992; López Montaño 1992b; Ocampo 1992; Ruiz Llano 1992).

One legal question concerned the draft's apparent lack of concern for and even violation of the constitutional principles of universal coverage and solidarity. Another issue was that the reform should be global (by including health care), and not limited simply to pensions, because relationships between the two programs already exist and there is a need to assess the total cost of reforms. One expert claimed that the total payroll contribution (combining pensions, health insurance, and employment injury) would be as high as 25 percent. Colombia would switch from having the ninth highest percentage contribution in Latin America to the fifth, thus equaling Chile; however, Chile ranks fourth in population coverage within the region, whereas Colombia is ranked twelfth, and the increase in contributions would not improve that situation (see below). A third general point was that the key impact of the government proposal would be the result of a toughening of entitlement conditions and benefits and a substantial raise in contributions, rather than an outcome of either institutional- or financial-regime changes (such as privatization or capitalization). Maintaining the ISS but with the proposed tougher conditions would achieve similar results.

The legal draft ignored the urgent need to expand population coverage. In the case of Chile such coverage prior to the reform was about 75 percent of the labor force, but in Colombia it is 30 percent. Furthermore, the informal sector in Colombia is considerably larger than in Chile (Chile, which offers voluntary coverage for the self-employed, as in Colombia, has been unable in the last 12 years to incorporate that segment of the population to a significant degree). Finally, Colombia has a poverty incidence of 40 percent (about half of Colombia's urban population age 60 and over does not receive any income), whereas Chile's is considerably lower. The government proposal claimed that liberal economic policies would ultimately lead to the complete "formalization" of the labor force: as all workers got stable salaried jobs they would become incorporated into the private scheme. Even if that optimistic scenario were feasible it would take a long time to materialize. The proposed reform would therefore consolidate the protection of one-third of the population (in middle- and lower high-income brackets) at the expense of the majority who are concentrated in the lowest income brackets. There are not enough resources to both consolidate protection for those in higher brackets and provide coverage for those in lower brackets.

The lack of equity was another important issue. The draft imposes considerable sacrifices on those currently covered by the ISS, but civil servants are allowed to keep their special benefits. One of those privileged groups includes congressional representatives; the proposal's creators did not dare restrict the representatives' benefits. In the new scheme inequality between male and female pensions (as explained in the Chilean case) should persist until the age of retirement becomes the same, but because women live longer and usually have lower retirement ages, the difference would not be completely eliminated.

According to data in the government proposal an average insured with 30 years of contribution (assuming a 4 percent real interest rate—see below) would have a salary replacement rate of only 41 percent (54 percent with a 5 percent interest rate); to receive 100 percent replacement, 45 years of contribution would be needed (40 years with a 5 percent rate). These calculations assume full compliance throughout the working lives of the insured, but the ISS record for compliance is about 50 percent (because of labor instability, evasion, etc.); hence, few of those insured would actually accumulate the required 30 years of contribution. Furthermore, about 80 percent of the ISS-insured earn a salary equal to twice the minimum wage or less. For these reasons a large majority of the insured could end up receiving a minimum pension, and the cost of the state subsidy would increase.

Finally, by increasing the number of salary years required to calculate the pension amount, the draft addressed the important issue of early underreporting. Because the amount of a pension under the ISS is based on the last two years' salary, many insured underreport for most of their working lives and then increase their contributions prior to retirement. Critics argue, however, that this is the case only for middle- and high-income insured (a minority) but not for low-income insured (the majority), whose payments are usually based on the minimum legal salary and so cannot be underreported.

Most criticism of the draft focused on its financial flaws, even if the critics had accepted the revised-downward figures that the government offered for the cost of the reform. The increase in contributions to 13.5 percent would allow the ISS to be self-financed, at least until 2010, and would leave a surplus to cover part of the ensuing deficit after that year. This estimate, however, assumed that none of those insured by the ISS would move to the private scheme. But if the large majority indeed moved (as happened in Chile), such a level of contribution would be grossly insufficient (because the ISS would still have the old affiliates but would lose young contributors). Hence, either the contribution would have to be increased or the state would have to pay the difference. The draft tried to reduce that problem by banning those currently insured who are age 55/50 and over from switching to the private scheme (unless they decided to contribute until they became 65), but the above projection apparently already had taken this modification into account. Furthermore, the financial situation in CAJANAL (and other public pensions) is much worse: in 1993 the estimated level of contribution needed to cover expenses is 21 percent—well above the previously projected 13.5 percent. Thus the *combined* private-public system would start with a deficit because it would require a level of contribution of almost 14 percent in 1993, and this level would rise to 17.6 percent in 2000 and 31 percent in 2020. Estimates of the debt generated by the entire reform by 2025 ranged from 20–64 percent of GDP (depending on whether only some of the ISS-insured would move to the new scheme or whether some of those insured in the public funds would also move); only 8–45 percent of that debt would be financed by the private pension funds. In 1991 Colombia considered having 7.4 percent of GDP in central bank securities to be too high, but that figure would look small compared with the forecasted pension debt burden. The draft lacked a clear formula for calculating the recognition bonds (it had three different alternatives) and did not fix the interest rate; it was therefore impossible to calculate accurately the future cost of such bonds: estimates ranged from 8.5–46.5 percent of GDP in 2025 (Ocampo 1992; López Montaño 1992b). These rough projections of the costs of the entire system suggested that the 45 percent limit set in the draft for SAFP investment in central bank securities would be too low to finance the debt, particularly if a good portion of those insured in public funds moved to the new private scheme.

Three different types of interest rates were considered in the draft, and there were important contradictions among them: the rate earned by the SAFPs, the rate to be fixed by the government for recognition bonds, and the rate the state would have to pay to get the resources needed to finance such bonds and other reform costs. If the overall interest rate happened to be low, the government would benefit (its cost would be lower), but the yields of the SAFPs would be harmed; in this case many insured would not meet the requirements for minimum pensions, thereby increasing the state subsidy. Conversely, if the interest rate happened to be high, the SAFPs' gain would be the government's loss, except for a lower cost of the minimum pension. The draft did not have consistent calculations based on the same rates. The real interest rates projected in the government proposal, which ranged from 5–8 percent, are considered to be too high. The purpose of such inflated figures might have been to project a higher salary-replacement rate, but, on the other hand, financing the debt would then be costlier. The average rate in Colombia from 1951–1992 was close to 4 percent (the draft improperly gave a value of 7.5 percent), and international real rates were 2–3 percent. With the opening of Colombia's economy domestic rates would have to decline in order to be competitive in the world market.

How will the cost of the old system based on pay-as-you-go compare with that of the new system based on capitalization? The draft assumed that the latter would be smaller and that a growing surplus would be generated, thereby leading to a higher capital accumulation. However, the Chilean experience does not provide evidence that a capitalization scheme increases national savings. A Colombian expert argues that the costs of each system depend on the relationship of the interest rate and economic growth: if both rates are equal, the costs are the same; if the interest rate is higher than the growth rate, a pay-as-you-go method would be costlier than capitalization; and the opposite would be true if the interest rate is lower than the growth rate. He believes that a lower interest rate is the most likely scenario as Colombia's economy becomes more open, and he argues that it is for that reason that U.S. and Western European pension schemes are not fully funded. If they were, the enormous accumulation of funds would be extremely difficult to invest (López Castaño 1992).

Because of limitations in Colombia's domestic capital market (more so than in Chile's) critics contend that there would be either (1) a very high proportion of funds invested in public debt instruments (a risky tactic for the private scheme, as events in Chile in the early 1980s demonstrated), (2) pressure to allow the insured to withdraw funds from the SAFPs (e.g., to buy homes or finance education as in Singapore), or (3) a sizable portion of investment in foreign instruments (as is beginning to happen in Chile). Finally, there were economic and political concerns about the enormous resources to be controlled by a likely private oligopoly of SAFPs, which would hold a substantial public debt.

The Fate of the Government Proposal and New Alternatives

Mounting criticism forced President César Gaviria in December 1992 to withdraw his proposal from the congress. All parties agreed to rewrite the draft; debate and resubmit it for congressional approval; amend it to cover both pension and health-care reform; and discuss it through an integrated commission of representatives from government, labor, and business. In the best-case scenario final approval of the revised draft was not expected until mid-1993.

In the meantime new proposals have been developed by congressional representatives and experts. One proposal basically resurrects the mixed approach summarized earlier but also incorporates some of the draft elements: (1) the merging of all public funds into a national fund that should standardize entitlement conditions and benefits to bring them in line with the tougher conditions imposed on the ISS (the national fund would have either public accounts with investment in the financial market or separate funds for each group under state supervision); (2) the ISS would develop a separate fund to manage the transition, and the payroll contribution would be gradually increased (instead of being abruptly raised) to finance the meager benefits; and (3) a fund for the dispossessed elderly would be established and financed by general taxes (López Castaño 1992).

Another proposal offers three alternatives, all of them arguably less expensive than the government's (such savings could then be used to finance public assistance pensions for the elderly or expand coverage to the informal sector): (1) the first option outlined on page 140 but with a portion of ISS resources channeled to the private capital market; (2) the mixed option (which I consider the best); and (3) a variant of the privatization option but with a new element of solidarity—a portion of the contributions to the SAFPs would be used to partly finance a basic pension fund (Ocampo 1992).

A third proposal introduces the following modifications to the draft: (1) facilitate the incorporation of the informal sector by making contributions more flexible (e.g., by allowing irregular, nonperiodic payments, some of them below the minimum contribution) and setting a 10 percent contribution by the worker and 3.5 percent by the state; (2) introduce solidarity elements, such as the elimination of the salary ceiling to contributions, and use the extra revenue to support pensions for low-income workers; and (3) authorize cooperatives and nonprofit organizations (e.g., family-allowance funds) to operate SAFPs in order to expand coverage to low-income groups (Ruiz Llano 1992).

The government resubmitted the first legal draft, with some modifications, in 1993, and in June it was approved by commissions of both chambers of congress, although it still needs full congressional approval. One important difference is that, according to the second draft, the reform embraces both health-care and pensions, whereas the first draft was limited to the latter. The pension component of the second draft basically reproduced the first draft, that is, privatization Chilean style, but with some changes either to respond to criticism against the first draft or to make its passage in congress easier. First, the cut-off age, below which those already insured have the option to move to the new private system, was reduced from 50/55 for females/males to 40/45. Second, within the old system the first draft was modified by the second draft as follows: (1) ages of retirement were decreased from 65 for both sexes to 57/62, which is only two additional years over the current statutory ages; (3) the minimum number of years of contribution for retirement was cut down from 30 to 20 (still twice the number currently required); (4) the salary base used to calculate the pension was increased from the last 10 years of work to the entire active life of the insured (currently it is the last two years of work); (5) the total wage contribution was initially decreased 2.5 percentage points (from 13.5 percent to 11 percent), but later on it was to be increased back up to 13.5 percent; and (6) a solidarity pension fund was created, financed by an additional salary contribution of 0.5 percent from the highest-income insured, in order to facilitate the incorporation of low-income workers (allowing for some expansion of coverage). The private system was reproduced in the second draft as it was in the first draft, except that the bond of recognition earned a 5 percent annual real rate of interest whereas such interest was unspecified in the first draft. (Botero 1993)

The changes described above did not avoid a repetition of the criticism against the first draft. The second draft has been substantially modified by congress, thus resulting in a third draft that goes back to the mixed model: the public system (centered on ISS) is retained and competes with the private system. (Details on the third draft were not available at the time this book was completed.) The senate approved the third draft in November, and the chamber of deputies passed it into law in December 1993.

Argentina: A Mixed Model

The Situation Prior to the Reform

Together with Uruguay, Argentina suffers the worst financial disequilibrium of pension schemes in the region. In the 1960s and 1970s multiple pension funds were unified, relatively standardized, and placed under the under secretary of social security. However, an administrative distinction among three branches or funds has continued: industry and commerce (salaried private workers), state (civil servants), and self-employed. Financially, though, there is a pooling of revenues for all three. Population coverage is almost universal, although some groups are not insured, such as the lowest-income self-employed and some rural temporary and seasonal workers. As the degree of informalization of the labor market increases there could be a growing noncovered sector, but the virtual lack of data on population coverage impedes any serious analysis.

Pension benefits have been excessively generous; for instance, in spite of one of the highest life expectancies in the region the overall age of retirement is 60 for males and 55 for females. Disability pensions are easily granted, and because of irregularities and a lack of control 30 percent of all pensioners under the legal age of retirement receive them (one-fifth of all self-employed pensions are for disability). Privileged special programs (e.g., for the judiciary, legislative branch, top executives) allow retirement after a minimum number of years of work regardless of age. According to law the pension should be set at 70–82 percent of the base salary, which is calculated as the average of the best three years of salary out of the 10 years prior to retirement, and pensions should be adjusted based on the average overall salary adjustment. These unrealistic norms were unable to be maintained in the long run (once the financial deficit of the system expanded dramatically and inflation skyrocketed), so the real level of pensions declined by 25 percent from 1981–1988 and by another 30 percent from 1988–1991. More than 20,000 judicial claims have been granted to collect retroactively the difference between the pension actually paid and that legally established, and another 60,000 claims are pending; all of these, however, account for only 4 percent of the total number of pensioners. In 1991 the government agreed to settle the debt to the pensioners for the previous 12 years at a cost of U.S. $7 billion (to be paid with public bonds), but since then the debt has continued to grow at a rate of U.S. $2.4 billion per year.

There are significant inequalities in the scheme. The privileged programs, which cover a tiny fraction of 1 percent of all pensioners, receive 2 percent of all expenditures; and the state branch, which has 0.7 percent of all pensioners, gets 6 percent of total pension expenditures. In the industry/commerce branch (the only one that generates a surplus) 80 percent of pensioners get the minimum pension, but in the state branch only 53 percent fall in that category. Some insured contribute all their working lives, but others (particularly the self-employed) underreport their income in the early years and concentrate their contributions on the last three years; thus both groups may end up receiving the same pension amounts. Multiple benefits that can legally be received by one person account for 12 percent of total expenditures. Grace and noncontributory pensions are paid to poor elderly people, but much better ones go to former judges of the supreme court and church dignitaries. In 1991 there were 150,000 of these pensions that cost a total of U.S. $16 million. In 1991 a law was passed abolishing privileged programs, but some of them have managed to maintain their perquisites.

Social security expenditures in Argentina equaled 9 percent of GDP in 1980 and an estimated 13 percent in 1991; about 80 percent of such expenditures goes to pensions. The total wage tax for social security is 56 percent (21 percent for pensions), the highest in the region. Since the mid-1980s there have also been taxes on gas and public utilities, but these revenues are grossly insufficient to finance the system. The state therefore has to subsidize 35 percent of pension expenditures, and that burden has been rapidly increasing. The industry/commerce branch surplus is used to cover the expanding deficit of the state and self-employed branches (the latter's revenue covers only 20 percent of its expenditures).

In addition to the above-mentioned largesse in benefits the deficit has been caused by a gradual decline in real revenues resulting from internal and external factors. The employers' contribution was eliminated in 1980 and replaced with a proportion of VAT (value-added tax) revenues, but these revenues turned out to be considerably lower than the previous amount, so the employers' contribution was re-established in 1984. Evasion is officially estimated at 30 percent and unofficially at 40 percent; payment delays are even worse. As lower-income groups have become covered by the pension scheme, their contributions have become smaller (but they are still entitled to a minimum pension). I have also noted widespread underreporting of income and salaries. Reserves used to account for as much as 28 percent of GDP, but they were invested in state securities at a fixed interest rate (which resulted in a 16 percent negative rate); when the state canceled its obligation in 1970 those funds had shrunk to 1 percent of GDP.

The economic crisis of the 1980s aggravated the deficit: industrial employment declined 39 percent from 1975–1988 and industrial real salaries by 25 percent, thus reducing revenues. The percentage of the population age 65 and over increased from 4 percent to 10 percent from 1950–1991, and life expectancy also grew significantly. Because coverage was almost universal, the ratio of contributors to pensioners rapidly declined to 1.62 in 1990 (and to 1 in the self-employed branch) and was projected to further decrease to 1.46 by 2025. To finance the pension scheme under current conditions the ratio should be 4. Projections for 1995–2025 show that the wage contribution would have to almost triple (to 55 percent) or the state subsidy would have to increase to 62 percent of expenditures to maintain payment of pensions. The cumulative deficit of the scheme in the next 30 years is estimated to become equal to the national debt with all foreign banks in 1991 (Schulthess 1990; Mesa-Lago 1991d, 1992a; Feldman 1992; El Poder Ejecutivo Nacional 1992).

Reform Proposal

For at least a decade the urgent need for a global radical reform (instead of a partial cosmetic one) has been obvious to experts and government officials, but several legal drafts to accomplish that task have failed. Part of the explanation is the absence of accurate knowledge about the population; another is the reluctance of politicians to "bite the bullet." Interviews conducted in 1990 with leaders of political parties, trade unions, associations of pensioners, and selected employer groups showed that they had a remarkable lack of information on both the current pension scheme and proposals for its reform. If this was true among a supposedly well-informed elite, the situation among the mass of the population had to be much worse (Isuani 1991).

A technical project prepared in 1988 by the statistical section of the under secretary of social security tried to save the old scheme through minor modifications (such as an increase in the age of retirement) and by securing an unrealistic 7 percent of GDP annually to finance the deficit. It never made it to the congress.

Another unsuccessful legal draft, developed by the under secretary of social security (Proyecto Estrada) in 1990, tried more seriously to solve the problem, mostly by tightening the conditions and benefits of the existing scheme: raising the age of retirement to 65/62 plus 35 years of contribution; reducing pensions to 65 percent of a base salary calculated as an average of the 10 years prior to retirement; increasing the contribution level by 1 percentage point; eliminating privileged programs; and converting the costly self-employed branch into a public assistance program under the charge of and totally financed by the state. The draft also allowed a private supplementary scheme to which those insured in the public scheme could shift as much as 2 percent of their own contributions (Feldman 1992).

The above two drafts were not preceded by substantial study and were virtually kept secret by the under secretary of social security. A new approach was followed by President Menem's administration and the new under secretary, Walter Schulthess. With external funding, some 30 technical studies were conducted from 1989–1991 covering virtually all legal, economic, and statistical aspects of the reform (Mesa-Lago 1992a). Several legal drafts were developed, but the one submitted to congress in May 1992 was voted down. A revised legal draft incorporating substantial modifications requested by legislators was ready in August of that year, and another draft with more (but minor) changes was delivered to the commission of pensions of the chamber of deputies toward the end of the year. The legal draft was submitted to the chamber of deputies in February 1993 and approved in April of that year, the senate approved it in October, and the president signed it the same month. It will enter in force in July 1994. (The text of the law was still unavailable at the time of this writing.)

General features of the proposed reform. The proposed system is mixed, a combination of (1) a permanent public scheme based on a pay-as-you-go approach and on paying a basic pension and (2) a supplementary private scheme; it is fully funded and very similar to Chile's. All those age 18 and over are mandatorily covered by the new system, as are future entrants in the labor force. (A previous version of the legal draft divided the insured population into two groups: those age 45 and over would stay in the old public scheme—with an option to join the new system—and those under 45 would mandatorily enter the latter.) Therefore the public scheme is not closed, and the private scheme supplements rather than replaces the public scheme. Another important feature is that in Argentina the self-employed are compulsorily covered (a situation that predated the new system), whereas they have voluntary coverage in Chile. Employer contributions are maintained in Argentina. There is no reduction in the insured's contribution and thus no increase in their salary (as in Chile).

All salaried workers in the private and public sectors (except provinces and municipalities that may choose not to enter the system) as well as the self-employed are covered; all differences among the three branches are eliminated. Voluntary coverage is available for members of co-ops, housewives, the church, and other minor groups. Contributions are uniform for the whole system: the salaried insured pay 11 percent of their wages and the employers 16 percent, whereas the self-employed pay 27 percent of their incomes (the sum of both percentages for salaried workers). The employers' contributions and 16 percent of the self-employed's salaries go to the public scheme, and the salaried insured's contributions plus 11 percent of the self-employed's salaries go to the private scheme.

(Note that the self-employed have a percentage contribution that almost triples that of the salaried worker; in Chile both percentages are identical, but compliance among the registered self-employed is still very poor—a situation that augurs a worse scenario in Argentina.) All contributions are collected by ANSES, the administrative arm of the unified system of social security, which transfers the corresponding portions to the public and private schemes. Payment of the public (basic) and private (supplementary) components of a pension are unified. The destitute who have reached a certain age but are not covered by the system are entitled to a public assistance pension (conditioned to a means test) that is directly paid and financed by the state out of general revenue. The age of retirement in both schemes will increase gradually in the next 20 years from 60/55 to 65 for both male and female salaried workers and from 60 to 65 for self-employed female workers; 30 years of work and contribution are also required. These conditions are tougher than Chile's: five more years for females—though this will eliminate statutory differences in the level of pensions—and 10 more years of contribution. But the current debt of the Argentinean system is considerably worse than that of Chile in 1980.

Public scheme. All those insured are entitled to a universal basic pension plus a compensatory benefit. The basic pension is equal to 2.5 AMPOs, i.e., 2.5 times the value that results from dividing the contributions going to the private scheme (basically those of the insured) by the number of those registered in the system; the value of an AMPO is estimated twice a year. If an insured has more than 30 and up to 45 years of contributions the basic pension is increased at a rate of 1 percent per year. The basic pension thus eliminates the need for a minimum pension as in the Chilean system.

The compensatory benefit is similar to Chile's recognition bond, but rather than being deposited by the state in an insured's individual private-scheme account (at the time of retirement) it is paid by the public scheme. It is calculated at the rate of 1.5 percent of the base salary (the salary average of the last 10 years prior to retirement) for each year of work/contribution, with a maximum of 36 years, and the resulting sum is adjusted for inflation. Therefore there is a ceiling of 60 percent of the base salary (as well as a maximum of one AMPO for each year of work), and there is no 4 percent interest payment as in the Chilean case. These factors should reduce the cost of this benefit. (A previous draft version excluded this benefit altogether, but legislative pressure forced its eventual inclusion.)

For those who are age 45 and older, disability and survivors pensions are paid by the public scheme, which might receive some compensation from the private scheme or insurance companies who cover a younger population. Adjustment of all public pensions to the cost of living will be based on the AMPO. All public pensioners are also entitled to two month's worth of extra pensions, a costly legacy from prereform legislation. The draft also eliminates the payment of more than one pension to an individual as well as pension payments to those with income from working. The entire public scheme is administered by ANSES.

The public scheme is financed by the insured's contributions of 11 percent (explained above) plus the following: up to 25 percent of IVA revenue, 100 percent of revenue from selling shares of the state petroleum enterprise, and 20 percent from the profit tax. (A previous draft included a tax on enterprises' "primary surplus" that was highly controversial and thus eliminated in the current draft.) In addition, the private scheme will buy state bonds, and there is the possibility of long-term loans from multilateral lending agencies. It is said that the federal government might reduce its financial contribution to the provinces and transfer those resources to the public pension scheme.

Private scheme. The private scheme is virtually identical to Chile's except for the differences noted above plus the following: (1) the private corporations administering the system are abbreviated as AFJPs instead of AFPs; (2) the mandatory insured's contribution rate of 11 percent for the old-age scheme is 1 percentage point higher than Chile's, and the voluntary additional contribution is not specified; (3) the contributions to pay for disability/ survivors premiums to the insurance companies are not listed separately from the commissions to the AFJPs; (4) the unified system of payment of contributions through ANSES reduces the burden on employers, particularly small ones, but if it is not efficient it may not be fast enough to transfer the funds and so could generate errors and legal claims; (5) the required capital of an AFJP is equivalent to U.S. $1.5 million, less than the U.S. $2 million now required in Chile but much more than the initially required sum of U.S. $100,000 in Chile; (6) changes among AFJPs are limited to two annually, which reduces the seller's gains but limits the insured's freedom of choice; (7) AFJPs are not allowed to have publicity without approval, and thereafter their publicity is subject to state control (an advantage over the Chilean system); (8) the maximum percentages allowed for AFJP investment in particular instruments are much more flexible than in Chile; for instance, as much as 80 percent can be invested in state securities and 30 percent in securities from provinces, municipalities, and public enterprises (the combined maximum in Chile is 45 percent), and the maximum for all enterprise shares is 70 percent (30 percent in Chile); (9) insurance companies must be dedicated exclusively to managing their disability/survivors insurance and life annuity programs (it remains to be seen whether companies with such narrowness are profitable or if that stipulation will increase the premiums; (10) trade unions, associations of entrepreneurs and professionals, cooperatives, mutual aid societies, and banks are allowed to operate AFJPs but only as separate enterprises, something prohibited in Chile, where only corporations (i.e., *sociedades anónimas*) may do so; (11) the superintendency of the private scheme is not financed by the state (as in Chile) but by the AFJP, a practice that should increase the latter's costs and commissions; and (12) the state provides some guarantees to the insured not available in Chile; for instance, if an insurance company goes bankrupt, the state is responsible for paying the life annuity to the pensioner.

Uruguay: The Reform of the Prototypical Welfare State

Uruguay is the prototypical welfare state in the Western hemisphere and the pioneer in the inception of social insurance. Its first pension programs were introduced early in the twentieth century. The combination of pressure from interest groups, a pluralistic democracy, and clientelistic politics in both traditional parties led in the 1960s not only to the most developed and generous social security system in LAC but also to the most stratified and costly. The system's heavy burden (15 percent of GDP, 62 percent of fiscal expenditures, and 65 percent of the wage tax) contributed to the economic stagnation suffered by Uruguay. Since the end of the 1960s there has been a process of reform that has unified the administration of multiple schemes and has fairly standardized the entitlement conditions and benefits of most of them. Nevertheless, the reforms have not corrected the fundamental problems of the system, which since the mid-1970s has been besieged by persistent deficits that require substantial state subsidies in spite of extremely high payroll contributions. Pensions have been taking an increasing percentage of benefit expenditures—from 66 percent in 1970 to 80 percent in 1990—and generate close to half the system deficit (Mesa-Lago 1978; Dixon 1990; BPS 1990; Saldaín 1992).

The Administrative Organization of Pensions

The general social security institute in Uruguay is the social insurance bank (Banco de Previsión Social—BPS), which in addition to pensions[9] also manages sickness, maternity, unemployment, and family-allowance programs. There are three major occupational groups within BPS (such groups previously had independent funds): (1) civil servants and teachers; (2) industry and commerce workers; and (3) rural workers and domestic servants (this group also includes pensions for the dispossessed). Outside of the BPS there are seven additional independent pension schemes: one each for banking workers, university professionals, notary publics, the military, and the police, and two for jockeys. About 87 percent of the insured and 90 percent of the pensioners are in the BPS (DGEC 1988; BPS 1990).

Coverage of the Labor Force

Statistics on the labor force, employment, and particularly the total number of insured are scarce; those on the total number of insured are fragmentary, suffer from wide gaps, and are often confusing and contradictory. Therefore the following estimates should be taken with caution. Social insurance coverage (all funds) declined from 81–82 percent of the labor force for 1975–1981 to a trough of 67–68 percent for 1984–1985 and then increased to 76 percent in 1987 (another estimate for 1987 is substantially lower: 63 percent). The decline was a result of the economic crisis; in the second half of the 1980s the modest economic recuperation, decreasing unemployment, and better control measures led to increased coverage, but not to the precrisis level. The degree of coverage varies significantly among occupational groups: it is universal among civil servants, teachers, the armed forces, and possibly banking workers; it effectively extends to at least three-fourths of industry and commerce but only half of rural wage earners, one-third of the self-employed, and one-fifth of the domestic servants. However, the noninsured dispossessed are entitled to assistance pensions, so coverage is virtually universal.

Because of the aging of the population, a net negative migration of the young, and generous entitlement conditions, the ratio of all contributing insured to all pensioners steadily decreased from 1.8 in 1975 to 1.2 in 1989 (Lacurcia 1990). Within the BPS the ratio declined from 1.7 to 1.0 from 1963–1988, or from 2.4 to 1.3 if one entire survivor pension is used (rather than the average three pensioners for this type of pension). Regardless of the quality of the data it can safely be said that at the beginning of the 1990s each active worker supported one pensioner in Uruguay—the lowest active/passive ratio in the entire continent. In 1986 the lowest ratios (ranging from 0.9–1.2) were found among rural workers, domestic servants, the police, civil servants, and teachers, whereas the highest ratios (ranging from 1.5–3.4) were registered among university professionals and industry and commerce workers (Mesa-Lago 1978, 1992c; Giral-Bosca and Diéguez 1988; DGEC 1988, 1989; BPS 1986–1990; República 1992).

Generous Entitlement Conditions, Benefits, and Adjustments for Pensions

Practically all pension programs in Uruguay were introduced in the first four decades of the twentieth century, when life expectancy at birth was considerably lower than the current 72 years. The population was also much younger then, but in 1985 15.4 percent of it was 60 years and older (23 percent among the urban population), and that proportion—the highest in LAC—is expected to increase to 17 percent by the year 2000. Almost one-fourth of the total population was under some type of pension at the end of the 1980s. The percentage of the population 60 years and older dependent on the working-age population increased from 19 percent in 1963 to 28 percent in 1990.

In spite of the aging of the population several pension programs reduced the age of early retirement or introduced seniority pensions based on years of service regardless of age. By the end of the 1970s the normal age of retirement for most insured was 50 for males and 45 for females; furthermore, in the special programs and some independent funds it was possible to retire after 20 or 25 years of services (10 under certain conditions), i.e., at age 40 or even earlier. These privileged schemes also granted pensions five times higher than the general average and allowed the accumulation of multiple pensions without a limit.

Legal reforms in 1979 and 1987 curtailed some of the liberal conditions and benefits. The first reform (1) increased the age of retirement in the general system from 50/45 to 60/55; (2) eliminated the pension granted after 10 years of service for women with children and dismissed workers; (3) tightened the calculation of benefits; (4) abolished an extra month of pension paid annually; and (5) standardized entitlement conditions to a certain extent for most groups under the BPS. But this reform maintained the privileged schemes for top political jobs, judges, and teachers and allowed generous conditions for retirement during a transitional period. As a result of this transitional period there was a wave of retirements in 1980 and 1981, at twice the rate of 1969–1979, and half of those who retired were below the higher ages established by the new rules. The 1979 reform failed to tackle the fundamental problems of the crisis, and its net outcome was negative, at least in the medium term, as shown by the worsening deficit of social security from 1980–1984 (as discussed below).

The 1987 legal draft raised the age of retirement from 60/55 to 65/60, a point rejected by the legislators. The enacted law (1) reduced some of the liberal conditions of the privileged schemes (but still maintained significant differences between them and the general system); (2) introduced a ceiling of 15 times the minimum wage for all pensions; (3) prohibited the accumulation of more than two pensions (one from the BPS and another outside); (4) established a minimum pension; (5) adjusted pensions based on the average salary index for the previous year; and (6) eliminated the salary ceiling for contributions and added new taxes (as discussed below). Contrary to the first reform, the 1987 reform had positive financial results (an estimated increase in revenue of 0.2 percent of GDP) but still did not raise the age of retirement.

At the end of 1989, despite the adjustments decreed by law, the average pension was 25 percent of the level in 1962 (Lacurcia 1990). The constitutional amendment, approved by 80 percent of the population in the 1989 plebiscite, mandated that starting in 1990 pensions be adjusted every time that salaries of the public sector are adjusted and that the adjustments equal the increase in the cost of living in the period immediately beforehand. That action partly offset the positive financial effects of the 1987 reform and required significant increases in taxation (as discussed below).

A devastating reversal occurred when the pension ceiling of 15 times the minimum wage, set by the 1987 law, was declared unconstitutional. The elimination of the ceiling will largely benefit civil servants and teachers, whose high pensions are the result of generous conditions but are grossly underfinanced. In 1986 the average old-age pensions for civil servants and teachers were 56 percent and 36 percent above the average BPS pension, respectively, whereas those of industry and commerce were 16 percent below and those of rural workers and domestic servants about 37 percent below. Outside of the BPS the average pension of military men in 1982 was 400 percent above the BPS average and that of the police and banking workers 300 percent above. Finally, the current average public assistance pension is close to half the average contributory pension (Giral-Bosca and Diéguez 1988; BPS 1990; Mesa-Lago 1991b).

The current entitlement conditions and levels of salary replacement for BPS pensions are summarized in part A of Table 3.1. In spite of the 1987 restrictions on privileged schemes, political officials and teachers retain advantageous conditions. The former can retire once the sums of their years of age and years of service equal 80; for instance, a 49-year-old official with 31 years of overall service (and a minimum of three in a political job) is eligible for an old-age pension (5–10 years earlier than in the general system). Teachers can retire with 25 years of service regardless of age—hence, at age 45 or even earlier (10–15 years earlier and with five years less service than in the general system)—or with 50 years of age and 20 years of service (a combined 20 years less than a male in the general system). The average period of an old-age pension for teachers and political officials (based on life expectancy at the age of retirement) is considerably higher than the period of work/contribution. Under the general system the female period of retirement is only six years less than the period of contribution, and under the advanced-age program the former is four years more than the latter. The average life expectancy of a female pensioner in the general system is 24.2 years, compared with 16.2 years for males; under special schemes those figures may be as high as 34 and 31 (BPS 1991).

Current pension adjustments in Uruguay are possibly the most generous in LAC for three reasons: the calculation of the pension is based on the average salary of the last three years, adjusted for inflation; the current pension is fully adjusted to the cost of living annually; and there is no ceiling to the adjusted pension. The question is how long the productive labor force and the nation will be able to support such a heavy burden and such a transfer of funds from the active to the passive population.

Deficit Financing

According to ILO data, in 1986 the cost of the entire social security system in Uruguay (all expenditures expressed as percentages of GDP) was

Table 3.1   Liberal Pensions and Heavy Costs in Uruguay: 1980–1992

A. *Entitlement Conditions and Average Periods of Retirement (1990)*

BPS Pension Programs	Retirement Age		Years of Service	% of Salary Replacement[a]	Additional Years of Life Expectancy at Retirement[b]	
	Male	Female			Male	Female
General	60	55	30	60–80	16.2	24.1
Advanced Age	70	65	10	40–70	6.2	14.1
Political Posts[c]	----80----		–	50–80	27.2[d]	25.1[d]
Teachers	----Any----		25	50–70	31.2[d]	34.1[d]
Teachers	----50----		20	50–70	26.2	29.1
Dispossessed	----65----		[e]	45[e]	11.2	14.1

B. *The Cost of Social Security and Pensions (% of GDP)*

	1980	1981	1982	1983	1984	1985	1986	1987	1988	1989	1990	1992[f]
Social Security Expenditures	9.8	12.6	15.4	12.7	11.2	10.3	10.7	11.3	11.8	11.7	13.4	14.0
BPS Expenditures	7.6	9.9	12.0	10.0	8.6	8.3	8.8	9.3	9.9	9.8	11.5	12.3
BPS Deficit (State Subsidy)	1.4	3.7	5.8	4.3	3.2	2.8	2.3	2.5	2.9	2.8	2.0	2.1
BPS Pension Deficit	1.1	3.0	4.6	3.1	2.4	1.5	1.2	1.5	1.8	1.6	1.0	1.7

Sources: Part A from BPS 1990 and Mesa-Lago 1991b; Part B from Giral-Bosca and Diéguez 1988, revised and updated with DGEC 1988, 1989, BPS 1988–1990, and BPS 1991b, 1991c.

Notes: a. Salary base is the average of the last three years of salary indexed to cost of living.
b. Based on 1980–1985 data.
c. Top political posts and political appointees *(personal de particular confianza)*; the required 80 "years" can be reached with any combination of years of age and years of service, but three of the latter must be in the job in question.
d. Based on retirement at age 49 for political posts and age 45 for teachers.
e. Lack of both resources and relatives who can provide support; requires means test; the percentage of salary replacement is actually the average assistance pension in relation to the average BPS pension (1989).
f. Projection.

the third highest in LAC (9.6 percent, compared with 14.7 percent in Cuba and 13.1 percent in Chile) but showed a decline from 11 percent in 1983 (see Table 2.16). But estimates based on Uruguay's statistics (see part B of Table 3.1) show significantly higher percentages: increasing from 9.8 percent to 15.4 percent of GDP from 1980–1982 (mainly a result of the wave of retirements after the 1979 reform and the adjustment of pensions to the cost of living), declining to 10.3 percent in 1985, and increasing thereafter to 13.4 percent in 1990 (a higher level than in 1980). Estimates for 1992 indicated an increase to 14 percent. The table indicates that the share of BPS expenditures in total social security expenditures steadily increased from 78 percent to 86 percent from 1980–1990. The proportion of pensions in total BPS benefit expenditures rose from 78.7 percent in 1985 to 80.2 percent in 1990 (BPS 1986–1990). The overall BPS deficit, covered with state transfers, jumped from 1.4 percent to 5.8 percent of GDP from 1980–1982 and thereafter oscillated but exhibited a declining trend to 2 percent in 1990. The BPS deficit was almost similar to the central government's fiscal deficit in 1985, but by 1987 it was twice as high, and by 1990 it was 25 times higher because the government conducted a successful program to reduce its deficit while the BPS deficit soared. The proportion of the BPS deficit generated by the pension programs increased from 51 percent to 68 percent from 1985–1988 but declined to 59 percent in 1989 and 50 percent in 1990. Two factors explain the downward trend in the last two years: the rising share of the deficit faced by the sickness/maternity scheme (and to a lesser extent the deficit of the unemployment scheme) and the significant increase in employers' contributions, to be explained below (BPS 1979–1991; República 1992).

Some independent pension funds generate surpluses, and the magnitude of disequilibrium varies among those schemes suffering from deficits. In 1988 the annual fiscal balance of each pension program per beneficiary was as follows (in U.S. dollars): military, -$696; police -$692; rural/domestic workers and public assistance, -$514; civil servants/teachers, -$422; notaries, +$48; industry/commerce, +$78; professionals, +$182; and banking workers, +$1,341 (based on DGEC 1989). Within the BPS the modest surplus generated by industry and commerce helps offset the deficits of both the civil servants/teachers program and the rural/domestic workers and public assistance program. The solidarity transfer to the latter program has a progressive effect on distribution (because rural workers, domestic servants, and the dispossessed have lower incomes than industrial and commerce workers); but the transfer to civil servants/teachers probably has a regressive effect, and in any case these groups (as well as the armed forces) enjoy more liberal entitlement conditions than industry/commerce. State subsidies to cover the deficit have similar progressive/regressive effects on distribution. Furthermore, an overall evaluation of the distributional impact of all state subsidies to social services (including social security, health, education, sanitation, housing) conducted in 1982 showed that (1) the state transfer to all health services had a high degree of progressiveness, but the transfer to pensions was regressive (because the bulk of the subsidies went to middle-income groups such as those in the armed forces, civil service, and teaching), and (2) the relative impact of the health subsidy on income distribution was lower than that of other subsidies, such as pensions, because the other subsidies were bigger. Therefore a redistribution of the state subsidy toward the lowest income group (rural/domestic and assistance pensioners) and health care not only would be fairer but also would improve the redistributional impact of such subsidies in favor of the most vulnerable groups (Davrieux 1987; Mesa-Lago 1992c).

Within the BPS the payroll contributions to pensions, which were quite different among occupational groups prior to the reform, have gradually been made uniform. The insured's payroll contributions for civil servants/teachers and industry/commerce were reduced, and those for rural/domestic workers were increased; thus by 1985 all three groups paid 13 percent (some rural workers had paid 10 percent since 1966). Notice that although teachers and some civil servants enjoy more liberal entitlement conditions than the rest, they pay the same percentage contribution. The employer's payroll contribution for civil servants and teachers in 1985 (15–20 percent) was higher—to support the liberal benefits of this group—than the contributions for the other groups (which were uniform at 12 percent, except for rural employers, who pay based on the size and productivity of farms). But the state contribution as an employer comes from general revenue, largely generated by regressive taxes, and thus adds to the regressive impact of the state subsidy. In 1989 the employer's contribution in all groups was increased by 1 percentage point and in 1990 by an additional 3.5 percentage points, for a total increase of 4.5 points. The resulting rates in 1990 were 19.5–24.5 percent for civil servants/teachers and 16.5 percent for the other groups (the insured's contributions were not increased). The total contribution for social security (via BPS) in Uruguay in 1990 ranged from 38.5–49.5 percent of wages (the second highest in LAC), but 20 percent of costs still had to be subsidized by the state. In 1991 the state subsidy to the entire social security system was U.S. $298 million, out of which U.S. $120 million went to BPS pensions.

Because of the heavy contributory burden, both employers and employees conspire to evade registration, and high inflation rates in the 1980s (and low fines) stimulated employers' delays in payment. In 1990 overall evasion in the BPS program was 55 percent; in industry and commerce it was 31.3 percent (65.5 percent among employers and 9 percent among insured); in the rural sector it was 36.5 percent (51.5 percent among the insured); and among domestic servants it was 77.2 percent. Payment delays among civil servants and teachers were estimated as 13.3

percent for 1989–1990. Among all evaders an estimated 68 percent are extremely difficult to control (Lacurcia 1990). In 1988 the BPS appeared to have given up the struggle to detect, register, and collect from evaders except for those in industry and commerce. BPS actuaries estimated that the cost of effectively incorporating noncovered domestic servants and rural workers would be extremely high. Furthermore, because of the low income of these groups the cost of providing benefits to them would be higher than their potential contributions, thereby aggravating the BPS deficit. Finally, BPS authorities believed that purely coercive methods of fighting evasion would not be effective without a drastic reform of BPS, particularly of the pension program. However, in 1989 a program began to expand computer facilities (with external aid) to do the following: (1) develop an up-to-date list of employers and contributors in order to cross-check that information with other sources such as tax records; (2) produce a registry and classification of agricultural producers in accordance with the special payment system of this group; (3) introduce an early warning system for detecting potential noncompliance (underpayment or late payment); (4) establish individual accounts for insured's contributions; and (5) improve the data on beneficiaries of the BPS (and possibly other programs) to eliminate the collection of multiple pensions above the legal maximum. In addition, there is a plan to unify the ID card for social security and taxes (Giral-Bosca and Diéguez 1988; BPS 1986–1990; Mesa-Lago 1992c).

From 1980–1984, in conjunction with the reduction in payroll contributions, the government increased the VAT by 8 percentage points (from 12 percent to 20 percent) and earmarked the revenue for social security. However, because of the economic crisis and difficulties in collection, VAT revenue did not offset the decline in payroll contributions, which worsened the growing deficit faced by social security and the BPS. In 1987 the VAT was increased by another percentage point, and a 20 percent tax was imposed on the registration of new vehicles to help finance the BPS deficit. In 1990 the VAT was increased by 5 additional percentage points and the income tax from 3.5 percent to 7.5 percent (together with an increase of 3.5 percentage points in the employer's contribution) to help finance the adjustment of pensions to the cost of living. In that year 16.2 percent of all BPS revenue came from the VAT and 81.6 percent from contributions (an increase of 10 percentage points over 1989); hence, state transfers were reduced to 2.2 percent of revenue. The actuarial payroll contribution rose from 31 percent in 1989, prior to the reform, to 41 percent in 1991 and is projected to be 50.5 percent in 2040. Because such payroll contributions are not feasible in practice, pensions will increasingly have to be financed by state subsidies (Mesa-Lago 1978; Giral-Bosca and Diéguez 1988; BPS 1990; Lacurcia 1990).

Reform Proposals

In 1990–1991 three alternative ways were reviewed to tackle the problems faced by pensions in Uruguay: (1) radically reform the current system but keep it on a pay-as-you-go basis (another version of this alternative was to introduce a new pay-as-you-go scheme to replace the current one); (2) completely replace the current system with a new one, for both current and future insured, based on capitalization (ie., the Chilean model); and (3) maintain the current system but make significant reforms and create a supplementary fully funded new system (i.e., a mixed model). (The following summary of the three approaches is based on Lacurcia 1990.)

1. The first alternative requires severe reforms of the current system. The possibility of eliminating the deficit with even higher contributions or taxes should not be considered because of the heavy burden that already exists and the potentially negative effects on employment creation. It is possible, however, to increase efficiency by reducing evasion and collecting the required contributions; the new computerization effort might be able to achieve that end if it is combined with individual ID numbers, improved inspection, and increased prosecution plus higher fines. These measures would be most effective only in the industry/commerce sector. A reduction of expenditures is therefore the principal task, and to that effect it is necessary to (1) increase the age of retirement to 65/60 or, even better, to 65 for both sexes (which could be done gradually); (2) require a minimum of 40 years of work as the salary base, instead of the last three years; (3) eliminate all the privileged entitlement conditions and benefits that still remain for high political posts and teachers; (4) reduce the percentage of salary replacement to 60 percent, reintroduce the pension ceiling, and establish an adjustment mechanism commensurate with the economic capacity of the country; (5) restrict the payment of survivors pensions to only the closest dependent relatives; and (6) introduce other cost reduction measures in the rest of the BPS schemes. There is little space to cut down administrative expenditures in the BPS because its share of total expenditures has declined from 6.1 percent to 4.5 percent, one of the lowest in LAC. The transition period should be brief in order to prevent a large proportion of the insured from retiring under the old system's norms. Several of the above measures will require a constitutional amendment and will be difficult to implement politically, particularly the increase in the age of retirement and the cut in the real level of pensions. In 1990 the government developed a proposal based on this approach. It maintained the last three years as the salary base but set a ceiling equal to the average salary of the last 10 years increased by 15 percent. The replacement rate was to be 50–55 percent for pensioners under the normal

retirement age but could be raised up to 75 percent thereafter. A pension ceiling of 15 times the minimum wage was to be established. The proposal cut 20 percent of expenses but was still found to be financially nonviable because the payroll contribution would remain very high (about 35 percent).

2. The second alternative (i.e., complete replacement by a fully funded private scheme) was considered by Lacurcia to be extremely costly because the state would have to recognize and guarantee each worker's number of years of contribution to the old system so that it counts in the new system. The cost of the recognition bonds alone would be U.S. $6.4 billion if the option of moving to the new scheme were given to all those in the old scheme. This cost would decline if limitations were set on the age before which people could move: U.S. $4.3 billion up to age 50, U.S. $2 billion up to age 40, and U.S. $510 million up to age 30. The total cost of the reform at the year 2030 would be U.S. $17.3 billion if all those less than 40 years old moved to the new scheme. This alternative worked in Chile, but the entitlement conditions in Uruguay are more liberal and the active/passive ratios considerably lower than in Chile. The public debt resulting from such costs has been estimated to be equal to the total external debt of the country. There is the additional problem that Uruguay's capital market might be less able than the Chilean market to absorb the flow of funds resulting from a national system of capitalization. The proportion of public securities in the Uruguayan stock market is very high and has been growing since 1983; it was 99 percent at the end of the 1980s. There are very few private shares and no private enterprise bonds. The number of enterprises with effective participation in the stock market declined from 24 percent to 21 percent from 1984–1990, and 95 percent of the transactions were done by only nine enterprises.

3. The third alternative (i.e., the mixed approach) combines a reformed public system (to whom all insured belong, based on a pay-as-you-go method) and a fully funded scheme that would pay supplementary pensions. The latter would be voluntary and state controlled, would offer defined benefits and a minimum pension (for those who do not meet the requirements for other benefits), and would be administered by public and/or private institutions. Access to the capitalization scheme could be given to all or some of those covered in the old system or only to new entrants in the labor force. If the second option is chosen, the scheme would grow slowly, so the capital market would gradually absorb the funds. A public assistance pension (for the elderly dispossessed not covered by social security) would be financed by the state. The problem with this approach is the heavy load of the old system: if the employers' contributions are geared to the old system (and the insured's contributions are transferred to the private scheme), it would cost U.S. $4.5 billion in 1989 dollars. If the employer's contribution is eliminated, the cost would be U.S. $10.2 billion.

The BPS conducted a series of studies in 1990–1991 that included an analysis of the three alternatives summarized above, statistical projections of their costs, simulation exercises, etc. A projection that assumed that the current system would not be reformed and would not increase its contributions resulted in the following alarming figures: (1) if economic growth were to continue at the same rate as in the past, by the year 2000 the pension deficit would be 33 percent of income and would increase to 75 percent by 2045; and (2) if a more optimistic economic growth scenario could be assumed, the respective deficits would be 27 percent and 58 percent. As a percentage of GDP the deficit in 2045 would be from 4.5–5.8 percent (BPS 1991b, 1991c). The crisis was considered to be of enormous magnitude and irreversible unless a reform was rapidly enacted. The government selected the third alternative (i.e., the mixed model) and developed a first draft in early 1992 that was discussed with leaders of political parties, unions, and employers' associations. The draft was revised and submitted to the congress in April 1991. The main aspects of the draft are summarized below (República 1992).

The mixed system is made up of three levels: (1) a reformed public contributory scheme, administered by the BPS and based on a pay-as-you-go method, with the addition of individual accounts on which the basic pension is based; (2) a noncontributory public assistánce pension paid directly by the state; and (3) supplementary pensions of a voluntary nature, based on capitalization and with different forms and administration.

The first-level, public contributory basic pension scheme administered by the BPS retained some features of the past but introduced several important reforms. Ages of retirement were maintained at 60/55 for males and females, but instead of 30 years of work a minimum of 10 years of work *and contributions* were required. Payroll contributions were not changed. A system of individual accounts would be introduced and become the essential base for determining all future pensions: contributions would be deposited in the account, which would accrue a 3.5 percent annual interest. The value of the deposits would be calculated in pension units (PUs) that are adjusted monthly according to the average salary index. The old-age pension was to be calculated as 60 percent of the average monthly deposit (in PUs) plus 0.5 percent for every year of contributions above 30 years, with a maximum of 65 percent (in PUs the maximum would gradually increase from 140 to 500 in the eleventh year after the system begins to operate). The minimum pension would be equal to the minimum national salary, 33 percent higher than the public assistance pension. A new "progressive" pension allowed retirement at the statutory age with 50 percent of the fund and full retirement later with the remaining 50 percent plus additional contributions and accrued interest. The pension amount therefore would basically depend on three variables: contributions paid over the working life of the insured, salary stability, and age of retirement. More contributions, greater salary stability, and a higher age would result in a higher pension, and vice versa. The scheme would also pay disability and survivors pensions.

The second-level noncontributory assistance pension was to be paid by the state out of general revenue. Eligible would be those 70 years and older or totally disabled who are not covered by the BPS, are without resources, and pass a means test.

The third level is a supplementary pension. Societies that administer supplementary pension funds (SAFCPs) were authorized by a 1984 law and regulated in 1989. The SAFCPs have been the subject of debate in Uruguay. Those in favor argue that the social security crisis is structural and will not be solved; hence, the SAFCP can provide an alternative means of protection. Those opposed believe that the state should be the only provider of social security and that private funds will go against the principle of solidarity. In 1986 the BPS acknowledged that SAFCPs can be established and managed independently. Actually there were 10 of those funds in operation prior to the enactment of such norms, e.g., for employees of state and private banks, telecommunications, ports, and so forth. Four types of SAFCPs can be created: (1) nonprofit funds organized by unions as well as professional and trade associations approved by the BPS; (2) funds established within BPS; (3) funds organized by the state insurance bank, which has a national monopoly on insurance; and (4) funds set by employers when they are the only contributors (these are considered deferred salary payments and are not subject to SAFCP regulations). Funds can be "closed" (available only for those in the same enterprise, economic branch, trade, or occupation) or "open" (accessible to all those registered in the BPS). The schemes could be of defined benefits and/or defined contributions. Contributions to the funds can be made by the insured only or by both the insured and employers; the latter are banned from transferring their contributions to prices. The capitalization system can be collective (for the group insured and covering a period of 20 years or more) or individual; a pay-as-you-go method is available but not for pension schemes. Administrative expenditures can be no higher than 8 percent of the fund's annual revenue. Investment should go mostly to public securities and deposits in state banks; in addition, up to 25 percent can go to real estate and up to 20 percent to personal loans, with strict regulations. In 1990 there were about 24 funds with 30,000 affiliates, only 4 percent of the number of contributors to the BPS. There is a high proportion of elderly insured in the funds; hence, their financial viability is still to be tested (MTSS 1989; Casares 1990; BPS 1979–1991; Lacurcia 1990).

The legal draft was submitted to congress but, despite the apparent consensus built, was rejected in May 1992. In November a new law introduced some changes to the system: (1) the salary base to calculate general old-age retirement is the average of the last six years of wages; (2) the salary replacement ratio is 55 percent to 75 percent but will gradually go up to 80 percent (the ceiling for advanced-age retirement is 65 percent of the salary base); (3) a pension ceiling is established, which gradually increases to 15 times the minimum monthly wage; and (4) an individual account (the only element taken from the legal draft) will become the base on which to estimate future pensions (Ley 16,320).

4

The Future Role of Social Security in Alleviating the Social Costs of Adjustment and Restructuring

Redefining the Roles of the Principal Actors

The State

The crisis of the 1980s and the probable continuation of adjustment and restructuring policies in the 1990s dictate that some changes be made in the role of the state in social security. In this section I review general socioeconomic policies as well as specific social security measures.

General policies. Adequate socioeconomic policies of a general nature would provide a sounder financial base for social security and facilitate its needed reforms. Successful policies to reduce the external debt, convert the net capital outflow into a net inflow, generate higher rates of economic growth and productive employment, increase real wages, and reduce inflation to reasonable levels would help to raise social security population coverage and revenue, provide better opportunities for investment of pension funds, make real positive investment yields more feasible, reduce incentives for evasion and late payments, cut unemployment compensation and public assistance benefits, and attain financial and actuarial equilibrium. But it should be recalled that social security confronted serious financial difficulties in various Latin American countries prior to the crisis of the 1980s. In addition, the prospects for a vigorous recuperation of the region in the 1990s (at least to the levels of the 1960s and 1970s) appear to be slim, but even if such a recuperation materializes, it would not solve some crucial social security problems.

Instead of passively waiting for a miraculous economic recuperation, social security should actively seek to alleviate the social costs of adjustment and restructuring, particularly among the most affected vulnerable groups. (The need to protect the poor of course predated the process of adjustment/restructuring, but the process has had a worse impact on the poor than on other groups.) Social security action, however, should be taken

169

cautiously to avoid hampering the process of recovery. I have noted that in some LAC countries compensatory measures (e.g., emergency employment programs, continuation of health-care coverage to the unemployed insured, expansion of coverage to lower-income groups, provision of public assistance health care and pensions for indigents) have ameliorated the adverse effects of readjustment/restructuring. In other countries a stabilizing social pact has been signed by business and labor to accomplish a fairer distribution of both the costs of the crisis and the potential gains of a future recovery. These positive approaches (rather than those of authoritarian regimes, which have placed the burden of the costs on labor and the poor) are more likely to continue with the current democratization trend in LAC. Finally, social security policies should be integrated with state actions to combat the crisis and relieve its hardships (e.g., antipoverty programs).

Social security policies. The state should continue to be in charge of social security guidance, policy regulation, coordination, and supervision. The following subsections recommend government action in the areas of organization, financing, benefits, and public education. Proposed measures to expand personal and contingency coverage are discussed thereafter.

• Organizational Measures. The central government of each country should plan social security more effectively than in the past, with increased participation of those involved in the system, in order to program social security reform, achieve functional integration among various social agencies, set the proper priorities for the allocation of scarce resources, expand population coverage, and determine which groups should be targeted for aid.

Integration of or a high level of coordination between social insurances and the services of the ministry of health—a goal long debated but rarely implemented—should be a key part of that plan. The plan must set a timetable for concrete targets for action—for instance, functional and progressive integration of resources and services in specific geographical areas, the establishment of joint basic units for the delivery of health care at the primary level, and designs for integrated hospitals. The successful experiences of integrating under social insurances programs (as in Costa Rica) and under ministries of health (as in the NLC, Cuba) should be models to study and follow. As part of integration a better balance in the allocation of resources between preventive and curative services must be sought. Decentralization in the organization, financing, and delivery of health services, as well as community participation, are highly recommended but only with the goal of improving such services, not as an excuse to reduce central government expenditures.

The state must also push for the integration of or coordination between social insurance and public assistance services. The experiences of a few countries that have successively accomplished that task under the social insurance institute (e.g., the Bahamas, Barbados, Costa Rica, Uruguay) have been positive: the two schemes, working together, have facilitated virtual universal population coverage, induced a compensatory antirecession effect (although coverage under the insurance component temporarily declined, it increased in the assistance component), and generated a progressive impact on distribution. But the analysis in Chapter 2 showed that it is important to follow some important rules: the two funds should be separate (instead of pooling their resources), the minimum insurance pension should be considerably higher than the assistance pension (although in principle there should not be discrimination for medical benefits), means tests must be effectively administered and tight control exercised to avoid free riders, and the state should honor its financial obligations to the assistance program fully and punctually. The positive experience of another country (Jamaica) that separated public assistance from social insurance—but put the two under the same ministry—ratifies both the positive effects of integration and the need to follow the listed rules.

The state should take the initiative in eliminating the inefficient, unfair, and costly multiplicity of social security institutions with different entitlement conditions, contributions, and benefits; and it must strictly prohibit the future creation of separate independent programs. Since the 1960s there have been several successful processes of unification and standardization in LAC, but severe cases of fragmentation persist (e.g., in Colombia). In the same vein the government should merge and simplify prolific social security legislation that has become too complex, contradictory, and difficult to understand and apply, and it should also disseminate clear information on rights and duties. In order to provide a solid basis for evaluation, policy formulation, and actuarial review the state should request that the social security institute (or the corresponding agency) gather data and develop statistical series on the covered and noncovered population (disaggregated by pertinent groups), evasion and payment delays, the state debt, real investment yields, real value of pensions, number of employees and their salaries, etc. A set of priorities must be established to select, gather, and publish data based on the institution's most urgent needs, as well as to provide clear differentiation in the data for evaluation and analysis. There should be better coordination among departments, financial statistics must be integrated, budgets must be developed in accordance with function, a clear relationship should be established between revenue and expenditure in each program, accounting techniques should be modernized, and bidding procedures should be made agile and flexible according to the nature of goods and services considered. State regulation of the administrative expenditures of social security institutions and the auditing of their expenses are also recommended to curtail excesses and trim costs.

Finally, the state should provide a favorable environment, with proper regulations and guarantees, for the creation and operation of private non-profit or for-profit providers (for health care, pensions, employment injury insurance) in order to have them fill gaps and perform functions that social security is unable to accomplish. In countries where social security covers a small fraction of the population and cannot extend coverage, the government should help intermediate bodies, NGOs, and self-help organizations tackle that task. In addition, the state should encourage insurance companies and HMOs to draw up low-cost policies and health packages affordable to uninsured low-income groups.

• Financial Measures. The state cannot and should not continue to subsidize large social security deficits during a crisis or even in a potential recovery, particularly in countries where only a minority of the population is insured. In pioneer countries, where coverage is universal, the state subsidies are so huge that they obviously cannot continue in the long run (e.g., in Argentina and Uruguay such subsidies equal one-fourth to one-third of total expenditures in spite of a 50 percent payroll tax). Furthermore, the subsidies often finance privileged pensions for relatively high- or middle-income groups whose contributions are nil or insufficient. A shift of the state subsidies toward more vulnerable groups (low-income informal and rural workers) or other types of programs (public assistance, primary health care) would not only be fairer but also help those most affected by the crisis and improve distribution as well.

The state should negotiate its past debt with the social security institution, set future government contributions as a third party at a reasonable level, and earmark these contributions for the expansion of coverage to lower-income groups or public assistance programs. A closer collaboration between fiscal agencies and social security (now in process in various LAC countries) can lead to the development of a single ID card for all tax purposes and the cross-checking of employment contributions with tax records. Other government measures to reduce evasion and late payments have been tried: conditioning employers' abilities to obtain import permits and participate in public bidding to their compliance, and requiring by law that budget approval of state agencies and autonomous institutions be conditioned to proof that they are up to date in their payments to social security.

State regulation of investment of pension funds should be made more flexible (but still providing minimum guarantees) to diversify the portfolio and thus move it away from government securities (unless they pay high real yields) and toward more profitable investment including commercial bank fixed deposits and enterprise shares and bonds. Classifying public and private shares by risk and setting adequate ceilings should ensure a minimum level of safety in that type of investment. Direct state interference in or control over social security investment should be eliminated. Finally, interest and other investment returns should be indexed to inflation.

• Benefit Measures. Legislation should be enacted to prevent the executive and the legislature from liberalizing entitlement conditions and expanding benefits without an actuarial assessment of their costs and the required implementation of adequate revenue sources.

The state should eliminate costly privileged benefits granted to civil servants and the armed forces, such as seniority pensions (as in Brazil, Uruguay) or lower ages for retirement (as in Colombia, Costa Rica, Uruguay). Entitlement conditions and contributions of those groups should be standardized with those of the general system, and state subsidies should be eliminated (except for government contributions as an employer). If such privileged conditions, contributions, benefits, and subsidies are meant as a substitute for inadequate civil servant salaries, then the salaries should be set at the proper level. These changes would help countries achieve much greater transparency and would reduce costs.

Low retirement ages in the general system should be properly adjusted according to life expectancy; if that is not politically feasible, early retirement should be discouraged by a drastic reduction in the percentage of salary replacement and/or an increase in the number of weeks of contribution required (as has recently been done in Costa Rica). Governments that currently intend to reduce the age of retirement in spite of significant increases in life expectancy (as in Jamaica) should seriously consider the damaging consequences that a similar measure has brought to other countries and the subsequent difficulties that these countries have confronted (as in Costa Rica and Uruguay).

Finally, adjustment of pensions to the cost of living should be standardized for the entire system and set at levels commensurate with the country's economic capacity, thus avoiding costly mistakes such as those made by Argentina and Uruguay.

• Public Education. Many of the corrective measures listed above will be difficult to implement if they are not preceded by a public campaign to educate the public, political leaders, and the social security bureaucracy on the unavoidable need for reform. The insured should be shown how little they actually pay for the benefits they receive and that many generous entitlement conditions and benefits simply cannot be financed. Younger generations should be alerted to the heavy burden they will bear if the system is not reformed. The noncovered population should be mobilized in support of the reform and the needed extension of personal coverage. Politicians should learn about the damaging effects of irresponsible behavior and also realize that the uninsured majority may carry more votes than the insured minority. The central government must take the initiative in this important area.

Intermediate Bodies: Cooperatives and Mutual Aid Societies

Cooperatives, mutual aid societies, unions, self-help organizations, and the like can play a fundamental role in LAC countries where social security covers only a minority of the population and the possibility of expanding protection is low. In those countries where a majority of the population is protected such intermediate organizations can play a subsidiary role: filling gaps, supplementing benefits, fostering efficiency, and improving the quality of services. The conventional definition of social security should be broadened to include intermediate organizations. Several examples of their actual performance or potential as providers follow.

Associations of self-employed have signed agreements with social security institutions in several countries (e.g., Costa Rica, Mexico) to incorporate their members: the association encourages affiliation, collects contributions, helps process benefits, and in some cases pays a contribution itself and/or guarantees the members' required payments. These types of agreements should be facilitated and extended to other groups of informal workers.

In some LAC countries intermediate organizations provide funeral, health-care, and life insurance services either directly or through contracts with private providers such as clinics and insurance companies. In Jamaica and Peru informal workers have developed their own "informal" means of mutual protection through rudimentary common emergency funds that are granted to members on a rotation basis in case of accident, grave disease, or death.

In Peru 250,000 inhabitants of Villa El Salvador (mostly low-income informal workers), a squatter village near Lima, organized a self-government system that developed and implemented an integrated health plan. It pulled together the available meager public health services as well as aid from international agencies. The program has immunized two-thirds of the children below five years, provided care for the majority of pregnant women, and significantly reduced the incidence of common diseases such as acute diarrhea. This is a successful model for similar communities in LAC.

Cooperatives perform such important functions in LAC as providing credit, performing production marketing, and transporting and selling consumer goods. However, they have so far played a minor role in the provision of social security services. They should be stimulated and aided by the government, NGOs, and international organizations to perform some social security functions.

Mutual aid societies flourished in the nineteenth century and early twentieth century before the introduction of compulsory social insurance but declined thereafter. However, in Europe many societies survived, and there is currently a trend (in Belgium, France, Germany) toward coordinating mutual aid societies with social security institutions to facilitate decentralization and improve services. In African and Asian countries, where social security has recently been introduced and personal coverage is low, mutual aid societies currently perform important functions, particularly in basic protection for agricultural workers, artisans, and the self-employed. In LAC (particularly in the Southern Cone and Cuba) mutual aid societies played an early key role in the provision of health services for immigrants and their families but later on declined or disappeared in some countries as the role of the state increased. However, in Argentina there are 3,700 of these societies in operation, with a membership of five million people; they offer pensions, health care, and other social services. With the decline in the role of the state as a result of restructuring, mutual aid societies should be revived or strengthened either as surrogate bodies of social security to reach certain groups of the population or as independent providers.

Many of these intermediate organizations, however, lack resources, leadership, and proper skills and have other priorities. In general they are too weak to set up a sustainable social network for their own members, much less to extend their scope to outsiders. Therefore to properly perform social security functions, they need help (from the government, international organizations, NGOs) in the form of guidance, training, and credit. Finally, cooperatives and self-management organizations have signed agreements with social security institutions (e.g., in Costa Rica, Colombia) to manage clinics that care for the insured. Reportedly they have reduced costs and improved the quality of services (Vázquez and Moles 1990; Schmidt 1991; Utrero 1991; Mesa-Lago 1992c).

The Private Sector

There is a trend in LAC for increasing participation of the private sector in social security functions to varying degrees, but this sector still covers only a minority of the population. Although there is an apparent wave of social security privatization in Latin America, the fact is that by the end of 1992 only two countries—Chile and Peru—had enacted a law creating a substitutive private pension scheme. Peru's law, however, was only passed in July 1992 and was modified thereafter, so only Chile has had significant experience (about a dozen years) with this type of reform. The proposal to privatize the pension system in Colombia was withdrawn because of strong criticism and is now under review. Two legal drafts under consideration in Argentina and Uruguay follow a mixed approach. Supplementary pension schemes currently exist in Ecuador, Guatemala, Mexico, and Uruguay, but in two countries they are voluntary and in two are exclusively administered either by the social security institute or by public or nonprofit organizations. Privatization of health care is even less important, as shown by the fact that the leading country, Chile, has only one-fourth of its population insured in private HMOs. In a few other countries there has been either marginal privatization (of nonmedical services as in Jamaica) or collaboration between a public scheme and the private sector (as in Costa Rica and Colombia). Several countries are studying reforms, but it is still too early to know what their style will be. The overwhelming majority of LAC therefore retains a public pension scheme, although a reformed one in some countries. But there is talk that toward the end of the century a wave of privatization may become a major threat to social security. Some countries see the Chilean model as a panacea, but they lack sufficient knowledge of its feasibility and implications for their own societies.

Is the Chilean model replicable in LAC? Political, economic, and social factors that differ from those of Chile can make the adoption of its privatization model much more difficult in other countries. The drastic Chilean reform was made feasible by an authoritarian government that banned political parties and controlled unions and the news media. Under such conditions any opposition to the reform either was eliminated or was very weak. Conversely, in the 1980s and the beginning of the 1990s there was a trend toward democracy in Latin America. Even with authoritarian regimes in power in Argentina, Brazil, and Uruguay (though not as radical and repressive as Chile's) full-fledged reforms were not possible. In an international seminar held in Santiago in October 1992 I questioned José Piñera, author of the Chilean reform, about whether such different political conditions made the Chilean model unsuitable for other countries. He answered by saying that it was as difficult to convince a group of congressmen as a group of generals. However, he did not actually have any experience with congressional representatives and basically had to convince only one general. It is significant that the only other country that has so far passed a substitutive private pension scheme, Peru, did so after a coup d'état and under suspension of constitutional rule. The first attempt of Colombia's president to pass a similar reform failed because of strong opposition from congress, political parties, other government agencies, and experts who were all freely able to voice their criticisms. Even moderate mixed-scheme reforms proposed in Argentina and Uruguay, preceded by careful study and public discussion (at least in Uruguay), were voted down by congress, and important modifications had to be introduced. Finally, the constitutions of several countries (e.g., Colombia, Peru) mandate the state's predominant role in social security and/or the principles of solidarity and universality, all of which conflict with a substitutive private scheme.

Different socioeconomic conditions also come into play. In 1980 Chile was experiencing a four-year economic boom that provided a comfortable base for the reform; however, the severe crisis of 1982 forced direct government intervention to save the reform from bankruptcy. Economies such as those of Peru are currently facing a severe crisis, and others are just emerging from the terrible recession of the 1980s. Capital markets in countries such as Colombia and Uruguay are considerably less developed than that of Chile at the time of the reform and so are less capable of properly absorbing a sudden, huge flow of funds.

Last but not least, social security conditions in many Latin American countries are less propitious than in Chile. In less developed countries such as Bolivia, Colombia, Ecuador, Peru, and most of those in Central America and the Latin Caribbean, less than one-fourth of the population is covered by social security; furthermore, poverty levels, the informal sector, self-employment, and the marginal peasant sector are much more significant than was the case in Chile. If public schemes have been unable to expand population coverage to a significant extent under a Bismarckian model, a private scheme will certainly be an insurmountable barrier to coverage because the majority of the population (nonformal, nonsalaried, rural) will not have access to the private scheme. Scarce public funds will be committed to consolidating the social security system of a minority at the expense of such desperately needed programs for the majority as public assistance, primary health care, and so forth. In the most developed countries of the region such pioneers as Argentina and Uruguay currently face a pension disequilibrium much worse than Chile's in 1980, so the cost of the reform would be higher. Demographic and other factors are similarly more limiting; for instance, the ratio of contributors to pensioners was 2 to 1 in Chile but is 1 to 1 in Uruguay. Even less developed countries such as Colombia suffer a worse disequilibrium (particularly in the civil service sector) than was the case in Chile (Mesa-Lago 1993).

Lessons learned from the Chilean experience. The Chilean pension reform has brought such important advantages as (1) a reduction of insured's payroll contributions; (2) higher benefits (so far) and easier and faster granting of pensions; (3) eradication of privileged programs (except for the armed forces); (4) recognition of previous contributions to the old scheme; (5) state guarantees to the insured; (6) very high investment yields; and (7) eventual disappearance of the costly old scheme. But contrary to the founders' expectations there are obvious disadvantages and unanswered questions concerning the reform: (1) about half of those registered do not contribute to the private scheme, and overall effective population coverage has declined; (2) coverage of nonformal groups of the labor force is minimal; e.g., 42 percent of employees in microenterprises, 29 percent of the self-employed, and 8 percent of unpaid family workers (these groups make up the majority of the labor force in many Latin American countries); (3) the number of AFPs has increased very little in 12 years, and the high concentration of coverage by the three major AFPs has grown from 60 percent to 68 percent; furthermore, selection of an AFP by the insured is more a result of marketing and publicity than of higher yields and lower commissions, implying that the insured do not have adequate knowledge to make decisions and that the system is not as competitive as was originally hoped; (4) it is not clear whether administrative costs in the private scheme are higher or lower than in the old system; (5) there are contradictory projections of future salary-replacement rates that range from a high of 80–86 percent for males (but only 53–56 percent for females) down to 30–40 percent, depending on whether optimistic or pessimistic assumptions are used for the calculations; (6) there are doubts about the ability of the domestic capital market to absorb the growing funds (currently equal to about 35 percent of GDP); high enterprise-share yields appear artificially inflated by the insufficient number of those that qualify in the stock market; the opening to investment in foreign instruments could be an indication of poor availability of domestic investment opportunities; and there is no evidence that the system has had any beneficial impact on national savings; (7) an overall actuarial balance for the whole system is lacking, and projections of future costs vary widely as a result of incomplete data. Supporters of the reform pinpoint its positive effects, whereas critics stress the negative outcomes. Countries that are considering a reform should be aware of both types of results.

Several lessons can be learned from the Chilean experience. One is that the cost of the transition must be very carefully evaluated. Maintenance of part of the old entitlement, recognition bonds, and minimum pensions are all humane elements of a reform but are extremely costly; hence, they must be balanced with an accurate assessment of the future burden on society and alternative costs to other public programs for lower-income groups. Another lesson is that the presence of a market and private administrators does not necessarily ensure competition, control of evasion and payment delays, and other efficiency improvements. Huge collective savings have not led to a corresponding expansion of the domestic capital market, either. Finally, the exclusion of part of the population (e.g., the armed forces) from the reform and the maintenance of its privileged entitlement conditions and benefits can be forced for political reasons, but eventually such obvious inequality must be eradicated.

The analysis in this text of two enacted laws (in 1991 and 1992 in Peru), three legal drafts (in Argentina, Colombia, and Uruguay in 1992) and several proposals (in Colombia in 1991) concerning pension reform shows that these countries have learned some of the above lessons and have attempted to correct several disadvantages of the Chilean model. The legal proposals of Argentina and Uruguay (as well as the 1991 law in Peru and the Colombian proposals) discarded the substitutive private scheme and followed mixed schemes. To reduce costs of the reform, some proposals divide the population of insured in the old scheme by age, restricting the right to move to the new scheme to those who are below a certain age (e.g., 55/50 or 50/45 in Colombia and 45 in an early legal draft in Argentina). In Peru a ceiling is placed on the value of the recognition bond, no interest is accrued to it, and no minimum pension is guaranteed. Tougher entitlement conditions have been established; for instance, five more years of age for women to retire and ten more years of contribution for both sexes in Argentina and Colombia (this is particularly important to Colombia, where the life expectancy is shorter than in Chile). To increase revenue and infuse some solidarity into the system, the employers' contribution has not been eliminated in Colombia (where the contribution has actually increased substantially), Argentina, and Uruguay (where the employers' contribution goes in solidarity to the old scheme); Peru maintained such contributions in its 1991 law but eliminated them in the 1992 law. The insured's contribution has not been reduced as in Chile but rather maintained unchanged (in Argentina) or increased (in Colombia's and Peru's 1992 laws).

The administration of private pension schemes is entrusted not only to AFPs (*sociedades anónimas*) but also to savings associations and public financing agencies (in Colombia) and to banks, cooperatives, unions, and employers or professional associations (in Argentina). The supplementary pension scheme of Uruguay is voluntary and is exclusively administered by the social security institutes or by nonprofit private organizations. In Argentina a unified state collection solves the problem of having multiple forms to be sent by the employer to different social security institutions. Changes from one AFP to another are legally limited to two annually (in Argentina and Colombia), and no publicity is allowed until the AFP is approved; in Argentina the state sets norms and supervises all publicity. Chile's early bad experience with an excessive concentration of AFP investment in state and debt instruments—which led to eventual portfolio diversification—appears to have been ignored by Argentina (where 100 percent of investment can go to public debt instruments) but taken into account by Colombia (which fixed a ceiling of 45 percent for such instruments, the same as currently in Chile).

The barriers to extending coverage are not being confronted in Peru, but in Colombia criticism about such a flaw was one of the reasons the government withdrew a legal draft (new modifications attempt to correct this problem). Finally, exclusion of the armed forces from the reform seems to be universal (in Argentina, Colombia, Peru, Uruguay), an indication of the limits of democratization in all those countries; furthermore, privileged programs for civil servants were left untouched in Colombia's first legal draft.

The urgent need for profound social security reform in most of Latin America cannot be denied, even by those apologists who refused to see the dangerous signs of the crisis that began unfolding a decade ago. Democratization in the region is a welcome trend that has allowed ample debate concerning the proposed reforms by many segments of society. But in some countries the new political openness has become an obstacle in the path of reform or has led to a perpetual watering down of proposals that were studied and debated for years. Paradoxically, the Chilean democratization process has transformed a model of reform that was looked down upon into one that is politically correct or at least palatable in Latin America. Nevertheless, there is a danger in advocating the Chilean approach as the only valid one for the region. The executives, political parties, congress, unions, employers' associations, and other groups must put aside their own narrow interests and responsibly reach a consensus to adapt and implement the type of social security reform best suited to national peculiarities and needs (Mesa-Lago 1993).

Extending Social Security Coverage
Within the Process of Adjustment/Restructuring

Personal Coverage: Informal and Rural Sectors

The two largest noninsured sectors in LAC are informal and rural workers; the former expanded in the 1980s (as a result of the process of urbanization and the economic crisis), whereas the latter proportionally shrank. Unless there is a very vigorous economic recovery in the 1990s the informal sector will continue its expansion and will present the main challenge for personal coverage.

Informal sector. Legally the informal sector is largely excluded from social security coverage in LAC: coverage does not extend to half of the self-employed, domestic servants, and temporary or casual workers and virtually 100 percent of unpaid family workers. Salaried employees in microenterprises are legally covered in most countries, but enforcement is extremely poor—as is also the case with nonsalaried categories of informal workers—because of difficulties in detection, registration, and collection. Mandatory legal coverage—compared with voluntary coverage—does not result in any significant increase in actual protection, except among domestic servants.

The experiences of several LAC countries indicate that the actual degree of protection of the informal group is positively related to the smallness of the informal sector, the commitment of the political leadership, a financially strong social security institution, the existence of a supplementary pension program for the indigents, and the integration or extensive coordination of health-care institutions. Specific measures to increase coverage of the informal sector are as follows: (1) set a reasonable contribution to account for the very low income of this group (the self-employed cannot pay the equivalent of the employer's contribution in addition to their own); (2) subsidize the costs of protection for low-income informal workers with state transfers, or provide public assistance pensions and free health care for the informal indigent population (as in Costa Rica, Jamaica, and Uruguay); (3) explore alternative sources of financing to cover this group such as the VAT, a lottery, gasoline/tobacco taxes, a payroll contribution earmarked for extending personal coverage, etc.; (4) simplify the process of registration and payment for microenterprises, and provide other stimuli for their affiliation; (5) promote associations of informal workers, mobilize them in the quest for coverage, and later utilize them as intermediaries to affiliate workers and collect contributions; and (6) identify other effective mechanisms to exercise those functions, such as commissions for registering/collecting agencies.

In those countries where the social security institute is financially weak and/or covers a small proportion of the population it is advisable to support other institutions (e.g., the ministry of health) or organizations (e.g., mutual aid societies, cooperatives, self-help associations, *igualas*) that are better able to extend coverage to informal workers.

Rural sector. Legal coverage of the rural sector is at least as low as that of the informal sector: permanent rural salaried workers are excluded from coverage in two-fifths of LAC countries. Furthermore, most of the agricultural labor force is either self-employed, temporary, or seasonal and has lower legal coverage than the informal labor force. Law enforcement is also weak. The rural sector is more difficult to incorporate than the informal one for the following reasons: it suffers from a higher incidence of poverty (and so has lower income, less literacy, and reduced access to basic social services, as well as higher morbidity and infant mortality rates and worse nutrition and housing); it is more dispersed and isolated geographically and culturally; and it has a lower degree of mobilization and a lesser capacity to exercise pressure to obtain coverage. Protection of this sector is therefore more difficult to finance, and its costs are higher, e.g., for the provision of health care. General factors that facilitate an extension of personal coverage to this sector are similar to those discussed for the informal sector.

Three different models in LAC have been successful in achieving health-care coverage for the rural sector, either universally or to a significant degree: (1) integrated national health systems that provide equal services for the entire population and are financed by the state (though some of them charge user fees to those who can afford to pay); (2) social insurance sickness/maternity schemes that do not discriminate between the insured and the noninsured indigent, with state financing for the latter, combined with a PHC program offered by the ministry of health (as in Costa Rica); and (3) dual social insurance systems that grant full benefits for the insured and PHC for the dispersed poor rural population, coordinated with ministry of health services at a higher level (as in Brazil, Mexico, and to a lesser extent Ecuador). The third model has been financed through different means: direct state subsidies, transfers from the urban sector (via a percentage of the payroll contribution), modest contributions from those covered (in cash or communal work), and taxes on agricultural production or consumption.

Significant expansion of pension coverage to the rural population has been achieved in a few countries that have relatively developed agricultural sectors and unions through a combination of contributory schemes and public assistance pensions for the rural indigent population (as in Chile, Costa Rica, Uruguay, and various NLC countries). The state usually finances the public assistance scheme, although in some NLC countries the public assistance scheme receives transfers from the contributory scheme.

A general strategy for expanding personal coverage. The above-described programs for expanding coverage to the informal and rural sectors are generally found in the most economically developed countries of the pioneer group. Some of those programs have been negatively affected by the economic crisis and the adjustment/restructuring policies. Mexico, a country in the upper level of the intermediate group, was able to develop successfully its innovative solidarity program for the rural sector with the aid of the phenomenal oil boom of the 1970s; but its progress was halted by the crisis of the 1980s, and a similar program for the informal sector is not financially feasible now. These approaches to extending coverage (even the nonconventional ones that break away from the traditional Bismarckian model) are very difficult to replicate in the least developed countries of the Latin American latecomer group, as well as in the lower level of the intermediate group. In these countries personal social security coverage reaches less than one-fourth of the labor force (in other words, the formal sector), though the majority of the labor force is in the informal and rural sectors.

The consolidation of universal protection in the pioneer group, the continuing expansion of coverage in a few countries of the intermediate group, and the initiation of expanding coverage in the rest of the intermediate group and in the Latin American latecomer group all require a social security reform to be successful. The maintenance of privileged systems, the liberal entitlement conditions and generous benefits in the general system, and the high administrative expenditures are obstacles to the expansion of population coverage. Obviously extension of coverage under the current structure would be economically impossible in the least developed countries that have low personal coverage, particularly because of the current economic situation. But such largesse also jeopardizes the financial stability of social security in the most developed countries that have already achieved universal coverage. The measures needed to cut expenditures and increase revenue, as discussed in this study, will be summarized later in this chapter. Suffice it to say herein that state contributions as a third party must be reserved for financing an extension of coverage to the most vulnerable groups.

But even if the reform is successfully implemented many countries may not be financially able to maintain or expand coverage. In these extreme cases alternative measures should be considered: (1) providing basic benefits only; (2) setting national priorities, starting with health-care benefits for the entire population and moving to uniform pensions when economic conditions allow it; and (3) increasing the role of intermediate organizations and the private sector. The cost of extending coverage should be calculated on the basis of various combinations of basic benefits and groups to be covered; priorities should be established with respect to the most urgent needs, and higher priority should be given to those programs that would have the greatest impact on improving living conditions (in relation to cost) and on helping the most vulnerable groups (Mesa-Lago 1989a, 1990, 1991b, 1991c, 1992c).

Contingencies: Unemployment

Chapter 2 showed the serious difficulties that exist in expanding unemployment insurance in most LAC countries. Only in those that are the most developed and are enjoying an economic recuperation would such a program be financially feasible. Less developed LAC countries that are currently considering the introduction of unemployment insurance (e.g., Jamaica) should first study the experiences of the few more developed LAC countries that have this program in operation, as well as their own more urgent social security needs (such as the effective incorporation of the self-employed into the system, an increase in the meager benefits, etc.). In most LAC countries an unemployment assistance program to cover the bulk of the labor force (unemployed, underemployed, seasonal, informal) and pay uniform basic benefits would be more equitable than having unemployment insurance that covers only a small proportion of the labor force, but it would be impossible to finance. Therefore whatever resources are available to help the unemployed should be maximized in terms of their socioeconomic impact and coordinated with an antipoverty program to promote both employment generation and basic social protection for the most vulnerable groups.

The first priority should be the creation of productive employment in both the public and private sectors. Special public employment programs could rapidly create a high number of jobs at a relatively low cost and with a positive contribution to production or services (examples are found in Bolivia, Chile, Mexico). To achieve those results it is important to plan these programs carefully, provide a minimum of training and inputs to the participating workers, and assign the workers to areas of crucial need such as rural roads, irrigation, sanitation, and low-income housing.

Emergency social funds such as those created in Bolivia, Honduras, El Salvador, Chile, and Guatemala can provide a safety net and promote employment; this can be done through the mobilization of domestic and external resources to finance small, technically simple projects undertaken by NGOs, credit for microenterprises, rural infrastructure programs, and local expansion of primary health care and sanitation. Social funds should be promoters and intermediaries but should not undertake those projects directly (Mesa-Lago 1993b).

The state, NGOs, and external aid agencies should support the informal sector by eliminating or reducing existing legal barriers that make entry into the formal market very difficult and by providing credit tied to completion of a training program.

Facilities should be given to workers in bankrupt enterprises to reorganize them in cooperatives or to develop individual microenterprises. Private enterprises should be urged to hire more workers through subsidies or tax reductions or by promoting multiple work shifts to expand utilization of the installed capacity.

The current formal educational system should be reformed because those who now graduate at the elementary and secondary levels have few or no skills valuable to the labor market; hence, more emphasis and additional resources should be given to vocational education programs adapted to labor demand in urban and rural areas.

The current system of employment services and placement offices should be improved and more public funds devoted to it. Retraining programs should be developed or expanded, taking into account current labor needs and the characteristics of the unemployed, such as young, new entrants and civil servants and industrial workers dismissed as a result of the adjustment/restructuring process. Private firms that develop their own in-service training should be entitled to a deduction from the payroll tax. Labor mobility (either geographically or among trades) should be facilitated by a social security system that does not tie the workers to a specific occupation or place of employment. To facilitate mobility, aid could be provided for those in need to cover a portion of any moving expenses.

An expansion of social security coverage to unprotected segments of the labor force, in terms of primary health care and basic pensions (as discussed previously), should be given priority over an extension of unemployment insurance to a small segment of the labor force. The insured who become unemployed should be granted continuous protection in terms of sickness/maternity (already in force in at least three countries) and pensions. Policies recently introduced by industrialized Western countries to ameliorate unemployment, such as a reduction in the statutory age for early retirement, are inadequate for many Latin American countries where the age of retirement is already too low vis-à-vis life expectancy. In those countries where the unemployed are entitled to both severance payments and unemployment insurance, either the former should be eliminated (and a minimum benefit guaranteed in the latter) or both should be coordinated to avoid exceeding a ceiling.

In more developed LAC countries that have the capacity to introduce new unemployment insurance programs (and have achieved universal coverage concerning priority risks) it is advisable first to provide a basic uniform benefit and later on, when the program is consolidated, to link it to wages. In addition, benefits should be tied to the acceptance of retraining and any proper job offer.

Finally, a study should be conducted to evaluate the effects of unemployment programs based on savings that go to an individual account (and could be withdrawn in case of dismissal) versus conventional programs that replace part of the salary or pay a lump sum. Brazil would be a good case because it has both types of programs. (ILO 1986–1987; IDB 1987; García 1991; World Bank 1991).

Other Measures to Alleviate
the Impact of the Adjustment/Restructuring Process

Review of the Sources of Financing to Ensure Equilibrium

To ensure equilibrium it is necessary to raise revenue but also reduce expenditures. In fact, in some countries reducing expenditures should be given higher priority. An effort should be made to avoid increasing payroll taxes (except in those countries where they are quite low) unless there is no other option. Alternative sources of financing of a more neutral nature should be carefully considered.

Numerous policies to increase revenue have been discussed in this study. The first step is to improve detection of those required to contribute, registration, collection, auditing, execution of legal procedures against cheaters, and prosecution in order to reduce evasion and payment delays. Specific measures suggested are computerization of registration, contributions, individual accounts, and updated debtor lists; establishment of a single ID for all fiscal and social security payments; close collaboration between social security systems and tax authorities; fixing of interest and fines for noncompliance at a higher rate than inflation and commercial bank rates; conditioning of important enterprise activities (e.g., imports, bidding, contracts with public agencies) to proof of compliance; improvement of inspection, simplification of judicial procedures for trials, and effective prosecution of evaders and late payers (combined with wide publicity); and simplification of the procedures and requirements for microenterprises to become affiliated.

The state debt has been a major cause of disequilibrium in many countries, so the contribution of the state as a third party should be set at a level commensurate with the country's economic capacity, and diverse techniques should be used to ensure that the state contribution as an employer is included in the corresponding budgets and made effective. Payment of the state debt should be negotiated on the basis of bonds indexed to inflation, agreements to pay the debt with imported equipment, and other means to avoid debt devaluation. The social security institute should be obliged to release information periodically on the fulfillment of state obligations in order to mobilize public opinion on meeting such obligations.

In those countries that have partly funded programs it is crucial to improve efficiency through various steps: raising the skills of the staff in charge of investment, diversifying the portfolio by giving priority to high-yield and relatively safe instruments, indexing interest and yields to inflation, and periodically publishing data on investment policies and results. The principal source of revenue in most of LAC are the contributions of employers and the insured. In addition to enforcing compliance, the following actions are recommended to increase contribution revenue: gradually eliminate the wage ceilings for both entry into the system and payment; use the entire salary as the tax base; and eliminate contribution exemptions among civil servants, the armed forces, and employees of social security institutions.

Where the payroll contribution is relatively low it should be augmented if necessary. In those countries with a low population coverage preference should be given to increasing the insured's contribution (which averages less than one-fifth of social security revenue in LAC) to avoid the potentially negative effects of an increase in employers' contributions on employment or distribution. (Although there is no solid evidence, there are indications that in most of LAC there is no "backward" transfer of the employer's contribution to the worker.) In Chile a modest contribution from employers (who currently do not pay any) should be considered to help finance the deficit of the public pension scheme and the recognition bonds and minimum pensions in the private scheme (this action would also infuse some element of solidarity into the system). Where both the payroll contribution and level of personal coverage are already very high, an effort should be made to achieve equilibrium from the expenditure side. If such a policy does not work then alternative financing sources that are neutral in terms of employment effects should be considered.

The ideal alternative source of financing would be a progressive income tax because of its positive distributive effects and neutrality in terms of employment. However, such a tax faces problems in many LAC countries because of inefficient tax structures and the fact that a very substantial part of the labor force is nonsalaried and its income is difficult to assess. No country in LAC currently finances social security out of an income tax. Income tax collection should therefore be improved before it is used as an alternative revenue source.

The value-added tax (VAT) has various advantages: it neither discriminates between capital and labor nor creates incentives for the employer to report a smaller number of employees or lower salaries, it is relatively easy to collect, and it saves the cost of operating a bureaucracy to enforce compliance, particularly in countries with large informal and rural sectors. However, the VAT has regressive effects on distribution unless the poor are exempted, but implementing such exclusion complicates its administration. Two countries that have experimented with the VAT as an alternative source to the payroll tax are Argentina and Uruguay. The VAT faced serious difficulties in Argentina, which promptly returned to the payroll tax, but Uruguay continues to partly finance social security through a VAT. State sales taxes on nonessential or luxury goods (particularly those with adverse health effects such as alcohol and tobacco) have the advantages of both easy collection and positive distributive effects (Mesa-Lago 1985, 1989c, 1991b; Musgrove 1985; Wilson 1985).

There was considerable debate in the 1980s on the advantages and disadvantages of user fees. They discourage overuse of services and generate revenue that can in turn be invested in improving the quality of services, which rebounds in favor of the users. The fees are neutral concerning employment, and their effects on distribution can be avoided by exempting the poor or by grading the fees according to income, but these practices create serious administrative difficulties. An alternative is to offer services such as prophylaxis, sanitation, and PHC for free and to charge fees for hospital services based on their type, complexity, and location. A growing number of LAC countries have introduced user fees in the public health sector, but very few have done so in the social insurance sector. A recent study of user fees in the Dominican Republic's public health sector shows that in hospitals the fees filled crucial gaps created by shrinking funds for public health; however, because of an unfavorable administrative environment and the relatively low level of the fees, they were unable to improve the quality of services (although they prevented any further deterioration). Conversely, in the national laboratory the fees resulted in a significant increase in the quality of services for the following reasons: a proper administrative environment was provided; fees were high and generated half of the total revenue that was retained by the institution; and fee revenues were utilized to hire managerial personnel, train existing personnel, offer better labor incentives, and buy supplies and equipment. A major common problem was the ineffectiveness of the means test in identifying who could pay a full fee and who had to be exempted (La Forgia 1989). In Jamaica the 1990–1994 plan recommends an increase in user fees to somewhat close the gap with the real costs of services; since 1990, 75 percent of the fee revenue has been kept by the hospitals; and the poor are exempted through certification by public assistance authorities.

A solid comparative study is needed in LAC to evaluate the above alternative sources of revenue in terms of their actual potential to finance social security; relative ease of administration; and effects on employment, distribution, and other areas.

In pioneer states with very high contribution rates and large financial deficits (e.g., Argentina, Uruguay, Brazil) financial equilibrium must be restored mainly by drastically reducing expenditures. This action is also necessary in other LAC countries, but their largesse is usually more restrained than in the pioneers, and they have lower payroll contributions and in some cases even financial surpluses.

A number of measures to reduce benefit expenditures have been discussed in this text: (1) eliminate overly liberal entitlement conditions and excessively generous benefits (e.g., seniority pensions, early retirement at a low age compared with life expectancy, extravagant medical benefits); (2) if early retirement cannot be terminated because of political obstacles, discourage it by increasing the number of contributions required and reducing the percentage of salary replacement; (3) make the retirement ages for men and women equal; (4) relate pensions more closely to the insured's life earnings by increasing the number of years of work used to calculate the base salary; (5) establish a basic pension (uniform or with a reasonable minimum and maximum), and allow the operation of supplementary pension schemes with additional contributions; (6) adjust pensions on the basis of wages instead of the cost of living; (7) eliminate or decrease to a minimum the so-called social benefits provided in some countries (e.g., recreational, sport, and vacation facilities; shops that sell consumer goods at subsidized prices; low-rent housing), which invariably end in a deficit and deplete resources needed to pay the fundamental benefits or expand coverage; (8) reduce health-care expenses by improving efficiency (see next subsection); and (9) impede the addition of new benefits or the liberalizing of entitlement conditions if adequate funding is not provided.

A drastic cut in administrative expenditures is also unavoidable in most LAC countries. It would be unfair and politically unacceptable to impose sacrifices to most of the population while leaving the social security bureaucracy untouched. Unnecessary and incompetent employees should be dismissed, or, if that is politically unfeasible, the corresponding posts should be frozen and eventually eliminated when they are vacated by retirement or reassignment. Privileged fringe benefits should be terminated or significantly trimmed. Such measures are difficult and painful to implement in the midst of a crisis, but it should be recalled that the first priority of social security should be the welfare of the insured and the beneficiaries rather than that of the employees (Mesa-Lago 1991b, 1991c).

Policies of Containing Cost Increases in Health Care

There is a worldwide trend of growing health-care costs that the LAC cannot avoid. In the 1980s public health-care expenditures per capita declined in the region with very few exceptions (although this has not been established in the case of social insurance). Both domestic and international inflation have contributed to these rising health costs, for instance, through increases in physicians' salaries and prices of imported medical equipment and drugs. These trends are likely to continue in the 1990s.

The combination of growing health-care costs and stagnations in the percentage contributions for social insurance sickness/maternity schemes led to growing deficits in the latter programs. The most common short-term stopgap policy has been to borrow from the reserves of the pension schemes, particularly in those countries where such schemes were introduced late and so the number of pensioners is low and the reserves high. However, in the long run these loans cannot be amortized (interest is usually not paid, either), so they gradually decapitalize the pension reserves. Laws enacted in the 1980s in Colombia, Costa Rica, and Peru prohibited the continuation of such loans, although in Peru the practice continued by means of obscure accounting transfers. Some countries, such as Costa Rica, raised the level of contribution to their sickness/maternity schemes and generated temporary surpluses that were rapidly depleted at the beginning of the 1990s by increasing personnel salaries. A special effort is therefore needed to contain health-care costs.

The first step should be to eliminate or moderate liberal entitlement conditions and generous benefits: for instance, by reducing the percentage of salary replacement for sick leave (currently 90–100 percent in many countries), establishing a waiting period to avoid fake illnesses, and abolishing travel and treatment abroad.

The integration of or extensive coordination between the social security institute and the ministry of health in each country would reduce service duplication and save personnel. The growing cooperation between the WHO and the ILO (as well as the regional branches of both organizations) in an effort to coordinate their health services is laudable, but a stronger effort is needed to produce more concrete results.

A change in the philosophy of care—giving more emphasis to lower-cost primary health care rather than more expensive curative medicine—would reduce the incidence of disease and the costs of curative treatment. More resources should therefore be allocated to PHC, potable water supplies, excreta disposal systems, immunization, nutritional supplements, and health education. A better balance in the allocation of resources among the three traditional levels of care, with an increase in funding to the first level (particularly outpatient consultation), would lower the number (and corresponding cost) of patients seeking treatment at the more expensive higher levels. More extensive use of lower-paid paramedic personnel instead of higher-paid physicians would not only diminish personnel expenditures but also cut down the bargaining power of physicians. Targeting vulnerable groups such as pregnant women and children would lessen both infant mortality and costs. Allocating resources according to local morbidity and pathology profiles (e.g., to prevent and treat diseases of underdevelopment) would maximize the use of such funds.

Investment plans should give more emphasis to building rural health posts and clinics in marginal urban areas than to building large hospitals. Higher priority should be assigned to remodeling, re-equipping, and maintenance rather than to constructing new facilities.

Low hospital occupancy and long periods of stay are typical in LAC. The former is usually the result of excessive hospital capacity (including duplication by the two major health-care institutions), poor quality of services, and/or cultural barriers that impede access. Integration or coordination of health facilities would release funds that could be used to improve the quality of services and educate the population on the proper use of such services. The number of days of stay could be diminished by better organization and coordination between admission, test, surgical, and dismissal services, thereby making more hospital beds available. Such improvements would save resources and facilitate an expansion of personal coverage.

Domestic production of some drugs, wholesale buying and distribution of medical supplies and medicines, and the introduction of a basic list of generic drugs could generate savings. Modest fees could reduce overprescription and overconsumption of drugs. User fees, when properly administered, can reduce both the overuse of services and costs.

Decentralizing the health-care administration can reduce costs and improve services because both services and the collection of revenue are better when the services and administration are closer to the users and better adapted to their resources and needs. However, decentralization of the public health sector has often been used as an excuse to cut resources to health care. In addition, it has the potential to increase inequalities between the most and least developed regions; hence, some of the resources must remain centralized in order to help the least developed regions. The positive effects of decentralization should be studied before being adapted to social security health services.

Finally, I have discussed the experiences of some countries in using private services to reduce costs of health care and improve the quality of such services.

In closing, a word should be said about the role of international organizations in social security. It is obvious that the ILO will continue offering technical aid in this field, but the demand for its services will undoubtedly expand if the proposed reforms are endorsed and implemented. Other international organizations (such as the WHO), associations (ISSA and the Inter-American Permanent Committee on Social Security), and international and regional institutions (such as the World Bank, the Economic Commission for Latin America and the Caribbean, and the IDB) should therefore try to coordinate their efforts to tackle this important task properly. Loans and financial assistance by lenders should be conditioned to the implementation of the needed reforms, and a program of technical training and public education should be launched and supported by these institutions.

If the reforms are successfully undertaken, the social security systems in LAC will come out of the current crisis strengthened and better adapted to the needs and economic realities of their societies.

Notes

1. Contrary to the positive experience of Ecuador, a peasant social insurance program tried in Colombia in 1971 covered only 0.1 percent of the target population and was suspended in 1978. A new experimental model tested in 1989–1991 attempted to extend coverage in three rural municipalities, but in the first six months only 2 percent of the target population of 36,000 had registered. Draft legislation, never enforced, has been developed in Bolivia and Peru (ISSA 1991; Mesa-Lago 1992c).

2. The distinction between unemployment insurance and assistance is not always clear in LAC. Argentina, Barbados, Ecuador, and Venezuela have typical insurance (which is based on wage contributions and covers only the insured), but in the other three countries (in Brazil before 1987) the system is financed entirely by the state, although only the insured are eligible for benefits; however, in Brazil coverage is conditioned on the lack of other means.

3. The total contribution to the sickness/maternity program averages 9 percent in 14 Latin American countries, higher than the contributions in Australia, Austria, Canada, Ireland, and Luxembourg and similar to those of Belgium, Israel, and Sweden (US-SSA 1989).

4. In 13 out of 23 LAC countries the retirement age for women is 5 years lower than for men, although women live an average of 2–4 years longer than men.

5. This phenomenon is typical of lower-income groups covered by social insurance sickness/maternity schemes (e.g., in Costa Rica), but in those countries where such groups are protected by special, separate social insurance health services (e.g., peasants in Mexico) they are entitled to restricted benefits that are cheaper.

6. Chilean data combine both the old system (which suffers a hugh deficit covered by the state) and the new system (which generates a substantial surplus).

7. The recognition bond was created to compensate for the short periods of contribution to the private system by older affiliates who contributed sums to the public system. It is payable by the state in one lump sum at the time of retirement. The bond is based on the needed capital to pay a pension equal to 80 percent of insured earnings between June 1978 and June 1979, multiplied by the proportion of the insured's working life contributed to the old system, plus an annual interest of 4 percent accrued from the time of transfer, and all adjusted to the cost of living.

8. The 1 percent *encaje* has apparently not been used yet, and it reportedly limits the entry of new AFPs because of its proportionally heavier burden for new AFPs. It is not clear on what basis the 1 percent was chosen, and it has been sug-

193

gested that it is tied to the average yield of all AFPs in the entire system.

9. Uruguay uses the terms *jubilación común* for old-age retirement; *jubilación especial* for disability; and *pensiones* for survival pensions and also for public assistance old-age and disability pensions. In this text I use the general term *pension* for all those forms, qualifying it by the specific type of contingency.

Bibliography

Abel-Smith, Brian, and Andrew Creese. 1988. *Recurrent Costs in the Health Sector: Problems and Policy Options in Three Countries.* Geneva: WHO.

Abril Ojeda, Galo. 1991. "El Sistema Previsional Ecuatoriano: Los Fondos de Pensión como Fuente de Inversión." In Uthoff and Szalachman, eds., *Sistema de Pensiones,* 65–118.

"Anteproyecto de la Ley Sobre el Sistema Privado de Administración de Pensiones y su Reglamento." 1992. *El Peruano,* (July 16): 1–23.

Arellano, José Pablo. 1989. "La Seguridad Social en Chile en los Años 90." *Colección Estudios CIEPLAN,* no. 27 (December): 63–82.

Arrau, Patricio. 1991. "La Reforma Previsional Chilena y su Financiamiento Durante la Transición." *Colección Estudios CIEPLAN,* no. 32 (June): 5–44.

———. 1992. "El Nuevo Régimen Previsional Chileno." In FESCOL 1992a: 37–65.

Baeza, Sergio, and R. Manubens. 1988. *Sistema Privado de Pensiones en Chile.* Santiago: Centro de Estudios Públicos.

———. 1979–1991. "Normas de Seguridad Social." Montevideo: BPS.

———. 1986–1990. *Boletín Estadístico,* nos. 22–39.

———. 1991a. "Proyección del Comportamiento del Sistema Proyectado en Diversos Escenarios." Mimeo. Montevideo: BPS.

———. 1991b. "Proyección Financiera Fondo de Seguridad Social, Participación en el PBI." Mimeo. Montevideo: BPS.

———. 1991c. "Situación y Perspectivas Financieras del Fondo de la Seguridad Social." Mimeo. Montevideo: Informe del Grupo Técnico, July–September.

Barbeito, Alberto, and Rubén M. Lo Vuolo. 1992. *La Modernización Excluyente: Transformación Económica y Estado de Bienestar en Argentina.* Buenos Aires: UNICEF/CIEPP/Losada.

Bonilla García, Alejandro. 1991. "Informe de Misión Santiago de Chile." Unpublished manuscript. Geneva: ILO, October 5–12.

Borzutzky, Silvia. 1991. "The Chicago Boys, Social Security and Welfare." In Howard Gleenerster and James Midgley, eds., *The Radical Right and the Welfare State: An International Assessment.* Hertfordshire: Harvester Wheatsheaf, 79–99.

Botero, Libardo. 1993. "Seguridad Social: Capitalización Individual y Descapitalización Social." *Deslinde,* 14 (September–October): 29–50.

Boyd, Derick A.C. 1988. *Economic Management, Income Distribution and Poverty in Jamaica.* New York: Praeger.

Bronstein, Arturo S. 1990. "Protection Against Unjustified Dismissal in Latin America." *International Labour Review*, vol. 129, no. 5: 593–610.

Bustamante Alvarez, Rodrigo. 1990. "La Seguridad Social en Colombia." Oral presentation at PAHO, Washington, D.C., February 12.

Bustamante Jeraldo, Julio. 1991. "El Sistema de Pensiones en Chile." In *Seminario Fondo de Pensiones*. México D.F.: Bolsa Mexicana de Valores.

Caja Costarricense de Seguro Social (CCSS). 1988. *Memoria 1988*. San José: CCSS.

———. 1989. *Anuario Estadístico 1989*. San José: CCSS.

———. 1990. "Reformas al Reglamento del Seguro de Invalidez, Vejez y Muerte." Mimeo. San José: CCSS.

Cárdenas, Miguel Eduardo. 1992. "Seguridad Social y Régimen Pensional: Balance de Argumentos para una Reforma." In FESCOL, 1992a: 263–286.

Cartin Carranza, Ronald. 1991. "Sistemas de Pensiones en Costa Rica: Descripción, Opciones de Reforma y una Propuesta Integral." In Uthoff and Szalachman, eds., *Sistema de Pensiones*, 27–63.

Casares Mora, Luis. 1990. "Los Regímenes Complementarios como Estructura Integrante de los Régimenes de Pensiones: Experiencias en el Uruguay." In ISSA 1990a: 81–98.

Castañeda, Tarsicio. 1987. "El Sistema de Salud Chileno: Organización, Funcionamiento y Financiamiento." *Boletín de la Oficina Sanitaria Panamericana*, vol. 103, no. 6 (December): 544–570.

Castelblanco de Castro, Beatriz. 1991. *Sistema Nacional de Salud: Ley 10 de 1990 y Disposiciones Complementarias*. Bogotá: Biblioteca Actualidad Jurídica.

Castellanos, Jorge. 1986. "Coordinación Entre las Entidades del Sector Público que Prestan Servicios de Atención de Salud." In ILO/PAHO/CPISS 1986.

Castro-Gutiérrez, Alvaro. 1989. "Pension Schemes in Latin America: Some Financial Problems." *International Social Security Review*, no. 1: 35–61.

———. 1979–1991. "Normas de Seguridad Social." Montevideo: BPS.

———. 1990. "Los Regímenes Complementarios." *Previsión Social*, no. 1: 243–261.

Castro Jiménez, Maria, et al. 1990. "Los Seguros Privados en Chile: ¿Evolución o Extinción de la Seguridad Social?" *Seguridad Social*, no. 173 (October–December): 77–125.

Centro de Investigaciones Económicas Nacionales (CIEN). 1992. "El Sistema de Previsión Social en Guatemala." *Informe al Congreso*, no. 19.

Cheyre Valenzuela, Hernán. 1991. *La Previsión en Chile Ayer y Hoy: Impacto de una Reforma*. Santiago: Centro de Estudios Públicos.

Coke & Coke Associates. 1990. "5–Year Development Plan 1990–1994: Social Security and Welfare." Mimeo. Kingston: Coke & Coke.

Contraloría General de la República. 1992. *La Reforma de la Seguridad Social en Colombia: Una Aventura Económica*. Serie Estudios Ocasionales, no. 3. Bogota: Contraloria.

Corporación de Investigación, Estudio y Desarrollo de la Seguridad Social (CIEDESS). 1992. *12 Años de Modernización de la Seguridad Social en Chile: Evaluación Crítica y Proyecciones*. Santiago: CIEDESS.

"Crean el Sistema Privado de Salud . . ." *El Peruano* (November 10): 101589–101592.

"Créase el Sistema Privado de Pensiones Complementarias . . ." *El Peruano* (November 11): 101613–101618.

Cruz-Saco, María Amparo. 1993. "El Instituto Guatemalteco de Seguridad Social (IGSS): Evaluación Económica y Alternativas de Reforma." Washington, D.C.: IDB.

Davrieux, Hugo. 1987. *Papel de los Gastos Públicos en el Uruguay (1955–1984)*. Estudios CINVE, no. 9. Montevideo: CINVE.

Departamento Nacional de Planificación (DNP). 1991. "Seguridad Social Colombiana." Mimeo. Bogotá: DNP.

Dirección General de Estadística y Censo (DGEC). 1988, 1989. *Anuario Estadístico Uruguay 1988, 1989*. Montevideo: DGEC.

Dixon, John, and Robert Scheurell, eds. 1990. *Social Welfare in Latin America*. London: Routledge.

Dumont, Jean-Pierre. 1986. "L'Impact de la Crise Economique sur les Systèmes de Protection Sociale." Geneva: ILO.

Economic Commission for Latin America and the Caribbean (ECLAC). 1988. *The Evolution of the External Debt Problem in Latin America and the Caribbean*. Santiago: ECLAC.

———. 1990a, 1991a. *Preliminary Overview of the Economy of Latin America and the Caribbean*. Santiago: ECLAC.

———. 1990b. *Magnitud de la Pobreza en América Latina en los Años Ochenta*. Santiago: ECLAC.

———. 1991b. *Economic Panorama of Latin America 1991*. Santiago: ECLAC.

El Poder Ejecutivo Nacional. 1992. "Mensaje de Elevación del Anteproyecto de Ley de Reforma del Sistema Nacional de Previsión Social" and "Ley Nacional de Sistema Integrado de Jubilaciones y Pensiones." Mimeos. (August 25) Buenos Aires:

Feldman, Jorge. 1992. "El Sistema Previsional Argentino: Orientaciores y Alternativas para la Reforma." In FESCOL 1992a: 67–86.

Ferrara, Peter J. 1989. "The Privatization of Social Security in Chile." *Journal of Economic Growth* (Spring): 18–27.

Fundación Friedrich Ebert de Colombia (FESCOL). 1992a. *Regímenes Pensionales*. Bogotá: FESCOL.

———. 1992b. *La Reforma del Régimen Pensional en Colombia*. Bogotá: FESCOL.

Gamboa Patrón, Emilio. 1991. *Informe: LXVIII Asamblea General Ordinaria*. México D.F.: IMSS.

García, Norberto E. 1991. "Reestructuración Ecónomica y Mercado de Trabajo en América Latina." Mimeo. Buenos Aires: Instituto Internacional de Estudios Laborales-OIT.

Gillion, Colin, and Alejandro Bonilla. 1992. "Analysis of a National Private Pension Scheme: The Case of Chile." *International Labour Review*, vol. 131, no. 2: 171–195.

Giral-Bosca, Juan, and Héctor Diéguez. 1988. *Uruguay: Estudio de la Seguridad Social: Su Evolución, Actuales Problemas y Perspectivas*. Washington, D.C.: World Bank.

Government of Jamaica. 1988. "The Social Well-Being Programme: A Programme for Social Development." Mimeo. Kingston: Government of Jamaica.

Gwynne, Gretchen, and Dieter Zschock. 1989. "Health Care Financing in Latin America and the Caribbean, 1985–1989: Findings and Recommendations." Mimeo. HCF/LAC, no. 10. Stony Brook, N.Y.

Habitat. 1991. *10 Años de Historia del Sistema de AFP, 1981–1991*. Santiago: Habitat.

Iglesias P., Augusto, and Rodrigo Acuña R. 1991. *Chile: Experiencia con un Régimen de Capitalización 1981–1991*. Santiago: CEPAL/PNUD Sistemas de Pensiones en América Latina.

Instituto de Seguros Sociales (ISS). 1991. *Informe Estadístico 1990*. Bogotá, D.E.: ISS.

Instituto Mexicano de Seguridad Social (IMSS). 1983, 1988. *Diagnóstico de Salud en las Zonas Marginadas Rurales de México*. México D.F.: IMSS.
———. 1990a. *Memoria Estadística 1989*. México D.F.: IMSS.
———. 1990b. *Ley del Seguro Social*. México D.F.: IMSS.
———. 1991a. "Reformas a la Ley del Seguro Social." México D.F.: IMSS.
———. 1991b. "La Situación de Salud de la Población de México." In ISSA 1991: 203–231.
———, and COPLAMAR. 1987a. "Budget Summaries." México D.F.
———, and COPLAMAR. 1987b. *Anuario Estadístico* (1982–1986). México D.F.: Coordinación Médica.
———, and COPLAMAR. 1987c. "Estudio de Opinión Sobre la Calidad de los Servicios y la Participación de la Población como Respuesta a las Acciones de Salud del Programa IMSS-COPLAMAR."
———, and COPLAMAR. 1988a. "El Programa Nacional de Solidaridad Social por Cooperación Comunitaria (IMSS-COPLAMAR)." Managua: II Simposio Internacional de Extensión de Seguridad Social al Campo.
———, and COPLAMAR. 1988b. "Anexos del Documento Básico." Managua.
———, and Solidaridad. 1991. "México: Programa IMSS-Solidaridad." In ISSA 1991: 232–238.
Inter-American Development Bank (IDB). 1980–1991. *Economic and Social Progress in Latin America*. Washington, D.C.: IDB.
———. 1987. "Social Protection for the Unemployed in Latin America." *Economic and Social Progress in Latin America*. Washington, D.C.: IDB.
International Labour Office (ILO). 1976. *Employment, Growth and Basic Needs*. Geneva: ILO.
———. 1986–1987. *Employment Promotion and Social Security. Report IV (1), (2)*. Geneva: ILO.
———. 1988. *The Cost of Social Security, 1981–1983*. Geneva: ILO.
———. 1991a. *The Cost of Social Security, 1984–1986*. Geneva: ILO.
———. 1981–1991b. *Yearbook of Labour Statistics, 1980 to 1989/90*. Geneva: ILO.
———. 1991c. "Questionnaire and Answers from Jamaica for 14th Inquiry (1987–1989)." Mimeo. Geneva/Kingston: ILO.
———. 1992. *Report of the Director General*. 13th Conference of American States Members of the ILO, Caracas, Sept. 30–Oct. 7. Geneva: ILO.
International Labour Office, Pan American Health Organization and Comité Permanente Interamericano de Seguridad Social (ILO/PAHO/CPISS). 1986. *Atención Primaria y Estrategias de Salud en la Seguridad Social en América Latina*. Geneva: ILO.
International Social Security Association (ISSA). 1985. "Seguridad Social, Desempleo y Jubilación Anticipada." *Estudios de la Seguridad Social*, no. 54/55: 1–88.
———. 1989–1990. "Social Security News." *International Social Security Review*.
———. (Oficina Regional para las Américas). 1990a. *Grupo de Trabajo Regional Americano sobre Pensiones: Quinta Reunión Guatemala, 1989*. Documentación de la Seguridad Social Americana, Serie Actas, no. 11. Buenos Aires: ISSA.
———. 1991. *La Protección Social Rural*. Documentación de la Seguridad Social Americana, Serie Actas, no. 13. Buenos Aires: ISSA.
ISS-OIT-PNUD. 1992. *Elementos Conceptuales para una Reforma Integral a la Seguridad Social en Colombia: Experiencias Recientes en América y Europa*. Bogotá: ISS.

Isuani, Aldo E. 1985. "Social Security and Public Assistance." In Mesa-Lago 1985: 9–108.

———. 1991. "Opiniones y Posicionamiento de Actores Sociales Frente a la Reforma Previsional." Mimeo. Buenos Aires: CIEPP.

———, et al. 1989. *Estado Democrático y Política Social*. Buenos Aires: EUDEBA.

———, Ruben Lo Vuolo, et al. 1991. *El Estado Benefactor Un Paradigma en Crisis*. Buenos Aires: CIEPP.

Jaime González, Volmar. 1991. "Algunos Elementos Conceptuales para una Reforma de la Seguridad Social Colombiana." Bogotá.

Jaramillo Antillón, Iván, and Guido Miranda. 1985. *La Integración de Servicios de Salud en Costa Rica*. San José: Ministerio de Salud.

Lacey, Robert. 1987. "Chile: Privatization of the Social Security System." Mimeo. Washington, D.C.: World Bank.

Lacurcia, Hugo. 1990. "El Sistema de Pensiones en el Uruguay." *Regulación del Sistema Financiero y Reforma del Sistema de Pensiones: Experiencias de América Latina*. Santiago: CEPAL/PNUD.

La Forgia, Gerard. 1989. "User Fees, Quality of Care and the Poor: Lessons from the Dominican Republic." Mimeo. Washington, D.C.: Inter-American Foundation.

———. 1990. "Challenging Health Service Stratification: Social Security-Health Ministry Integration in Panama, 1973–1986." University of Pittsburgh, Graduate School of Public Health, Doctoral Dissertation.

———. 1991–1992. *Health Financing and Management in Belize,* (vols. 1–4.) Washington, D.C.: The Urban Institute.

"La Reforma al Régimen de Pensiones." 1992. *Debates de Coyuntura Económica*, no. 26. Bogotá: FEDESARROLLO-Fescol.

Lewis, Maureen A. 1988. "Privatization in the Jamaican Health Sector." Mimeo. Washington, D.C.: Resources for Child Health (REACH).

Ley 16, 320. November 1, 1992.

López Castaño, Hugo. 1992. "La Propuesta Gubernamental al Sistema Previsional Colombiano: Evaluación y Alternativas." November 26. Medellín.

López Castaño, Hugo, and Fernando Tobón Bernal. 1990. *Trabajadores Urbanos Independientes: Ciclo de Vida Laboral y Seguridad Social en Colombia*. Bogotá, D.E.: Instituto de Seguros Sociales and Universidad de Antioquia.

López Castaño, Hugo, and Jaime Martínez. 1991. *Propuestas de Reforma al Sistema de Seguros IVM: Una Evaluación General (Informe Elaborado para el ISS)*. Bogotá, D.E.

López González, Rosa, and Gustavo Céspedes Garay. 1992. Private correspondence, Lima, September 19 and December 8.

López Montaño, Cecilia. 1992a. "Elementos para un Debate sobre la Reforma a la Seguridad Social en Colombia." In FESCOL, 1992a: 193–198.

———. 1992b. "La Necesidad de una Reforma a la Seguridad Social en Colombia." *Nueva Frontera*, no. 907 (November): 12–17.

López Montaño, Cecilia, et al. 1991a. "La Seguridad Social y la Salud." Mimeo. Bogotá.

———. 1991b. "Ponencia Presentada al Primer Congreso de Ahorro." Mimeo. Bogotá.

Mackenzie, G. A. 1988. "Social Security Issues in Developing Countries: The Latin American Experience." *IMF Staff Papers*, vol. 35, no. 3 (September): 496–522.

Marcel, Mario, and Alberto Arenas. 1991. "Reformas a la Seguridad Social en Chile." Inter-American Development Bank, Series Monografías, no. 5. Washington, D.C.: IDB.

Marcos Rueda, Eduardo. 1992. "Seguridad Social Peruana de 1936 a 1992." *Estudios de la Seguridad Social*, no. 71: 62–68.

Margozzini, Francisco. 1991. "El Sistema Privado de Pensiones Chileno." Mimeo. Santiago.

McGreevey, William. 1990. *Social Security in Latin America: Issues and Options for the World Bank*. World Bank Discussion Papers, no. 110. Washington, D.C.: World Bank.

Meller, Patricio. 1990. "Revisión del Proceso de Ajuste Chileno en la Década del 80." *Colección Estudios CIEPLAN*, no. 30 (December): 5–54.

Mesa-Lago, Carmelo. 1978. *Social Security in Latin America: Pressure Groups, Stratification and Inequality*. Pittsburgh: University of Pittsburgh Press.

———. 1983a. "Social Security and Health: Final Report to World Bank SAL Mission to Costa Rica." Unpublished manuscript. Pittsburgh.

———. 1983b. "Social Security and Extreme Poverty in Latin America." *Journal of Development Economics*, no. 12: 83–110.

———, ed. 1985. *The Crisis of Social Security and Health Care: Latin American Experiences and Lessons*. Latin American Monograph and Document Series, no. 9. Pittsburgh: Center for Latin American Studies. University of Pittsburgh.

———. 1987a. "Social Security in Bahamas, Barbados and Jamaica." Mimeo. Geneva: ILO.

———. 1987b. "Chile SAL III Report on Pension System." Mimeo. Pittsburgh.

———. 1988a. "Review of Chile SAL III Conditions: Pension System." Mimeo. Pittsburgh.

———. 1988b. "Análisis Económico de los Sistemas de Pensiones en Costa Rica y Recomendaciones para su Reforma." Washington, D.C.: Development Technologies, Inc.

———. 1988c. "Informe Económico sobre la Extensión de la Cobertura Poblacional del Programa de Enfermedad-Maternidad del IPSS" (IPSS-USAID). Stony Brook, N.Y.: State University of New York.

———. 1989a. *Financiamiento de la Atención de la Salud en América Latina y el Caribe con Focalización en el Seguro Social*. World Bank, Institute of Economic Development, no. 42. Washington, D.C.: World Bank.

———. 1989b. "Financial and Economic Evaluation of Social Insurances (IESS) in Ecuador." Mimeo. Washington, D.C.: World Bank.

———. 1989c. *Ascent to Bankruptcy: Financing Social Security in Latin America*. Pittsburgh: University of Pittsburgh Press.

———. 1990. *La Seguridad Social y el Sector Informal*. Investigaciones sobre Empleo, no. 32. Santiago: PREALC.

———. 1991a. *Portfolio Performance of Selected Social Security Institutes in Latin America*. World Bank Discussion Papers, no. 139. Washington, D.C.: World Bank.

———. 1991b. *Social Security and Prospects for Equity in Latin America*. World Bank Discussion Papers, no. 140. Washington, D.C.: World Bank.

———. 1991c. "Social Security in Latin America." In IDB 1980–1991: 179–216.

———. 1991d. "Social Security and Economic Adjustment-Restructuring in Latin America and the Caribbean: A Study for the International Labour Office." Mimeo. Pittsburgh.

———. 1992a. "Evaluación de Proyectos Macroeconómicos y Comentarios al Ante Proyecto de Ley de Previsión Social de la Secretaría de Seguridad Social." Buenos Aires: PRONATASS.

———. 1992b. Instituto Ecuatoriano de Seguridad Social (IESS) Evalución Económica y Opciones para Reforma. Informe Técnico de HFS, no. 8. Washington, D.C.: Abt Associates/USAID.

———. 1992c. *Health Care for the Poor in Latin America and the Caribbean.* Pan American Health Organization and Inter-American Foundation. PAHO Scientific Publication, no. 539. Washington, D.C.: PAHO.

———. 1993a. "Social Security and Pension Reform in Latin America: Importance and Evaluation of Privatization Approaches." La Jolla: Institute of the Americas, Seminar on the Economic and Social Impact of Privatization in Latin America, January 28–29.

———. 1993b. "Safety Nets and Social Funds to Alleviate Poverty: Performance, Problems and Policy Options." Geneva: UNCTAD.

———, and Willy De Geyndt. 1987. "Colombia: Social Security Review." Mimeo. Washington, D.C.: World Bank, HRD.

Ministerio de Trabajo y Seguridad Social (MTSS). 1989. "Reglamento de las Sociedades Administradoras de Fondos Complementarios de Previsión Social, Uruguay." *Diario Oficial*, Montevideo, August 17: 407–409.

Ministerio de Trabajo y Seguridad Social, Colombia. (MTSS). 1990. *Políticas, Legislación y Estadísticas 1986–1990.* Bogotá: MTSS.

———. 1992. "Proyecto de Ley por el cual se Crea el Sistema de Ahorro Pensional y se Dictan Otras Disposiciones en Materia de Seguridad Social." Document. Bogotá: MTSS.

Ministry of Labour, Welfare and Sports (MLWS). 1990a. *National Development Five-Year Plan 1990– 91/1994–95: Social Security and Welfare.* Kingston: MLWS.

———. 1990b. *All About National Insurance.* Kingston: MLWS.

———. 1990c. *Contribution Tables.* Kingston: MLWS.

Miranda, Guido. 1991. "Repercusión de la Crisis Económica en la Caja Costarricense de Seguro Social." San José: IDB.

Musgrove, Philip. 1985. "The Impact of Social Security in Income Distribution." In Mesa-Lago 1985: 185–208.

———. 1986. "The Economic Crisis and its Impact on Health Care in Latin America and the Caribbean." Mimeo. Washington, D.C.: PAHO.

———. 1989. "Health, Debt and Disease: The Links Between Economics and Health." *The IDB* (December): 4–8.

Ocampo, José Antonio. 1992. "La Propuesta Gubernamental del Reforma al Régimen Pensional: Análisis y Alternativas." In "La Reforma del Régimen . . . " 1992: 28–51.

Pan American Health Organization (PAHO). 1981. "Coordinación Entre los Sistemas de Seguridad Social y la Salud Pública." Mimeo. Washington, D.C.: PAHO.

———. 1987. "Coordination of Social Security and Public Health Institutions." Washington, D.C., 99th Meeting of PAHO.

———. 1989. "Los Sistemas de seguridad social y salud." Mimeo. Washington, D.C.: PAHO.

———. 1990. *Health Conditions in the Americas*, vols. 1–2. Washington, D.C.: PAHO.

Piñera, José. 1991. *El Cascabel al Gato: La Batalla por la Reforma Previsional.* Santiago: Zig-Zag.

Planning Institute of Jamaica (PIJ). 1988–1991. *Economic and Social Survey Jamaica 1987–1990.* Kingston: PIJ.

———. 1990a. *Jamaica Five Year Development Plan 1990–1995.* Kingston: PIJ.

Quirós Coronado, Roberto. 1991. *Costa Rica: La Atención Médica en la Seguridad Social: Métodos para Mejorar la Relación Costo/Eficiencia de los Programas.* Ottawa: ISSA-5th Regional American Conference.

Raso Delgue, Juan. 1981. "Nueva Ley sobre Prestaciones por Desempleo en Uruguay." *Estudios de la Seguridad Social*, no. 39: 56–63.

————. 1983. *La Desocupación y el Seguro de Desempleo*. Montevideo: Ediciones Jurídicas.

República Oriental del Uruguay, Cámara de Representates. 1992. "Proyecto de Ley con Declaración de Urgente Consideración. Régimen de Seguridad Social." Mimeo. Montevideo. April.

Restrepo, Mauricio, et al. 1991. "Seguro Obligatorio de Salud Integral." Mimeo. Bogotá.

Ruiz Llano, Jaime. 1992. "La Reforma Pensional." In "La Reforma al Régimen . . ." 1992: 13–27.

Saldaín, Rodolfo. 1992. "Cobertura de los Riesgos de Invalidez, Vejez y Sobrevivencia en Uruguay: Un Análisis en Perspectiva y Bases de Cambio." *Estudios de la Seguridad Social*, no. 71: 15–46.

Santamaría, Marco. 1992. "Privatizing Social Security: The Chilean Case." *Columbia Journal of World Business*, vol. 27 (Spring): 38–51.

Scarpaci, Joseph L. 1990. *Primary Medical Care in Chile*. Pittsburgh: University of Pittsburgh Press.

Schmidt, Sönke. 1991. "Social Security in Developing Countries: Basic Tenets and Fields of State Intervention." Mimeo. Eschborn: GTZ R & D Project-Social Security Systems.

Schulthess, Walter. 1990. *Sistema Nacional de Previsión Social: Su Evolución y Situación a Fines de la Década del 80*. Buenos Aires: PRONATASS.

Sherraden, Margaret. 1989. "Primary Health Care for the Rural Poor in Mexico: The Case of IMSS-COPLAMAR (1979–1988)." St. Louis: Washington University.

"Sistema Privado . . . " and "Administradoras Privadas . . . " 1992. *El Peruano* (December 6): 110939–110952.

Solimano, Andrés. 1992. "Diversity in Economic Reform . . . " Mimeo. Washington, D.C.: World Bank.

Soto Pérez, Carlos. 1990. "Impacto de la Crisis Económica en las Instituciones de Seguridad Social." *Seguridad Social*, no. 172 (July–September): 143–160.

————. 1991. "Pensiones: Diagnóstico y Medida del Impacto Financiero." *Seguridad Social*, no. 174 (January–March): 110–124.

————. 1992. "Seguro de Retiro." *Cuestión Social*, no. 24 (January–March): 56–60.

Superintendencia de Administradores de Fondos de Pensiones (SAFP). 1981–1992. *Boletín Estadístico Mensual*, nos. 1–110.

Superintendencia de Seguridad Social (SSS). 1982–1992. *Seguridad Social, Estadísticas 1980–1990*. Santiago: SSS.

The Statistical Institute of Jamaica (SIJ). 1989. *Jamaica Survey of Living Conditions*. Kingston: SIJ.

————. 1990a. *Statistical Yearbook of Jamaica 1990*. Kingston: SIJ.

————. 1990b. *Statistical Abstract 1990*. Kingston: SIJ.

————. 1991. *Pocketbook of Statistics Jamaica 1991*. Kingston: SIJ.

Tokman, Víctor. 1986. "Adjustment and Employment in Latin America." *International Labor Review*, vol. 125, no. 5 (September–October): 533–543.

Ugalde, Antonio. 1985. "The Integration of Health Care in a National Health System." In Mesa-Lago 1985: 109–142.

United Nations Development Program (UNDP). 1991. *Human Development Report 1991*. Oxford: Oxford University Press.

United States Social Security Administration (US-SSA). 1989. *Social Security Programs Throughout the World—1989*. Washington, D.C.: GPO.

Uthoff, Andras, and Raquel Szalachman. 1991. *Sistema de Pensiones en América Latina: Diagnóstico y Alternativas de Reforma.* Santiago: CEPAL/PNUD.
Utrero, Roberto. 1991. "Las Cooperativas y la Protección Social: Su Incidencia en el Medio Rural." In ISSA 1991: 68–79.
Vázquez Riquelme, Gabriela, and Ricardo Moles. 1990. "Evolución y Tendencias del Mutualismo." *Estudios de la Seguridad Social,* no. 69: 93–101.
Velázquez, Georgina. 1989. "Diez Años de IMSS-COPLAMAR." *Cuestión Social,* no. 15 (Summer–Fall): 11–14.
———. 1990. "La Atención Primaria: Un Logro." *Cuestión Social,* no. 18 (Fall): 35–42.
———. 1991. "Calidad de la Atención a la Salud de la Población Rural." *Seguridad Social,* no. 175 (April–June): 55–71.
Williamson, John, ed. 1990. *Latin American Adjustment: How Much Has Happened?* Washington, D.C.: Institute for International Economics.
Wilson, Richard. 1985. "The Impact of Social Security on Employment." In Mesa-Lago 1985: 245–278.
World Bank. 1990, 1991. *World Development Report 1990, 1991: The Challenge of Development.* Oxford: Oxford University Press.
Zschock, Dieter, ed. 1988. *Health Care in Peru.* Boulder, Colorado: Westview.
Zulueta, Hernando. 1992. "El Régimen Pensional de Colombia: La Necesidad de Un Cambio Radical." In FESCOL 1992a: 199–221.

Index

About the Book and the Author

Social security, argues Mesa-Lago, should play a crucial role in alleviating the severe social costs of economic adjustment and restructuring in Latin America, but it has been hampered by a series of problems. After discussing these problems, the author concentrates on the process of social security reform occurring in the region.

Several types of reform—all intended to create mechanisms that can more effectively cope with the costs of economic adjustment—are analyzed in eight countries (Argentina, Chile, Colombia, Costa Rica, Jamaica, Mexico, Peru, and Uruguay). The data are current through early 1993. Mesa-Lago's concluding policy recommendations address such issues as the new roles of the state and the private sector and the extension of social security coverage to the rural population, the informal sector, and the unemployed.

Carmelo Mesa-Lago is Distinguished Service Professor of Economics and Latin American Studies at the University of Pittsburgh. He has conducted research on social security in Latin America for more than thirty-five years and has served as a consultant to virtually all international organizations dealing with the subject.